Barbara

MW00574098

TWENTY-FIRST CENTURY
BIBLICAL COMMENTARY SERIES

THE GOSPEL OF

MARK

CHRIST THE SERVANT

JAMES
McGOWAN

GENERAL EDITORS

MAL COUCH & ED HINDSON

Copyright © 2006 by Scofield Ministries
Published by AMG Publishers.
6815 Shallowford Road
Chattanooga, TN 37421

All Rights Reserved. Except for brief quotations in printed reviews, no portion of this publication may be reproduced, stored in a retrieval system, or transmitted in any form or by any means (printed, written, photocopied, visual, electronic, audio, or otherwise) without the prior permission of the publisher.

Unless otherwise noted, Scripture quotes are taken from the NEW AMERICAN STANDARD BIBLE, Copyright © 1960, 1962, 1963, 1968, 1971, 1972, 1973, 1975, 1977, by the Lockman Foundation. Used by permission. (www.Lockman.org)
Scriptures marked KJV are from the King James Version of the Bible.
Scriptures marked NIV are from the HOLY BIBLE NEW INTERNATIONAL VERSION®. NIV®. Copyright© 1973, 1978, 1984 by International Bible Society. Used by permission of Zondervan.

ISBN-13: 978-0–89957-821-7
ISBN-10: 0–89957-821-7

First Printing, September 2006

Cover Design by ImageWright, Inc.
Text Design by Warren Baker
Typesetting by Jennifer Ross
Edited and proofread by Warren Baker, Patrick Belvill, and Weller Editorial Services, Chippewa Lake, MI

Printed in the United States of America
11 10 09 08 07 06 –R– 8 7 6 5 4 3 2 1

Twenty-First Century Biblical Commentary Series

Mal Couch, Th.D., and Ed Hindson, D.Phil.

The New Testament has guided the Christian Church for over two thousand years. This one testament is made up of twenty-seven books, penned by godly men through the inspiration of the Holy Spirit. It tells us of the life of Jesus Christ, His atoning death for our sins, His miraculous resurrection, His ascension back to heaven, and the promise of His second coming. It also tells the story of the birth and growth of the Church and the people and principles that shaped it in its earliest days. The New Testament concludes with the book of Revelation pointing ahead to the glorious return of Jesus Christ.

Without the New Testament, the message of the Bible would be incomplete. The Old Testament emphasizes the promise of a coming Messiah. It constantly points us ahead to the One who is coming to be the King of Israel and the Savior of the world. But the Old Testament ends with this event still unfulfilled. All of its ceremonies, pictures, types, and prophecies are left awaiting the arrival of the "Lamb of God who takes away the sin of the world!" (John 1:29).

The message of the New Testament represents the timeless truth of God. As each generation seeks to apply that truth to its specific context, an up-to-date commentary needs to be created just for them. The editors and authors of the Twenty-First Century Biblical Commentary Series have endeavored to do just that. This team of scholars represents conservative, evangelical, and dispensational scholarship at its best. The individual authors may differ on minor points of interpretation, but all are convinced that the Old and New Testaments teach a dispensational framework for biblical history. They also hold to a pretribulational and premillennial understanding of biblical prophecy.

The French scholar René Pache reminded each succeeding generation, "If the power of the Holy Spirit is to be made manifest anew among us, it is of primary importance that His message should regain its due place. Then we shall be able to put the enemy to flight by the sword of the Spirit which is the Word of God."

The Gospel of Mark is one of the foundational books of the New Testament. The eminent Princeton scholar, Joseph Addison Alexander, has observed: "This Gospel has always formed a part of the New Testament canon, being found in all the ancient catalogues as one of the undisputed books and quoted by the earliest Christian writers."

William Lane of Gordon-Conwell Seminary described Mark as a: "witness document that found its creative impulse in the early apostolic preaching of salvation through Jesus Christ." He also observed that Mark's gospel may be described as a "passion narrative with an extended introduction." He adds: "The reason that almost half of Mark's sixteen chapters describe the final period of Jesus' ministry is that it is in his suffering, death and resurrection that the revelation of God in Christ is most clearly seen."

One of the key features in Mark's gospel is the accelerated tension caused by the ministry of Jesus Christ. Mark pictures Jesus as accepted by the general Jewish public but rejected by the Jewish leadership. As this tension grows, the narrative propels the reader toward the final crisis (the crucifixion) and its ultimate resolution (the resurrection).

To my wife Sandra, who gave me two wonderful daughters and who shares my dreams, takings them as her own.

To Ivan Ker, of Waco, Texas, who recognized the call of God on my life back in 1977, licensed me to preach, and who continues to exemplify what it means to be a real Pastor.

To Mal Couch and John Baze who imparted to me their love for the Biblical languages.

Acknowledgement

With special appreciation to Dr. Jim Combs, Provost of Louisiana Baptist Theological Seminary, for providing and sharing his study notes for use in the creation of this volume.

Contents

Background of Mark

Theme and Purpose

The theme of Mark's gospel is succinctly summarized in 10:45, "For even the Son of Man did not come to be served, but to serve, and to give His life a ransom for many." With the emphasis on Christ's actions, as well as His death and resurrection, this gospel shows Jesus as the Suffering Servant.

R. C. H. Lenski writes:

> Although he was infinitely great himself, omnipotent to lord it over all, he came (in his incarnation) on a mission that is the very opposite. He could have compelled all men to be his *diakonoi*, yea, his *douloi*, but he came "not to be ministered unto," to say nothing of being slaved for, "on the contrary" (*alla*) to minister (an effective aorist) and to do even more. In both verbs we have diakonos (*diakonia*) and not (*doulos*); the latter would not fit the work of Jesus because it would not conserve the divine dignity of this great Minister, a dignity which remained during his service, and would thus also fail to fit the exalted character of the service he rendered. Some humble ministrations of his friends he did accept (Luke 8:2, 3; John 12:2, 3), but the purpose of his life was to give and not to receive or take."[1]

This presentation of Christ was most appropriate to Mark's Roman audience. Whereas Matthew taught the kingship of Christ to a Jewish audience, Mark had a predominantly Gentile audience, a large number of whom were probably slaves and slave owners. Jesus, therefore, as a servant, spoke to their need.

In this portrayal of Christ as servant, there is much in the way of evangel-
istic material as well as deeper writing for the maturing of young disciples.
This teaching is perfectly suited to the needs of a church, which caused David
Grassmick to conclude that:

> Mark's purpose was basically pastoral. The Christians in Rome had
> already heard and believed the good news of God's saving power (Rom.
> 1:8), but they needed to hear it again with a new emphasis to catch afresh
> its implications for their lives in a dissolute and often hostile environ-
> ment. They needed to understand the nature of discipleship—what it
> meant to follow Jesus—in light of who Jesus is and what He had done
> and would keep doing for them.

> Like a good pastor, Mark presented "the gospel about Jesus Christ, the Son
> of God" (1:1) in a way that would meet this need and continue to shape
> his readers' lives. He achieved this through his portraits of Jesus and the
> 12 disciples with whom he expected his readers to identify, . . . He showed
> how Jesus Christ is the Messiah because He is the Son of God, and His
> death as the suffering Son of Man was God's plan for people's redemption.
> In light of this he showed how Jesus cared for His disciples and taught
> them about discipleship in the context of His death and resurrection—the
> same kind of care and teaching needed by all who follow Jesus.[2]

Authenticity

Citations and/or allusions to the Gospel of Mark are found as early as the
Epistle of Pseudo-Barnabas (c. A.D. 70-79); the writings of Polycarp (c. A. D.
110-150), a disciple of John the apostle; and the Shepherd of Hermes (c. A.D.
115-140).

Defense of the authenticity of the Gospel of Mark is dated as early as
A. D. 120 when Papias (c. A.D. 70-163) wrote "five treatises entitled
Interpretation of the Oracles of the Lord . . . which included the four gospels."[3]
Later, around A.D. 140, Papias refers to information related to him by some-
one he refers to as "the presbyter—presumably someone who in his earlier life
had known one or more of the apostles."[4]

> And the presbyter said this. Mark having become the interpreter of Peter,
> wrote down accurately whatsoever he remembered. It was not, however,
> in exact order that he related the sayings or deeds of Christ. For he neither
> heard the Lord nor accompanied Him. But afterwards, as I said, he accom-
> panied Peter, who accommodated his instructions to the necessities [of
> his hearers], but with no intention of giving a regular narrative of the

Lord's sayings. Wherefore Mark made no mistake in thus writing some things as he remembered them. For of one thing he took especial care, not to omit anything he had heard, and not to put anything fictitious into the statements.[5]

Sometime after A.D. 165, Justin Martyr's disciple, Tatian, wrote a harmony of the four Gospels called the *Diatessaron.* This was to be "for centuries a very influential edition of the gospels."[6] It was written and widely circulated in both a Greek edition and a Syriac edition. The Syriac churches used it as their primary gospel document for more than two hundred years.[7]

As with the other three Gospels, it was recognized by all of the major canons, translations and church councils, which authenticated the canon of Scripture.

Authorship

Nowhere in the Gospel of Mark is the name of the author given. The title *Kata Markon* ("According to Mark"), was given to the book later, before A.D. 125, by a copyist. However, all of the early church fathers agreed that the author was Mark, who they believed was an associate of the apostle Peter (as evidenced above by Papias). With this external evidence, and the internal, biblical evidence, the logical conclusion of authorship would fall to John Mark.

Mark is first introduced in Acts 12:12, "And when he realized this, he went to the house of Mary, the mother of John who was also called Mark, where many were gathered together and were praying." This passage is referring to Peter's movements following his miraculous deliverance from Herod's prison. Much is learned from this passage. Since Mark's house is referred to as the *"house of Mary,"* it would appear that his father was deceased. The fact that *"many were gathered together"* in her house tells us that it was a large house, which gives the impression that they were a wealthy family. This is also supported by the fact that they had a servant (Acts 12:13). Furthermore, it appears that Peter had visited Mary's house before since the servant recognized his voice when he knocked at the gate (Acts 12:14). This supports the source and authenticity of Mark's gospel. Bruce Wilkinson and Kenneth Boa make this observation:

> Barnabas was Mark's cousin (Col. 4:10), but Peter may have been the person who led him to Christ (Peter called him "Mark my son" I Pet. 5:13). It was this close association with Peter that lent apostolic authority to Mark's gospel, since Peter was evidently Mark's primary source of information.[8]

Next, we find Mark going to Antioch with Barnabas and Paul (Acts 12:25) and leaving with them on their first missionary journey. However, for a reason not revealed in Scripture, Mark left Barnabas and Paul in the midst of their first missionary journey and returned to Jerusalem (Acts 13:13). This resulted in Paul rejecting Barnabas' idea to take Mark with them on their second missionary journey (Acts 15:38) and the eventual split of Paul and Barnabas into two missionary teams (Paul going with Silas and Barnabas going with Mark), traveling in two different directions.

The rift between Mark and Paul was eventually healed, as evidenced by Mark's presence when Paul was imprisoned the first time in Rome (Col. 4:10; Philem. 1:24), and by Paul's statement to Timothy toward the end of his life:

> Make every effort to come to me soon; for Demas, having loved this present world, has deserted me and gone to Thessalonica; Crescens has gone to Galatia, Titus to Dalmatia. Only Luke is with me. *Pick up Mark and bring him with you, for he is useful to me for service.* (2 Tim. 4:9–11 [emphasis mine])

R. C. H. Lenski offers this summary of these final scriptural references to Mark and his place among the gospel writers:

> Now Col. 4:10, written in the year 62 toward the end of Paul's first imprisonment, plus Philemon 24, show that Mark was at that time associated with Paul. We know that after that Mark was with Peter in Rome, and that Mark wrote his Gospel at the request of the Romans. That Gospel is composed of what Mark had heard Peter present to his hearers again and again so that Mark's writing earned him the designation Peter's "interpreter." In the year 64 Peter was crucified in Rome. Now we discover that Mark is again the assistant to Timothy, surely by direction of Paul; and Paul wants him as well as Timothy to hurry to Rome.
>
> We see why Paul says that Mark is useful to him "for ministry" . . . Mark had been in Rome with Paul (Col. 4:10; Philemon 1:24) and after that with Peter and knew Rome and the Roman Christians, as many as were still left, so well that he was certainly a most useful man for Paul to have about him in Rome under present conditions. Would that we had the pertinent details! Yet those that are indicated seem assured.[9]

When and Where was the Gospel of Mark Written?

Though the exact date of writing is unknown, many scholars believe that Mark was the first gospel written. Since Mark 13:2 gives a prophecy regarding the destruction of the temple, the gospel was apparently written sometime before

A.D. 70 The early date is traditionally set sometime around the martyrdom of Peter, which occurred in A.D. 64.

David Grassmick offers this detailed analysis:

Because of conflicting external evidence the question of date remains problematic. Two options are available. One view is that the Gospel can be dated between A.D. 67–69 if one accepts the tradition that it was written after the deaths of Peter *and* Paul. Advocates of this view usually hold either that Matthew and Luke were written after A.D. 70 or that they were written before Mark. A second view is that the Gospel can be dated prior to A.D. 64–68 (when Peter was martyred) if one accepts the tradition that it was written during Peter's lifetime. On this view one can accept the priority of Mark (or Matt.) and still hold that all the Synoptic Gospels were written before A.D. 70.

The second view is preferred for these reasons: (1) Tradition is divided though the more reliable evidence supports this view. (2) The priority of Mark . . . , particularly Mark's relationship to Luke, which antedates Acts (cf. Acts 1:1), points to a date before A.D. 64. The fact that Acts closes with Paul still in prison prior to his first release (ca. A.D. 62) pushes the date for Mark before A.D. 60. (3) It is historically probable that Mark (and perhaps Peter also for a short time) could have been in Rome during the latter part of the 50s. . . . Thus a plausible dating would seem to be A.D. 57–59 during the early part of Emperor Nero's reign (A.D. 54–68).[10]

As for where this gospel was written, the general consensus among the early church fathers is that it was written in Rome, to a primarily Gentile, Roman congregation. This view is supported by a large body of evidence from the gospel itself:

(1) Jewish customs are explained (cf. 7:3–4; 14:12; 15:42). (2) Aramaic expressions are translated into Greek (cf. 3:17; 5:41; 7:11, 34; 9:43; 10:46; 14:36; 15:22, 34) (3) Several Latin terms are used rather than their Greek equivalents (cf. 5:9; 6:27; 12:15, 42; 15:16, 39). (4) The Roman method of reckoning time is used (cf. 6:48; 13:35). (5) Only Mark identified Simon of Cyrene as the father of Alexander and Rufus (cf. 15:21; Rom. 16:13). (6) Few Old Testament quotations or references to fulfilled prophecy are used. (7) Mark portrayed a particular concern for "all the nations" (cf. comments on Mark 5:18–20; 7:24–8:10; 11:17; 13:10; 14:9), and at a climactic point in the Gospel a Gentile Roman centurion unwittingly proclaimed Jesus' deity (cf. 15:39). (8) The tone and message of the Gospel are appropriate to Roman believers who were encountering perse-

cution and expecting more (cf. comments on 9:49; 13:9–13). (9) Mark assumed that his readers were familiar with the main characters and events of his narrative, so he wrote with more of a theological than a biographical interest. (10) Mark addressed his readers as Christians more directly by explaining the meaning for them of particular actions and statements (cf. 2:10, 28; 7:19).[11]

Mark's Unique Writing Style

Two of the defining qualities of Mark's gospel are brevity and action. Whereas Luke is the longest gospel, having twenty-four chapters and more than 1,100 verses, Mark is the shortest, having sixteen chapters with less than 700 verses.

Mark is also known as the gospel of action. It is the fastest paced of the Synoptic Gospels (the word "immediately" occurs forty times) and deals more with the actions of Jesus than with His teachings. John MacArthur points out that:

> Mark omits the lengthy discourses found in the other gospels, often relating only brief excerpts to give the gist of Jesus' teaching. Mark also omits any account of Jesus' ancestry and birth, beginning where Jesus' public ministry began, with His baptism by John in the wilderness.[12]

Wilkinson and Boa add:

> With few comments, Mark lets the narrative speak for itself as it tells the story of the Servant who constantly ministers to others through preaching, healing, teaching, and, ultimately, His own death. Mark traces the steady building of hostility and opposition to Jesus as He resolutely moves toward the fulfillment of His earthly mission. Almost 40 percent of this gospel is devoted to a detailed account of the last eight days of Jesus' life, climaxing in His resurrection. The Lord is vividly portrayed in this book in two parts: to serve (1–10); to sacrifice (11–16).[13]

Mark's fast-paced style is also enhanced by the rich, vividly descriptive manner in which he portrays the works of Christ and the people He encountered. Grassmick observes that

> Mark's writing style is vivid, forceful, and descriptive, reflecting an eyewitness source such as Peter (cf., e.g., 2:4; 4:37–38; 5:2–5; 6:39; 7:33; 8:23–24; 14:54). His use of Greek is nonliterary, close to the everyday speech of that time with a recognizable Semitic flavoring. His use of Greek tenses, especially the "historical present" tense (used over 150 times), simple sentences linked by "and," frequent use of "immediately"

(*euthus;* cf. comments on 1:10), and the use of forceful words (e.g., lit., "impelled," 1:12) lend vividness to his narrative.[14]

He adds:

Mark portrayed his subjects with unusual candor. He emphasized the responses of Jesus' hearers with various expressions of amazement (cf. comments on 1:22, 27; 2:12; 5:20; 9:15). He related the concern of Jesus' family over His mental health (cf. 3:21, 31–35). He candidly and repeatedly drew attention to the disciples' lack of understanding and failures (cf. 4:13; 6:52; 8:17, 21; 9:10, 32; 10:26). He also highlighted Jesus' emotions such as His compassion (1:41; 6:34; 8:2; 10:16), His anger and displeasure (1:43; 3:5; 8:33; 10:14), and His sighs of distress and sorrow (7:34; 8:12; 14:33–34).[15]

Mark's Impact On The Twenty-first Century

The Gospel of Mark is incredibly well suited as an evangelistic tool in our times. We live in the days of fast computers, extreme sports, and an ever-increasing pace to be met in society. Mark meets this need. Its pace is quick yet its message is focused and intense. The supernatural power of Christ is copiously displayed in the eighteen miracles noted in Mark, yet His humanity is emphasized as well. John MacArthur notes:

Mark demonstrated the humanity of Christ more clearly than any of the other evangelists, emphasizing Christ's human emotions (1:41; 3:5; 6:34; 8:12; 9:36), His human limitations (4:38; 11:12; 13:32), and other small details that highlight the human side of the Son of God (e.g., 7:33, 34; 8:12; 9:36; 10:13–16).[16]

The Eighteen Miracles in Mark
- *Removing an unclean spirit (1:23–26)*
- *Healing Simon Peter's mother (1:30–31)*
- *Healing a leper (1:40–42)*
- *Healing a paralytic (2:3–12)*
- *Healing a withered hand (3:1–5)*
- *Calming the stormy sea (4:37–39)*
- *Healing the Gerasene demoniac (5:2–13)*
- *Healing a woman's hemorrhage (5:25–34)*
- *Healing Jairus's daughter (5:22–43)*
- *Feeding the five thousand (6:41–44)*
- *Walking on water (6:48–51)*

- *Removing an unclean spirit (7:25–30)*
- *Restoring hearing to a deaf man (7:32–35)*
- *Feeding the four thousand (8:2–8)*
- *Healing a blind man (8:22–26)*
- *The transfiguration (9:2–8)*
- *Removing an unclean spirit (9:17–27)*
- *Healing Blind Bartimaeus (10:46–52)*

Finally, the large amount of text (almost 40 percent) devoted to the last eight days of Jesus' life provides an intense message regarding His mission, His devotion, and His miraculous accomplishment. "His willingness to bear countless human sins is the epitome of servanthood."[17]

A most impressive example of this servanthood was Jesus praying in the Garden of Gethsemane (Mark 14:32–36). Scripture tells us that He was "very distressed and troubled." Jesus, Himself said, "My soul is deeply grieved to the point of death." We know that this anguish brought Him to His knees, probably even prostrate on the ground, in prayer to His Father, asking that this "cup," this task, this mission of death may be taken from Him. He knew that, not only would He suffer the most painful form of death devised by humans to that time, but that He would also bear all of the sins of humanity at the same time. We cannot begin to imagine the pain and horror of this divine knowledge. Yet, knowing all of this, Jesus still ended His prayer by saying, "yet not what I will, but what Thou wilt." Above all, knowing the soon coming pain, agony, suffering, heartache, and death, Jesus remained true to His commitment, His duty to the Father. This is the type of message—fast-paced, intense, with great commitment and meaning—that speaks to people, especially young people, today.

CHAPTER 1

The Servant Begins His Ministry
Mark 1:1-45

Preview

While Matthew sets forth Christ's majesty as king, showing that He is the fulfill-ment of Old Testament prophecy, Mark's gospel depicts Christ's mastery as the Servant-Son of God with few quotations from the Old Testament. A servant needs no genealogy or description of early background, but this servant was and is the Son of God. This chapter touches on Christ's baptism by John and Christ's temptation, then plunges into a rapid fire account of His ministry. He calls disciples to follow Him, then manifests His authority over demons, fever, leprosy and other diseases, healing many as a servant to humankind. The account of His great Galilean ministry begins. Notice the words "immediately," "forthwith," and "straightway" (all the same word in Greek). The servant has tasks to perform and does them according to the Father's plan.

The Servant: His Identity Established (1:1)

It is fascinating to observe how each of the four Gospels is introduced. Matthew uses the expression "the book of the genealogy." *Genealogy* is from the Greek word *genesis* (Matt. 1:1). Mark uses the Greek word *archē*, meaning "to be first." Luke speaks of those who, "from the beginning [*archē*]" were eyewitnesses (Luke 1:2), while John reverts back before time saying, "In the beginning was the Word" (1:1). Thus all four Gospels declare that Jesus Christ Himself in all of His multifaceted persona is the supreme subject of each portrait of His life and work.

Mark's was the first gospel written and it is clear that from the formative days of the Christian church, Jesus was recognized and worshiped as the unique Son of God. In fact, in the last book of the New Testament, the glorified and risen Lord Himself proclaims, "I am . . . the beginning (*archē*) and the end" (Rev. 21:6; 22:13).

This gospel begins abruptly. This is probable due to the fact that the Romans were men of action and would respond to clear-cut and emphatic simplicity. The deity of Jesus Christ is initially stated. Mark begins by declaring that Jesus is "the Son of God." Then toward the close of the book he records the Roman centurion's remarkable assertion, "Truly this man was the Son of God" (15:39). Even demonic forces acknowledged Him as "the Son of God" (3:11; 5:7).

Mark's opening verse also identifies the "gospel," or "good news" as pertaining specifically to Jesus Christ for it is uniquely about Him. The word "gospel" (*euangelion*) signifies glad tidings, good news, the glorious proclamation that at last the Messiah had come. James A. Brooks notes:

> The "gospel" is an important subject in Mark. The word *euangelion* appears seven times (also 1:14–15; 8:35; 10:29; 13:10; and 14:9. Cf. also 16:15) versus only four times in Matthew and none in Luke and John (but Matthew has the cognate verb once and Luke ten times). By his frequent use of the term, Mark emphasized the freshness and even revolutionary character of the message of Jesus. This message offered hope to the neglected and oppressed.[1]

The Servant: His Coming Announced by John the Baptist (1:2–8)

(Compare Matthew 3:1–11; Luke 3:1–18; John 1:19–30)

As Mark introduces John the Baptist and his short but powerful ministry, he refers to two Old Testament prophecies, the first from Malachi 3:1, which reads "Behold I send my messenger, and he will clear the way before Me." Malachi, the last prophet in the Old Testament Scriptures, prophetically looked forward and spoke of John, the cousin of Jesus (cf. Luke 1), who would be the forerunner of the Messiah. In this manner, he linked the new message of Jesus to its roots in the past history of Israel and the writings of Israel's great prophets. Between Malachi (whose name means "messenger" in Hebrew), and John (whose name means "Jehovah is gracious" in Hebrew), was a period of four hundred years—four hundred years of spiritual famine, without any revelation of God. In his second quotation Mark references Isaiah 40:3, and speaks of the "voice of one crying in the wilderness" who would command, "Make ready the way of the Lord," two powerful predictions fulfilled in John's lifestyle and his message.

The principle theme of John's ministry was "a baptism of repentance for the forgiveness of sins" (v. 4). The prepositional phrase, "for the forgiveness of sins" is introduced with the Greek preposition *eis*, and would be better translated "with reference to." This baptism is not altogether unlike other Jewish "washings" for purification (cf. Heb. 6:1–3), however, it is unique in that: (1) it symbolizes a cleansing from sin and the close of a sinful lifestyle, and (2) it forecast the death, burial, and resurrection of Christ.

John's baptism was not designed to provoke repentance, nor was it causal—that is, it did not produce remission of sins. It was administered to those souls who had already repented (cf. Matt. 3:7–10).

Empowered by the Spirit, John brought a message to bring people under conviction for sin. As they came to recognize their sins, he spoke of remission, forgiveness, and the cancellation of their sins. Observe that repentance (*metanoia*), a change of heart and mind, is the prime requirement. Biblically, a repentant person is one who turns from trusting in himself to solely trusting in God, from serving self to serving the Lord (cf. 1 Thess. 1:9). Eventually, from those who heard and heeded John's call for repentance, Jesus gathered His initial disciples.

Like Elijah who lived some eight hundred years before him, John's food consisted of locusts and the honey made by wild bees (cf. Lev. 11:22; Deut. 32:13). As his short ministry of perhaps only a year or two proceeded, he announced that he was indeed only the forerunner of "one mightier than I," one who "will baptize you with the Holy Spirit." R. A. Guelich remarks:

> The phrase "Spirit-baptism" that has become prominent in certain circles today owes its derivation to this element inherent in the Baptist's message (Matt 3:11; Luke 3:16; John 1:33; cf. Acts 1:5; 19:1–7). John, focusing on his baptism as the trademark to his ministry, used baptism metaphorically to contrast his ministry with that of "the Greater One." The bestowal of the Spirit expressed metaphorically as a baptism signified God's eschatological act of salvation promised long ago by the prophets (e.g. Isa 32:15; 44:3; Ezek 11:19; 36:26–27; 37:14; Joel 3:1–2 [2:28–29]); *T. Jud.* 24.3; *T. Levi* 18.11). Therefore, the Baptist was declaring the dawn of a new day of salvation, not simply a new baptism.[2]

The outpouring of the Spirit was understood traditionally as an established characteristic of the messianic age (Isa. 44:3; Ezek. 36:25–27; Joel 2:28); however, John's use of the expression "baptize you with the Holy Spirit" here, was both new and unique.

The Servant's Baptism and Anointing (1:9–11)

(Compare Matthew 3:13–17; Luke 3:21–22; John 1:31–34)

"In those days" Jesus Himself appeared, historically, coming down from Nazareth where He had lived for thirty years. Up until this time Jesus, insofar as we know, had never preached, proclaimed His messiahship, performed miracles, or developed a following.

Mark does not address the reason that Jesus came to be baptized, but it was certainly not due to any personal sin. Jesus made it clear that His actions were to "fulfill all righteousness" (Matt. 3:15). By so doing, Jesus identified Himself with sinful humanity. Furthermore, His baptism pictured His voluntary acceptance of His role as the suffering servant.

Suggested Reasons Why Jesus Was Baptized
- *to identify Himself with John the Baptist's ministry*
- *to give divine approval to John's service*
- *to indicate the need of humankind to repent and gain forgiveness*
- *to manifest His identification with human beings, whose sins He would take upon Himself*
- *to set forth His baptism of death and resurrection (see 10:38–39)*
- *to inaugurate His own ministry*
- *to then receive His special anointing by the Holy Spirit in the form of a dove descending upon Him, as the Father's voice from heaven proclaimed His divine Sonship*
- *to leave an example for His followers to imitate after believing on Him as Savior*

As Jesus came up out of the Jordan River, "the Spirit like a dove descending upon him" anointing Him for ministry (cf. Acts 10:38). This was followed by a heavenly voice that declared, "Thou art My beloved Son, in Thee I am well pleased." D. Edmond Hiebert explains that this was

> the Father's confirmation to the incarnate Son, as He stood upon the bank of the Jordan. *Thou* is emphatic: "you yourself, in contradistinction to all others." *Thou art*, not "Thou hast become," acknowledged His unique sonship, not as a newly established relationship but as an abiding reality. *Beloved* stands emphatically at the end with the article—"Thou art my Son, the beloved"—stressing the love relationship.[3]

On two other occasions God spoke from heaven about Christ (Mark 9:7)—at the Transfiguration and during the last week at the temple (John 12:28). Contrary to some teaching, Jesus did not "become the Christ" at His baptism. He was already the Messiah, already God manifest in the flesh. This event dramatically inaugurated His public ministry.

The Servant Tempted by Satan (1:12-13)

(Compare Matthew 4:1-11; Luke 4:1-13)

Mark records that after His unique baptism, "immediately the Spirit impelled Him . . . into the wilderness," there to be tested and tempted by Satan. Full details are found in Matthew 4:1-11 and Luke 4:1-15.

For the first time since events in the Garden of Eden, Satan confronted a completely sinless person. However, whereas Adam was *created* a sinless being, Jesus was sinless by virtue of His being the very Son of God! In this instance, instead of dealing with an innocent *created* being, Satan came against the God-Man who was indwelt by the Holy Spirit and empowered for service. This in no way diminished the temptation, it was real, Satan was real, and Jesus' triumph was real. We know that the temptation was real, for Hebrews 4:15 declares that Jesus, "has been tempted in all things as we are, yet without sin." Other temptations would come as His ministry continued, but this was the great temptation that revealed Christ's impeccability.[4] Concerning Jesus' temptation, H. A. Ironside remarks:

> It was fitting that He should be tested before He began His gracious ministry. **His temptation was not to see if perchance He might fail and sin in the hour of stress, but rather to prove that He would not fail, because He was the absolutely sinless One**. Those who impute to Jesus either a sinful nature or the possibility of sinning do Him a grievous wrong. Scripture guards against any such misconceptions when it tells us that He "has been tempted in all things as we are, yet *without* sin"– or literally, apart from sin (Hebrews 4:15, italics added). There was in Him no inward tendency to sin. The temptations were all from without and found no response whatever in His heart. (emphasis added).[5]

At the close of the forty days, angels came and, "were ministering to Him." It is most likely that their ministry consisted in bringing food and water to Jesus, for that was His greatest need at that time. However, it is also likely that they brought Him spiritual encouragement. As a result of Jesus' temptation, we now have a high priest who can, "sympathize with our weaknesses" (Heb. 4:15) who offers grace, mercy, and help in our hour of temptation.

The Servant Begins His Ministry (1:14,15)

(Compare Matthew 4:12-17; Luke 4:14-15)

Mark records that, "after John had been taken into custody, Jesus came into Galilee, preaching the gospel of God." Between verses 14 and 15 of this chapter almost a year elapses. Events during this period are recorded in Matthew 4:18–22; Luke 5:2–11; and John 1:19—4:42.

The Kingdom of God

Use	Meaning
Generically	The kingdom of God is that sovereign rule over the hearts of people through the King of Kings, involving their obedience to the will of God and in the Son of God.
Spiritually	The kingdom of God includes all believers, both those in heaven and those on earth, who have been "born again" and thereby enter into a special spiritual relationship as sons and daughters of God (John 3:3, 5; Acts 8:12; 19:8; 28:23; Rom. 14:17; Col. 4:11; 1 Pet. 1:3–5, 23).
Historically	The kingdom of God in both a spiritual and political sense was offered to Israel but was rejected when the Messiah was rejected (Matthew 21:43).
Dispensationally	The kingdom of God/Heaven is present in "mystery form." (Matthew 13:11; Mark 4:11; Luke 8:10): the sphere of Christian profession on earth, consisting of "tares and wheat" and "good fish and bad fish" (Matt. 13:24–30; 47–50), genuine Christians and professing Christians throughout the world, the realm of Christianity and influence, Christendom.
Prophetically	The kingdom of God is that messianic and worldwide millennial reign of Jesus, the King of Kings, heir to the Davidic throne, as prophesied in the Old Testament and in the New Testament for Israel and the world (see Acts 1:6; Rev. 11:15; 12:10).
Universally	God reigns over the entire creation: "His sovereignty rules over all" (Psa. 103:19). Ultimately after God's grand plan for time merges into eternity future, "Then comes the end, when He delivers up the kingdom to the God and Father, when He has abolished all rule and all authority and power. For He must reign until He has put all His enemies under His feet." (1 Cor. 15:24–25). Then the eternal triune God will be "all in all" (15:28) and the eternal throne will be that "of God and of the Lamb" (Rev. 22:1).

It is important to consider the expression "kingdom of God," which appears some sixty times in the four Gospels and fifteen times in the remainder of the New Testament. "Kingdom of heaven" can be found thirty-one times in the Gospel of Matthew, and not in any other gospel. Obviously the two expressions are interchangeable in many contexts, as a close examination of parallel passages reveals.

Unquestionably Jesus' pronouncement that "The time is fulfilled, and the kingdom of God is at hand" emphasized the real presentation and offer of the Davidic kingdom to Israel. "The time fulfilled may refer to the 483 years (69 weeks of years) which Daniel prophesied would end with the first advent of the Messiah. The 'kingdom' here is concerned with the dominion of the Messiah over Israel.[6]

But Jesus' offer was much more than political. It was also spiritual and required acceptance of Jesus as the Messiah. It was this spiritual dimension of the kingdom that prompted Jesus to call upon the people to "repent . . . and believe in the gospel."

Here we have the actual "beginning of the Gospel," as preached by Jesus. The Good News was revealed in a process, which culminated in the death, burial, and resurrection of Christ, which we now preach to the world, but the first stage of that process was to proclaim "the kingdom of God." Had the Jews received Him, that glorious millennial kingdom would have been established. Since Jesus was ultimately rejected as Israel's Messiah, the Davidic kingdom, that is, the literal earthy reign of Messiah—has been temporarily postponed.

The sense in which we understand the "kingdom of God" as it exists today is as the sphere of Christian profession on earth (see the parables of chapter 4). Those who respond to the message of the gospel are brought into this kingdom by means of the new birth. This aspect of the kingdom of God was revealed to Nicodemus early in Jesus' ministry (John 3).

When discussing the "kingdom of God," it is important to differentiate what is meant by this phrase. One must determine the use of the phrase in its context to understand its meaning.

The Servant Calls His First Disciples (1:16–20)

(Compare Matthew 4:18–22; Luke 5:1–11; John 1:35–42)

All but one of the twelve apostles to be chosen were from Galilee, a place that had been referenced by Isaiah (Isa. 9:1–2) as the place from which the light of the gospel would emerge when Messiah came (Matt. 4:15–16). During these initial contacts in what is sometimes called the early Perean ministry,

Jesus began the process of choosing His disciples. Twelve of these men would later become His apostles.

This was not the first time that Jesus had spoken with Andrew and Peter. Following His baptism, Jesus was approached by two of the disciples of John the Baptist, one of whom was Andrew, who brought his brother Peter to meet Jesus (cf. Matt. 16:16–20). Together they met with the Lord and evidently some others (John 1:35–42). This was at the Jordan River, north of the Dead Sea about sixty miles south of the Sea of Galilee.

In this pericope two sets of brothers are called. Without hesitation, they actually left their successful fishing business to follow Jesus full-time. First Andrew and Simon responded to the call, "Follow Me, and I will make you become fishers of men." Then James and John, the sons of Zebedee, likewise "left their father Zebedee in the boat with the hired servants" to become disciples and constant companions of Jesus as He continued His Galilean ministry.

The Servant Cures the Demoniac (1:21–28)

(Compare Luke 4:31–37)

Because of an earlier experience of rejection by the people of Nazareth (Luke 4:16–30), Jesus moved to Capernaum, a town some twenty miles north of Nazareth, which lay on the northwest shore of the Sea of Galilee. This became His base of operations and was referred to as His "own city" in Matthew 9:1.

Prior to the rise of opposition by the Jewish religious leaders, Jesus was welcomed in the synagogues where, "on the Sabbath He entered . . . and began to teach." But Jesus' teachings were unlike anything they had ever heard and, "they were amazed at His teaching; for He was teaching them as one having authority, and not as the scribes."

On this particular Sabbath morning, a demon-possessed man was present. When the unclean spirit within this man was confronted with the authoritative teaching of the "written Word of God," by the "living Word of God," it cried out, "What do we have to do with You, Jesus of Nazareth? Have You come to destroy us? I know who You are—the Holy One of God!" Because the timing of the revelation concerning His identity was premature, Jesus authoritatively rebuked the unclean spirit commanding, "Be quiet and come out of him!" Jesus issued these commands because the unclean spirit had no authority to announce who Jesus was nor did it have the right any longer to possess the man's mind and body.

Awed by this marvelous deliverance, the people pondered both Jesus' "new teaching" and the authority by which He commanded even the unclean spirits to leave victims. As a result of their exchanges about this event, "the news about Him went out everywhere into all the surrounding district of Galilee."

The Servant Heals Peter's Mother-in-law (1:29–31)

(Compare Matthew 8:14–15; Luke 4:38–39)

Upon leaving the synagogue, Jesus proceeded to Peter's house, no doubt invited by him to rest and share a meal. As they entered the house, Jesus was told that Peter's mother-in-law was "lying sick with a fever." Mark notes that Jesus, "came to her and raised her up . . . and the fever left her." This healing was instantaneous, final, and complete. Totally restored with no after effects, the healed woman immediately arose and "waited on them." Regarding healing, Lawrence O. Richards writes:

> Mark records a stream of healings in the opening chapters of his Gospel. Christians have often wondered, is there healing for us today? The Bible clearly indicates that God *can* heal. But in New Testament times God did not always heal even His most faithful servants (see 2 Cor. 12:7–10). When one of Paul's dearest friends was ill, the apostle did not "heal" him, but rather prayed and waited for God's answer (cf. Phil. 2:26–28). What Jesus' healings assure us of is that, whatever our need, God cares![7]

The Servant Heals Various Diseases (1:32–34)

(Compare Matthew 8:16–18; Luke 4:40–41)

When the word got out that Jesus had healed Peter's mother-in-law, the whole city responded by bringing to Him "all who were ill, and those that were demon-possessed." While only some thirty-six miracles performed by Jesus are described in the Gospels in any detail, there must have been hundreds, if not thousands, of cases in which Jesus healed and cured the sick. With a true servant's heart, He worked. Matthew Henry observes:

> How powerful the Physician was; he *healed all* that were brought to him, though ever so many. Nor was it some one particular disease, that Christ set up for the cure of, but he healed those that were *sick of divers* diseases, for his word was a *panpharmacon—a salve for every sore*.[8]

In eight places in the Gospels it is recorded that He healed a great many in a community with no further details given. He was truly the Great Physician.

JESUS WITHDRAWS FOR PRAYER

First Withdrawal (1:35)	*Following the initial year of preaching, performing miracles and summoning disciples, Jesus withdrew into a desert place for prayer before preaching in many synagogues of Galilee and performing additional miracles. (see Matt. 4:18–25; Luke 4:42, 44)*
Second Withdrawal (3:7–12)	*After the first confrontations with the Pharisees over the Sabbath and their initial alliance with the Herodians to destroy Him, Jesus withdrew to the sea before naming His twelve disciples and sending them forth to preach. (see Matt. 10:1–42; Luke 6:12–16)*
Third Withdrawal (6:30–7:23)	*After receiving a detailed report on the murder of John the Baptist and hearing the reports from the Twelve's preaching, Jesus withdrew by ship across the Sea of Galilee.*
Fourth Withdrawal (7:24–30)	*This time Jesus and His disciples withdrew to the north of Galilee around Tyre and Sidon.*
Fifth Withdrawal (7:31–8:13)	*Withdrawing from Phoenicia (Tyre and Sidon area), Jesus returned to the Sea of Galilee but went east of the lake and the Jordan to the area of Decapolis (Ten Cities).*
Sixth Withdrawal (8:13–9:29)	*After ministering again around the Sea of Galilee, the Lord went north to the Mediterranean coastal area west of Mount Hermon, where the Transfiguration occurred.*
Seventh Withdrawal (9:30–10:1)	*Jesus and His entourage passed through Galilee and Capernaum, quickly proceeding on east of Jordan and of Jerusalem and then to an area called Perea. (See Luke 13–18.) Now far from Galilee, He preached, taught, and heals the sick in this area.*

The Servant Withdraws for Prayer (1:35)

Mark records the next morning that "while it was still dark, [Jesus] arose and went out and departed to a lonely place, and was praying there." This was a pattern Jesus would repeat many times in His ministry. If Christ the God-man felt the need for solitude and prayer, how much more do we need, like Him, to arise before dawn to pray or spend an afternoon or even a whole night in prayer. Time spent with Jesus is always time well spent. In His prayer life, Jesus left us an example for us to follow in his steps (cf. 1 Pet. 2:21).

The Servant Travels through Galilee (1:36–39)

(Compare Luke 4:42–44)

Finding Jesus, Peter and the other disciples declared, "Everyone is looking for You." But Jesus told them, "Let us go somewhere else to the towns nearby in order that I may preach there also; for that is what I came out for." Although Jesus was presenting Himself as Israel's Messiah, He was also presenting Himself as Savior. It was important that He so present Himself throughout all of Israel and not only in Capernaum. D. A. Carson correctly notes: "Jesus refused to be sought out as a mere miracle-worker; he wanted to be recognized as a saviour. The way to achieve this was to *preach* the good news, and Jesus committed himself to doing that in the *nearby villages.*"[9]

Another reason it was important for Jesus to keep moving about was that the people were easily excitable and prone to taking things into their own hands. On more than one occasion, they would attempt to force Jesus into becoming their political king.

The Servant Heals a Leper (1:40–45)

(Compare Matthew 8:1–4; Luke 5:12–16)

Leprosy in biblical times was a dreaded disease; like a living death, it caused deterioration of the body over a long period of time. Quarantine and isolation were the fate of the leper (Lev. 13:45). Because of the possibility of contagion, touching a leper was considered ceremonially defiling and physically dangerous. In spite of this, Jesus touched the leper who came with faith, humility and urgency, requesting, "If You are willing, You can make me clean." Jesus' short response, "I am willing; be cleansed" resulted in an immediate and complete cure.

The Lord then commanded the former leper, "See that you say nothing to anyone; but go, show yourself to the priest and offer for your cleansing what

Moses commanded, for a testimony to them." The command not to mention the healing was not a complete censure but was in force until the man had followed the Jewish law and custom (Lev. 13:45; 14:1–32). This law required that the priest should acknowledge his condition, followed by the appropriate Levitical offerings. Remember that Jesus came to "fulfill the law," not to destroy it.

Contrary to Jesus' command, the former leper did not remain quiet, but publicized his healing to such a degree that Jesus was forced to withdraw to the desert for solitude. However, once the people discovered where He was, "they were continually coming." The word *coming* (*ērchonto*) is in Greek an imperfect middle indicative from *erchomai* meaning, they *continually came, kept coming,* to hear and see Him.

Wherever Christ went, He saw those who were in distress and brought gracious relief to multitudes of people, many of whom would come to recognize that He was God's great gift to humankind. At this point, however, no one realized the full scope of the gospel, the good news of Jesus' coming. No one could grasp its magnitude until after Jesus' supreme sacrifice for sins and His resurrection. That message of salvation crystallizes the gospel for this dispensation. Let us proclaim it until Jesus returns.

Study Questions

1. Give some of the evidence that shows Mark wanted to set Christ forth as a faithful servant. Why is it important to present Him as servant to the Gentile world?

2. What was involved in "John's baptism"? What was the meaning of baptism to the Jews at that time?

3. Why was Jesus baptized? Was it because He was a sinner?

4. If Christ's forerunner lived the life of an aesthetic in the wilderness, why not Jesus?

5. How does Jesus' message differ from John's focus on repentance?

6. Could Jesus Christ have sinned when He was tempted by Satan? If He could not, what does this tell us of His person?

7. What was the importance to the Jewish people of all of the miracles Christ was performing in chapter 1? How did they impact the Jews spiritually?

8. Why did Christ touch the leper but not the demon possessed man?

CHAPTER 2

The Servant Responds to His Critics
Mark 2:1-28

Preview

In this second chapter, Christ comes again to Capernaum, which becomes his Galilean base of operations, but He meets growing hostility early in His ministry. When Christ speaks of forgiving sins, the scribes question Him in their hearts (v. 7). When Christ goes to Levi the publican's home, the scribes criticize Him (v. 16). When the Pharisees notice that Jesus does not practice fasting, their question contrasts Jesus with John the Baptist (v. 18). When Jesus and His disciples pluck ears of corn to eat on the Sabbath day, the Pharisees again raise a question (v. 24). Jesus responds to each criticism and question with spiritual wisdom and truth.

The Servant Heals the Paralytic (2:1-12)
(Compare Matthew 9:1-8; Luke 5:17-26)

Once Jesus had completed His itinerate ministry in the surrounding area, He came "back to Capernaum." By this time, many reports of the amazing ministry of this new preacher had been circulated and many desired to see Him. This being the case, it was impossible for Jesus to remain hidden and finally "it was heard that he was at home." This was more than likely Peter's house near the Sea of Galilee and was well known to the townspeople.

Upon discovering that Jesus was in town and "at home" the people immediately began to gather together, "so that there was no longer room, even near

21

the door." No doubt many of the townspeople were curious and came to see if what they had been hearing about the Nazarene was in fact true.

Jesus' popularity was a two-edged sword, and because of it, He encountered conflict very early in His ministry. This conflict came from the "Pharisees and teachers of the law sitting there, who had come from every village of Galilee, and Judea, and from Jerusalem" (Luke 5:17). Whereas the common folk were there to hear Jesus and welcomed His ministry, these Jewish leaders were there with malicious motives.

On this occasion Jesus had likely come to Peter's house to rest, but seeing the great need of the people, "He was speaking the word to them." We are not told how long He had been preaching, but at some point during His message, four men came "bringing [literally "carrying, bearing"] to Him a paralytic."

Mark records that the crowd was so thick that they were "unable to get to Him [Jesus]," but this did not dissuade them. Hauling the sick man along with them, they climbed up onto the top of the house. Once they were sure that they were just above Jesus, they "removed the roof" and carefully, "let down the pallet on which the paralytic was lying." Concerning these four men, Warren Wiersbe remarks:

> We must admire several characteristics of these men, qualities that ought to mark us as "fishers of men." For one thing, they were deeply concerned about their friend and wanted to see him helped. They had the faith to believe that Jesus could and would meet his need. They did not simply "pray about it," but they put some feet to their prayers; and they did not permit the difficult circumstances to discourage them. They worked together and dared to do something different, and Jesus rewarded their efforts. How easy it would have been for them to say, "Well, there is no sense trying to get to Jesus today! Maybe we can come back tomorrow."[1]

Each of the Synoptics specifies that "Jesus saw their faith." What was it exactly that Jesus saw? Simply put, it was their unstoppable, unashamed determination to get their friend to Jesus. This act in and of itself spoke volumes. These four unnamed men gave evidence to their faith in Jesus' power to heal their friend. He who came to serve was moved. Mark records that upon seeing the evidence of their faith, Jesus said to the sick man, "My son, your sins are forgiven."

As they were "reasoning in their hearts," the assessment of the Jewish leaders, "who can forgive sins but God alone?" was correct (cf. Exod. 34:6–9; Psa. 103:3; 130:4; Isa. 43:25 ; 44:22; 48:11; Dan. 9:9), but their conclusion, "Why does this man speak that way? He is blaspheming" was wrong.

Perceiving, "in His spirit that they were reasoning that way within themselves," Jesus did not wait for them to voice their thoughts but immediately addressed them saying, "Why are you reasoning about these things in your hearts?" This statement alone should have caused them to realize that He was no mere mortal. How many men had they encountered who could read their thoughts?

Jesus continued, "Which is easier, to say to the paralytic 'Your sins are forgiven'; or to say, 'Arise, and take up your pallet and walk'?" This question was designed to compel them to reflect upon Jesus' ministry. They were well aware of His ability to heal and cast out demons, but they had not yet put the facts together regarding who He really was. These questions forced these Jewish leaders to reconsider their theology. Lawrence O. Richards comments:

> Jesus answered their unspoken objection in a graphic way. Which is easier: to tell a paralyzed man that he is forgiven, or to heal him? The answer is clear. It is far *easier* to speak of forgiveness. Who could possibly look into a man's heart to see if he was forgiven? It's easy to say, "You're forgiven," because who could really tell? How different to say, "Take up your bed and walk." Everyone can see, then, if the speaker has authority![2]

Jesus had these religious leaders right were He wanted them and as they meditated upon His words, He took the next step in revealing who He was by saying, "But in order that you may know that the Son of Man has authority on earth to forgive sins" [this was the principal question which Jesus set out to answer]—He said to the paralytic—I say to you, rise, take up your pallet and go home." This is the first of fourteen times that the title "Son of man" is used in Mark's gospel (cf. 2:28; 8:31, 38; 9:9, 12, 31; 10:33, 45; 13:26; 14:21, 41, 62). This title comes from Daniel 7:13–14 and in due course became a designation of the Messiah. It is the title that Jesus most often used when referring to Himself.

Jesus had cunningly set the stage and maneuvered the religious leaders into facing the fact that His authority to heal and His authority to forgive sins not only came from God but revealed that He *was* God. Royce Gordon Gruenler explains:

> The charge that Jesus is blaspheming is their reply to what is ironically a true theological statement. They understand Jesus' syllogism: (1) only God can forgive sins; (2) I am forgiving sins; (3) therefore, I am claiming to stand in the very place of God and to exercise his authority.[3]

This confrontation over authority served as an opportunity for Jesus to reveal His true identity as the Son of God. The Jewish leaders understood this and could not respond. Lawrence O. Richards points out: "Those who argue that Jesus never claimed to be God ignore this passage. The religious experts of His day did not. Jesus claimed a divine prerogative and thus laid claim to be God. Forgiving and healing are equally impossible for man, equally easy for God."[4]

The truth of Jesus' claim was confirmed in what happened next. "He rose and immediately took up the pallet and went out in the sight of all; so that they were all amazed and were glorifying God, saying, 'We have never seen anything like this.'" It should be noted that while the religious leaders stumbled at Jesus' words and actions, the common people were amazed and glorified God.

The Servant Calls Levi (Matthew) (2:13–15)

(Compare Matthew 9:9; Luke 5:27–28)

Mark often introduces new circumstances by mentioning Jesus' surroundings (eg. Mark 1:16; 2:13; 4:1; 7:31). In the preceding pericope, Mark presents Jesus as the "forgiver of sins." To further drive home the point that Jesus has God's authority, Mark shifts to another instance where this authority comes into play. Here he records that some time later, Jesus, "went out again by the seashore; and all the multitude were coming to Him, and He was teaching them."

Apparently, as Jesus was walking on the shore of the sea of Galilee, He noticed, "Levi [Matthew] the son of Alphaeus sitting in the tax office." Levi, a Jew, served Rome as a publican, or tax collector (cf. Matt. 10:3; Luke 5:27). As such, he was considered a traitor by his countrymen. This is understandable given that tax collectors often profited from their position through extortion. Furthermore, publicans were often grouped by others with "sinners" (cf. Matt. 9:10–11; 11:19; Mark 2:15–16; Luke 5:30; 7:34; 15:1) and prostitutes (cf. Matt. 21:31–32).

Interestingly, Jesus called out to him, "Follow Me" and without wavering, this man so despised by his Jewish countrymen "rose and followed Him." D. A. Carson appropriately notes the impact of this act:

> We miss the wonder of Levi's call if we do not remember all that "tax collector" meant in those days. It meant all that "loan-shark" means to us today, with the added idea of collaborator, for it usually involved working for the hated imperial power or the equally hated local dictator, Herod. Tax collectors were usually greedy, dishonest and immoral. Worse still, to a Jew, they were ceremonially unclean through mixing continually with non-Jewish people.[5]

As if Levi's call was not scandalous enough, Jesus later went to his home and reclined "at the table in his house" (cf. Luke 5:29–39). Normally in Middle Eastern culture a special invitation to eat at someone's home was considered an honor for the guest. However, the acceptance by someone of Jesus' reputation of an invitation to dine was considered an even greater honor for the host and his family. Add to this the fact that dinner was eaten while in a reclined position, with the guest given the most honored position at the table, and you have a level of intimacy that is unknown in western culture.

Mark records that along with Levi, "many tax-gatherers and sinners were dining with Jesus and His disciples." Although we are not specifically told, it is possible that Jesus' acceptance of Levi, and Levi's subsequent calling, may have influenced this large group of publicans to follow Jesus. No doubt as they saw the divine Servant's love in action, they realized that while it was one thing to forgive someone whom He would never see again, it was another thing entirely to welcome a well-known sinner as one of His very own disciples!

The Servant Answers the Pharisees' Criticisms (2:16–28)

(Compare Matthew 9:10–17; Luke 5:29–39)

Mark inserts Levi's call (cf. Matt. 9:9) and the subsequent criticism of the scribes and Pharisees here because it theologically parallels the scenario with the healing of the paralytic above. As in the previous situation, Jesus' actions flew in the face of Jewish tradition, and this could not go uncontested.

In this situation there were scribes and Pharisees (perhaps even some of the same ones) present who were gathered outside Levi's house to keep from becoming "defiled." When they saw that Jesus and His disciples ate with "tax-gatherers and sinners,"[6] they were greatly offended and questioned His disciples, asking them, "Why is He eating and drinking with tax-gatherers and sinners?" Luke records that they asked the disciples the same question (Luke 5:30). James R. Brooks explains why this was a problem for the scribes and Pharisees:

> Those who live in modern, Western society with comparatively few social distinctions have difficulty realizing just how scandalous it was for Jesus to associate with outcasts. In Semitic society table fellowship was one of the most intimate expressions of friendship. For this reason the religious leaders could not understand how Jesus could be a religious person and dine with "bad characters" (v. 15, NEB).[7]

In reality this was a formal attack on Jesus Himself, but instead of directing their question to Him as they should have, the scribes hoped to sow discord among the disciples. Regarding these Jewish leaders, R. C. H. Lenski remarks:

> They were out to spy upon Jesus, having come to Capernaum from far and near for that very purpose. Some were from Judea and Jerusalem, Luke 5:17. So they saw the company gathering at Levi's house. They themselves, of course, did not enter the place, for that would have contaminated them. They waited outside until the guests came out and then assailed the disciples, for despite all their hostility to Jesus they never show any real courage in facing him on the issues they feel constrained to raise.[8]

Jesus did not subscribe to the "high morals" of the scribes and the Pharisees, and this became a point of contention for them. As they began questioning His disciples, Jesus overheard what they were saying and said to them, "It is not those who are healthy who need a physician, but those who are sick."

By giving this response, Jesus artfully turned the tables on these religious hypocrites. He made it very clear that in His mind, these sinners were like sick people in need of a doctor. Since a doctor's purpose is to bring healing and restoration to those who are sick, it would be ridiculous for the doctor to spend his time with those who were well. Moreover, Jesus added that His purpose was not to "call the righteous, but sinners." This statement played upon the fact that these Jewish leaders considered themselves "the righteous" and all others "sinners." Jesus was saying that if they were truly righteous, they too would be reaching out to those in need.

The scribes questioning of Jesus and the disciples revealed that they did not put themselves in a position to be ministered to by Jesus. As the apostle Paul put it, they "judged themselves unworthy of eternal life" (Acts 13:46). Matthew records that Jesus also said, "But go and learn what this means; I desire compassion, and not sacrifice" (Matt. 9:13). Though these men were famous for their personal (yet hypocritical) sacrifices, they were devoid of mercy and compassion and went about to justify their evil attitudes (cf. Luke 16:15). Jesus' response to their questions was intended to expose their impious hearts by showing them that they were even worse than the publicans and sinners they denounced because they refused to (1) acknowledge their need and (2) accept Jesus' ministry.

Mark introduces the third confrontation in this periscope, by noting that "John's disciples and the Pharisees were fasting." Although John had actual disciples, the Pharisees did not, and therefore it is probably best to understand the use of "disciples" here in a broader sense to refer to those who had heeded John's preaching and those who although not Pharisees themselves, followed their strict regimen. The phrase "were fasting" is an imperfect peri-phrastic construction (*ēsan . . . nēsteuontes*) and probably suggests that these "disciples" were actively fasting when they came to Jesus.

Confronting Jesus, they asked Him, "Why do John's disciples and the disciples of the Pharisees fast, but Your disciples do not fast?" D. Edmond Hiebert explains the reason for their question:

> During the time of Jesus, the pious Pharisees fasted twice a week (Luke 18:12), on the second and fifth day. If the feast of Levi fell on the evening beginning either of their weekly fast days, the disciples of Jesus were feast-ing at the very time the pious Pharisees were fasting. Since Jesus and His disciples formed an earnest religious group, it was regarded as astonish-ing that they did not adhere to the pious practice.[9]

Strictly speaking, neither Jesus nor His disciples were breaking the law by not fasting, and one cannot determine from the context whether there was a hostile motive behind the question. Jesus' answer does not seem to be correc-tive in nature, and so it would seem that their question was genuine.

Jesus responded by using a metaphor that was clearly understood in Jewish circles, namely, a wedding. He said, "While the bridegroom is with them, the attendants of the bridegroom do not fast, do they? So long as they have the bridegroom with them, they cannot fast." Isaiah and Jeremiah both had previously used the marriage relationship as an illustration of Israel's being married to Jehovah (Isa. 54:5; Jer. 31:32). Now Jesus, using veiled lan-guage, directly identifies Himself as Israel's husband (cf. Hos. 2:14–23) and therefore as Jehovah!

When identifying Jesus, John the Baptist had likewise announced that Jesus was the Bridegroom. "He who has the bride is the bridegroom; but the friend of the bridegroom, who stands and hears him, rejoices greatly because of the bridegroom's voice. And so this joy of mine has been made full" (John 3:29). Jesus answered John's disciples by using a metaphor that they should have remembered and understood. Accepting the Baptist's own explanation of who He was, Jesus further developed this concept by equating His disci-ples with members of the wedding party, "the attendants of the bridegroom," or more literally, the groomsmen. Although the disciples of John were fast-ing (perhaps because of the arrest of John), it was not appropriate for "the attendants of the bridegroom" to fast because the Bridegroom was in their presence.

Jesus continued, "But the days will come, when the bridegroom is taken away from them, and then they will fast in that day." The disciples of Jesus were presently rejoicing because of Jesus' presence, but it would not be long before the Bridegroom would be taken away (the first hint of Jesus' coming death in Mark's gospel), then they would fast. In the Greek, the phrase "is taken away" (aorist, passive, subjunctive of *apairō*) suggests a violent removal (cf. Isa. 53:8). This word is used in each of the Synoptics (cf. Matt. 9:15; Luke 5:35) but is found nowhere else in the New Testament.

Jesus terminated this confrontation with John's disciples and the Pharisees by using an analogy with which they would be familiar, a torn piece of cloth. No one in their right mind would attempt to repair an old garment by sewing a fresh, new piece to it, because the new piece of fabric, which had not been preshrunk, when it did shrink, would easily tear away from the rest of the garment, making the original hole much worse. Similarly, no wise person would put new wine into an old wineskin, because the internal gases would cause the old wineskin to burst.

The disciples of John and of the Pharisees had come to Jesus complaining about His failure to accept and follow the common fasting "tradition," but His comments uniquely addressed a much broader need, namely, that "one puts new wine into fresh wineskins." What did Jesus mean by this?

Matthew recorded that Jesus came to fulfill the law (cf. Matt. 5:17). As the fulfillment of the law, Jesus' presence signified both the transitory nature of the dispensation of law and the forthcoming introduction of a new dispensation of grace (cf. John 1:17). Any endeavor to unite the new dispensation of grace with the previous dispensation of law would be like sowing a new piece of cloth onto an old, wornout garment or like putting new wine in old, wornout wineskins. Jesus' message of salvation could not and must not be mixed with the Mosaic Law or traditional Judaism. This was later echoed by the apostle Paul in his epistle to the Galatians (cf. Gal. 1:6–9).

At this stage in His ministry, Jesus had demonstrated that He did not adhere to the Sabbath traditions, having delivered the man possessed by demons (Mark 1:21–28) and having healed Peter's mother-in-law on the Sabbath (Mark 1:29–31). He had also healed the lame man at the Pool of Bethesda on the Sabbath (John 5:1–9). The fourth confrontation that Jesus experienced specifically dealt with this failure to conform to the traditional Sabbath observances. Warren Wiersbe explains why this was important:

> The Sabbath was cherished by the Jews as a sacred institution. God gave the people of Israel the Sabbath after they came out of Egypt (Exod. 20:8–11; Neh. 9:14), and it was a special sign between Israel and Jehovah (Exod. 31:13–17). There is no record in Scripture that God ever gave the Sabbath to any other nation. So, when Jesus began openly to violate the Sabbath traditions, it was like declaring war against the religious establishment.[10]

Mark records, "It came about that He was passing through the grainfields on the Sabbath, and His disciples began to make their way along while picking the heads of grain." The Law of Moses specifically established certain acts that were forbidden on the Sabbath (see, e.g. Exod. 20:10; 35:3; Num. 15:32–36; Jer. 17:21–27; Neh. 10:31; 13:15, 19), but over time rabbinical tradition stepped into the picture and added many extra requirements, changing the Sabbath from a day of rest and reflection upon God to a day of religious bondage.

Upon seeing the actions of the disciples, the Pharisees charged them with breaking the Sabbath, saying "See here, why are they doing what is not lawful on the Sabbath?" In reality they were not breaking the Sabbath, for the Law of Moses also stated that a hungry person could pass through his neighbor's field and "eat his fill" of fruit or grain, as long as he did not put any of it into a vessel or use a sickle to harvest it (Deut. 23:24–25). The issue came down to the fact that the Pharisees were forcing their traditional interpretation of "working on the Sabbath" into the text.

Instead of debating traditional interpretation with them, Jesus went directly to the Scriptures to support the actions of His disciples, reminding them that when David and his men had need, they partook of the showbread. Moreover, He then claimed to be the Lord of the Sabbath. Royce Gordon Gruenler explains:

> Jewish law forbade reaping on the Sabbath (one of thirty-nine works forbidden on the Sabbath), but Jesus replies by citing two higher levels of authority than Pharisaic tradition. First, in the time of Abiathar who later became high priest (the likely meaning of the reference), David and his companions ate the consecrated bread in the house of God when they were hungry (1 Sam. 21:1–6) and were not condemned for it, though they had technically broken the law. *Their need invoked a higher law and a special dispensation that took precedence over ritual law.* Second, by analogy, but in an even greater sense, the source of the law itself, the Son of man, has given permission to his followers to pluck grain on the Sabbath, for he is Lord of the Sabbath and restores its true intent as a day designed to benefit, not deprive man of well-being and health (emphasis mine).[11]

With these words, Jesus revealed two things: that He condoned David's actions and, that as Lord of the Sabbath, He was not constrained by it. The One who had demonstrated that He had power to forgive sins also had authority over traditional Sabbath observances! The Pharisees had twisted God's original intent for the Sabbath, and Jesus exposed this along with their evil hearts.

Study Questions

1. What are some of the more often repeated words in Mark?

2. Did the paralytic man who was carried by his four friends have faith of his own?

3. Can a person ask for forgiveness and yet not understand all it entails? Explain.

4. What did Christ do to make forgiveness available?

5. In chapter 2, how many false accusations against Christ are there here?

6. Why should believers fast now? What value is there in fasting?

7. What lessons is Christ teaching when He describes the old wineskins and the new wineskins?

CHAPTER 3

The Servant Chooses the Twelve
Mark 3:1-35

Preview

Our Lord, the Servant and Son of God, continued going about doing good and healing all who were oppressed (Acts 10:38), but He met rising opposition, criticism, and slander. He chose the Twelve, who would become part of the foundation of the church, which was yet to be established (Eph. 2:20). The Pharisees and Herodians plotted against Him. Enthusiastic crowds surrounded Him. The Twelve followed Him. His friends thought He was crazy and sought to restrain Him. The scribes attributed His power to Satan. His mother and brothers came to reason with Him, but He had established a wonderful new family.

The Servant: Healing a Withered Hand (3:1-6)

(Compare Matthew 12:9-14; Luke 6:6-11)

In the previous chapter the Pharisees had accused the disciples of breaking the law as they plucked some ears of corn on the Sabbath (2:23–28). This chapter begins with another Sabbath conflict. Each synoptic writer has these conflicts in succession, signifying the deep-seated antagonism of the religious leaders toward Jesus.

As was His custom on the Sabbath, Jesus once again went to the local synagogue to teach the people (cf. 1:21, 39; see also Luke 6:6). On this occasion, a man was present who had a withered right hand, an observation made only by Luke the physician. The Greek word translated "withered" is a perfect passive participle, suggesting that the man's hand had not always been in this condition. Moreover, the definition of this word suggests that the man's hand had become paralyzed as the result of some accident.

Like vultures flying over roadkill, the scribes and Pharisees "were continually watching" (imperfect active indicative) Him. This verb "watching" literally means "to lie in wait for." The idea is that these men were intently scrutinizing Jesus in the hopes that they might catch His words or actions so as to bring charges against Him. More specifically they were watching Jesus to see if He would heal this man's withered hand, "on the Sabbath, in order that they might accuse Him."

These men were very familiar with Jesus' healing ministry and His compassion; therefore they planted this man in the synagogue to entrap Jesus. The issue at hand was whether Jesus would maintain established tradition. Interestingly, rabbinical tradition did allow for healing on the Sabbath but only under specific circumstances. John D. Grassmick says: "They permitted healing on the Sabbath only if a life was in danger. This man's problem was not life-threatening and could wait till the next day; so if Jesus healed him, they could accuse Him of being a Sabbath violator, an offense punishable by death (cf. Ex. 31:14-17)."[1]

Luke records that Jesus "knew what they were thinking" (Luke 6:8) while Matthew records that these men actually asked Him, "Is it lawful to heal on the Sabbath?" (Matt. 12:10). Although the text does not tell us how, it is apparent that Jesus somehow maneuvered these hypocrites into articulating what they were thinking. "Apparently, when Jesus gave an indication that He intended to heal the man, they raised the legal question challenging the propriety of the act."[2]

Once this question was put to Him, Jesus followed it by giving the illustration of the lost sheep (Matt. 12:11-13) and stating that "it is lawful to do good on the Sabbath" (v. 12). As the dutiful Servant, Jesus always sought to correct the errant scriptural views of the Jews. Then He called upon the man with the withered hand to "Rise and come forward." Jesus was about to establish a Sabbath precedent, and it was imperative that everyone present understand it. Therefore He had the man stand up in the midst of the accusers so that everyone could see him.

While this pitiful man stood before the entire assembly, Jesus, in rabbinical fashion, responded to the religious leaders by asking His own question, "Is it lawful on the Sabbath to do good or to do harm, to save a life, or to kill?"

Jesus had established with the illustration of the lost sheep that doing good on the Sabbath was lawful. By turning the question upon them, He forced them to acknowledge the same because a man of greater value of a sheep (cf. Matt. 12:12). R. C. H. Lenski observes:

These Jews made the alternative either "to do" or "not to do on the Sabbath" and then decided that lawfulness required the latter and disregarded everything else and entirely misconceived the purpose of the Sabbath. They made it a law that was strictly imposed on man instead of a blessing bestowed on man. They thus allowed no work of mercy for suffering man on the Sabbath although they would inconsistently work to save a sheep on the Sabbath, for they would not want to lose the sheep. But some man they would treat heartlessly—his suffering meant no loss to them. So Jesus restates the question in the way in which it ought to be put: "Is it lawful to do good, namely what is morally excellent, on the Sabbath or to do harm, what is morally base?" Thus put, the question answers itself. Deeds that are morally excellent would only grace and honor the old Jewish legal Sabbath.[3]

The logical conclusion of doing good on the Sabbath required that the scribes and Pharisees should have acknowledged their hypocrisy, but instead, "they kept silent," refusing to admit their error.

Having put His question to them, Jesus then "looked around at them." His gaze went from one person to the next searching for any hint of repentance and compassion, but He found none. Then His gaze became filled "with anger" because He was grieved at "their hardness of heart." John D. Grassmick writes: "This is the only explicit reference to Jesus' anger in the New Testament. It was nonmalicious indignation coupled with deep sorrow (grief) at their obstinate insensitivity (*pōrōsei*, "hardening," cf. Rom. 11:25; Eph. 4:18) to God's mercy and human misery."[4]

Rarely did the Son of God become angry, but this was a just and righteous indignation, directed against hypocrisy and the elevation of human religious rules above the deep human and spiritual need of people. Regarding the fact that the divinity becomes angry, R. C. H. Lenski writes:

That God or that Jesus should ever become angry has been passionately denied. This denial is, however, based on the common conception of human anger, a passionate flaring up which is always sinful. *The divine anger is far different; it is the holy reaction in the heart of God or of Jesus against man's hardness of heart.* God and Jesus are not impassive; man's sin and wicked resistance stir them most deeply. Anger, in this sense, is ascribed to God throughout the Scriptures. Only wrong conceptions of both God as a person and of what holy anger really is can lead to the denial of the divine anger (emphasis added).[5]

Once it became obvious that no one was going to stand up for truth, Jesus commanded the deformed man to stretch out his hand. Again, this was done as a witness to all those present. Mark records that immediately upon doing as Jesus commanded, "his hand was restored." Regarding this healing, D. Edmond Hiebert writes:

> All eyes in the synagogue were fixed on that extended hand; as they watched, the hand was instantly, completely restored. The healing was an act of Jesus' own volition, wrought without a touch or the use of external means. Jesus thus did nothing that violated their trivial Sabbath regulations. The healing did not even have the appearance of work. It was unmistakably an act of supernatural power. His ability to heal the man's hand by the exercise of His will was proof that Jesus was more than a mere man.[6]

Having no means by which they could arrest Jesus, these hard-hearted religious leaders left the synagogue. So great was their hatred of Jesus that they set aside their precious legalism and immediately "began taking counsel with the Herodians against Him, as to how they might destroy him."

The Herodians represented a group of politically oriented Jews who supported King Herod and his rule. They were despised by patriotic Jews and ostracized by religious Jews. The fact that the Pharisees would enlist their aid speaks to the intense hatred they felt for Jesus. Normally these two groups would never have associated together but now they had a common enemy. This is the first of four references concerning the conspiracy to kill Jesus (cf. 11:18; 12:12; 14:1). Healing on the Sabbath was deemed a crime worthy of death by these religious bigots, but conspiring to have someone killed on the Sabbath was lawful.

The Servant: Withdrawing to the Sea (3:7–12)

(Compare Matthew 12:15–21; Luke 6:17–19)

Jesus' reaction to the threat of the Pharisees and the Herodians was to withdraw with His disciples from Capernaum proper eastward to the shore of the Sea of Galilee. This was not due to fear but rather because His time had not yet come and there was much work to be done. By this time Jesus' fame had reached such a level that wherever He went, great multitudes of people followed after Him. Mark notes that "a great multitude heard of all that He was doing and came to Him" from Galilee, Judea, Jerusalem, and Idumaea, and from beyond Jordan and the area around Tyre and Sidon.

Jesus was always ready to minister to the needs of the people, and Mark records that during the course of the day "He had healed many." The atmosphere must have been electric as Jesus moved among the people, for the witness of healing power incited hope within those who had plagues, and they too "pressed about Him in order to touch Him," believing that touching His person would secure healing for them too. Because of the press of the crowd, Jesus told the disciples to have a small ship ready in the event that He needed to free Himself from them.

Mark also records that among those needing healing, there were also many who had "unclean spirits." These demons, upon seeing Jesus, "would fall down before Him, and cry out, saying, You are the Son of God." It is fascinating to consider that right in the middle of this mighty move of God, demons manifested themselves and tried to deflect attention from Jesus to themselves. But it was not appropriate that demons should give testimony to who Jesus was, so He "earnestly warned them not to make Him known." Ironically, the demons recognized Jesus for who He was while the religious leaders and the multitudes that clamored after Him did not.

The Servant: Selecting the Disciples (3:13-19)

(Compare Matthew 10:1-4: Luke 6:12-16; Acts 1:13)

In preparation for the appointing of the Twelve, Mark notes that Jesus went up into a mountain in preparation for the appointing of the Twelve. Luke further explains that the reason for this seclusion was prayer. In fact, Luke records that Jesus, "spent the whole night in prayer to God" (Luke 6:12).

When daybreak finally came, Jesus then "summoned those whom He Himself wanted, and they came to Him." This is a significant statement. The choice of these men had nothing to do with their abilities, nor did they have any say in it. Their will in no way influenced Jesus' decision. The choice was His and His alone (see the table "Seven Observations from the Pericope," p.37).

Having personally called these men from among His larger group of disciples (cf. Mark 2:15), Jesus then publicly ordained them in the midst of the others, specifically naming them "apostles" (Luke 6:13). The purpose Mark gives for Jesus' choice of these apostles was twofold. First, it was for companionship, "that they might be with Him," and second, it was so that "He might send them out to preach." Included in their calling to minister was the "authority to cast out the demons."

It was supremely important that the order should not be reversed! It was imperative that the apostles should first learn from their master. This would best be accomplished by living with Him and studying under Him day and night. Only when they were sufficiently instructed, could they be sent out to minister. That day was not so very far off, and when it finally would come, their message would be identical to Jesus' message, namely, that "The kingdom of heaven is at hand" (cf. Matt. 10:7).

In listing the names of the apostles, Mark and Luke merely separate them with the conjunction and, while Matthew separates them into pairs. In each list Peter is first and Judas Iscariot is named last. Each list contains the same names although the order varies.

Comparative Listing of the Twelve Apostles

Matthew 10:2–4	Mark 3:16–19	Luke 6:14–16	Acts 1:13
1. Simon Peter	Simon Peter	Simon Peter	Peter
2. Andrew	James	Andrew	John
3. James	John	James	James
4. John	Andrew	John	Andrew
5. Philip	Philip	Philip	Philip
6. Bartholomew	Bartholomew	Bartholomew	Thomas
7. Thomas	Matthew	Matthew	Bartholomew
8. Matthew	Thomas	Thomas	Matthew
9. James of Alphaeus	James of Alphaeus	James of Alphaeus	Jas. of Alphaeus
10. Thaddaeus	Thaddaeus	Simon the Zealot	Simon the Zealot
11. Simon the Canaanite	Simon the Canaanite	Judas of James	Judas of James
12. Judas Iscariot	Judas Iscariot	Judas Iscariot	— — —

The first apostle named is Simon, whom Jesus surnames Peter ("a stone"). That is what he was to become under Jesus' mentoring. His name is first in all the lists, and he was the principle spokesman for the Twelve, as is clear from his involvement on the Day of Pentecost, in the house of Cornelius, and in his entire ministry. Andrew, Peter's brother, met Jesus first and later brought the future fiery leader to Christ (John 1:40–42). Next in order are James and John, two brothers Jesus surnamed Boanerges, sons of thunder, indicative of their energetic personalities. It was these two "energetic" disciples who approached Jesus with the desire to sit at His right and left hand in the kingdom age (Mark 10:35–37). James was the first apostolic martyr (Acts 12:1–2), while John outlived all of the other apostles and authored the book of Revelation in A.D. 95–96. These men made up the first grouping of apostles.

The second group of apostles included Phillip and Bartholomew (also called Nathanael) who were linked together with Andrew and Peter, the former bringing the latter to Christ (John 1:45–51). Matthew (also called Levi) was a hated tax collector who left all to follow Jesus. He later wrote the gospel bearing his name. Thomas (also called Didymus), both of whose names mean "twin" (John 11:16), is unfortunately best known because of his lack of faith (John 20:24–29). Tradition records that Thomas carried the gospel to India.

The final grouping of apostles includes James of Alphaeus, probably the same as James the Less. Also in this group is Thaddaeus, sometimes called Judas the brother of James, or Lebbaeus (the KJV adds the words "the brother of " when referring to this Judas in Luke and in Acts, however, these words do not appear in the Greek text [cf. Luke 6:16; Acts 1:13]). A better translation would be Judas, son of James.), Simon the Canaanite or Zealot (the Hebrew word [Canaanite] means "Zealot") who may have belonged to the radical Jewish party of patriots known as Zealots, and Judas Iscariot, "man of Kerioth," the only non-Galilean, who was doomed to eternal infamy as the betrayer of Christ. The Twelve formed the nucleus from which all of Christianity would eventually spring.

As is his custom, Mark now once again shifts scenes, leaving out many details that take place between verses 19 and 20. These include the Sermon on the Mount recorded in Matthew 5–7 and the events recorded in Luke 7:1–8:3.

Seven Observations from This Pericope

- *Jesus Himself was responsible for their being chosen*
- *They responded immediately.*
- *Jesus specifically appointed a limited group*
- *They Jesus' first companions—listening, learning, and beholding Him*
- *They were destined ultimately to preach*
- *They were given power to heal*
- *They were given authority over demons*

The Servant: Charged with Madness (3:20–21)

Mark frequently uses a literary device in which he introduces a subject and then interjects another topic. He will then come back to his original subject some verses later. This has been referred to as a "sandwich" structure and can be seen in numerous places throughout his gospel (cf. 5:21–43; 6:7–31; 11:12–26; 14:1–11, 27–52). The purpose for this device is usually to provide an emphasis or contrast. This is the case here. Mark introduces the topic of Jesus' family in verses 20–21 and concludes it in verses 31–35. However, in verses 22–30 he records the account of Jesus being accused of being in league with Beelzebub.

How much time elapsed between the appointing of the Twelve and the events recorded in this pericope is unknown but it seems that Jesus and the Twelve were "in the house" preparing to eat after having spent themselves ministering to the people. Meal preparation in those days was a lengthy process, and while they were waiting, the crowds again began to gather outside the house. The needs of the people were such that, "they could not even eat a meal."

Matthew records that among those needing help was a demon possessed man who was both blind and dumb. In compassion Jesus left the table, went outside, and "healed him, so that the dumb man spoke and saw" (Matt. 12:22–23; cf. Luke 11:14). Some of Jesus' relatives (*oi par autou* refers to family members here, not friends) had also shown up at the house, and seeing that He was not allowing Himself time to eat, "they went out to take custody of Him; for they were saying, 'He has lost His senses'." The Greek word for "to lay hold on "is *krateō* (literally "to take control of") and is also used in the sense of "to arrest" (cf. Mark 6:17; 12:12; 14:1, 44, 46, 49, 51). The NET Bible observes:

> It is probably Mark's intention in this structure to show that Jesus' family is to be regarded as not altogether unlike the experts in the law [scribes] in their perception of the true identity of Jesus; they are incorrect in their understanding of him as well. The tone is obviously one of sadness, and the emphasis on Jesus' true family in vv. 31–35 serves to underscore the comparison between his relatives and the scribes on the one hand, and those who truly obey God on the other.[7]

Perhaps Jesus' relatives were well meaning and sincere in their desire to help. After all, everyone needs to eat and rest. But Jesus told them, "I have food to eat that you do not know about " (John 4:32) nor were they as of yet "believing in Him" (John 7:5). In reality, it is more likely that they wanted to rescue Him from what they supposed were delusions of grandeur. Interestingly, it is only in Mark's gospel that we find this instance Jesus' relatives charging Him with madness.

The Servant: Accused of Using Satanic Power (3:22–30)
(Compare Matthew 12:22–32; Luke 11:14–23)

Mark does not record the miracle of the healing of the possessed man nor the reaction of the multitude but Matthew does, noting that "all the multitudes were amazed, and began to say, 'This man cannot be the Son of David, can He?'" (Matt. 12:23; cf. also Luke 11:14). The title "Son of David" was uniquely messianic in nature and reveals that at least on some level the people were beginning to think of Jesus in this manner. Matthew records that it was this questioning among the people that stirred up the scribes (v. 24). It is at this point that Mark picks up the narration.

That Jesus was doing incredible miracles was beyond question. His servanthood was undeniable. However, it had also been demonstrated that this Jesus was a Sabbath violator and did not adhere to the traditions of the rabbis. In fact, the Jewish leadership was secretly conspiring with the Herodians to put Him to death!

This was a serious problem for the scribes because the crowd was ready to declare Jesus to be the Messiah. The scribes had to find some way to acknowledge the miracles that were being done among the people while at the same time discrediting them.

Mark records how this was done, noting that the scribes declared before the people that Jesus Himself was possessed by Beelzebul, and "He casts out the demons by the ruler of the demons." The use of the imperfect (*elegon*, "they were saying") suggests that the scribes had been in the process of spreading this slander for some time. By so saying, the scribes thought that they had found the perfect way to defuse any claims that the people or Jesus might make concerning His messiahship. In effect they were saying that this man whom the people were claiming might be God's Messiah was in fact in league with Satan!

Matthew and Luke both record that Jesus knew what these scribes were thinking a point Mark does not include. Instead of waiting for them to come to Him, Jesus "called them to Himself." Previously Jesus had responded to charges brought against Him only after having been confronted. In this situation He takes the initiative and addresses these scribes in parables.

This is the first occurrence of the word *parable(s)* in Mark's gospel (see also 4:2, 10–11, 13, 30, 33–34; 7:17; 12:1, 12; 13:28). A parable is a unique literary device consisting of riddles, metaphors, similes, and other figures of speech, even at times allegory.[8] Jesus' use of parables was designed to present profound truth in understandable language.

As the scribes gathered around Him, Jesus began by addressing their second accusation concerning Him, namely, that "He casts out the demons by the ruler of the demons." He said to them, "How can Satan cast out Satan? . . . And if a kingdom is divided against itself, that kingdom cannot stand." The absurdity of the scribes' claims was incredible. These highly educated scribes wanted the people to believe that Satan was casting out Satan! Even the common people could see that if Satan fighting against his own house and his own kingdom, he would eventually cease to be effective in the world. Jesus' logic in this matter was beyond debate.

As if to drive home this point Matthew records that Jesus added, "And if I by Beelzebul cast out demons, by whom do your sons cast them out?" (Matt. 12:27). Jesus' authority and power over sickness, disease, and evil spirits far exceeded anything the Jewish exorcists could claim. Therefore the sons of the scribes would be their judges, for they never would have levied such an accusation against them! Contrary to what the scribes were saying, Jesus claimed that He was casting out devils by the power of the Spirit of God. Therefore the kingdom of God was in their midst and had come unto them (Matt. 12:28).

Then Jesus addresses the first accusation made by the scribes, namely, that "He is possessed by Beelzebul." He had already demonstrated the ludicrousness of their claims concerning where His power to cast out demons originated. Now He says, "No one can enter the strong man's house and plunder his property unless he first binds the strong man, and then he will plunder his house." The significance of the word play here does not come through in English. Beelzebul means "lord of the heavenly dwelling" or "lord of the heavenly house." This is equivalent to the idea expressed by the apostle Paul when he wrote that Satan was the "prince of the power of the air" (Eph. 2:2).

Jesus was asserting that by casting out demons He had entered into the strong man's house (Beelzebub, the lord of the heavenly house) and had spoiled his goods! He was able to do this because He was stronger than the "strong man" and had bound him. The logic here is unassailable. If Satan cannot cast out Satan, then one greater and stronger than Satan must be present! The only one greater and stronger than Satan is God Himself! Therefore, Jesus must be effecting healings and deliverances by the very power of God! (cf. Luke 11:20).

Having successfully argued that His power to cast out demons established His superiority over Satan, Jesus then changed the tenor of His address to the scribes from one of instruction to one of sharp rebuke and stern admonition.

He began by saying, "Truly I say to you." This expression is spoken only by Jesus and appears twelve more times in Mark's gospel (cf. 8:12; 9:1, 41; 10:15, 29; 11:23; 12:43; 13:30; 14:9, 18, 25; 14:30). "This manner of speaking has the effect of solemnifying Jesus' words by implicitly invoking God's sanction of them. Jesus thereby claims to be God's very spokesman." Jesus follows this solemn expression by stating that, "All sins shall be forgiven the sons of men, and whatever blasphemies they utter."[9]

When considering this passage, it must be remembered that the Jewish leaders had vilified Jesus because He did not fit into their preconceived concept of who and what the Messiah was to be. As they reflected upon Jesus' humble life, His appearance, and the fact that He was supposedly a Galilean, born in Nazareth (cf. John 7:52), they were perplexed because they could not deny that they had witnessed astounding miracles at His hands.

Moreover, the fact that Jesus was popular with the common people, being considered by many of them to be the "Son of David," compelled these men to call attention to what they deemed were inconsistencies in Jesus' qualifications. It was these blasphemies that Jesus was referring to when He made this statement. In other words, any and all blasphemies directed toward Him concerning His birth, lifestyle, appearance, and so on, could and would be forgiven if forgiveness was sought (cf. Matt. 12:32). Jesus did not stop there, however, but added, "whoever blasphemes against the Holy Spirit never has forgiveness, but is guilty of an eternal sin."

To understand the second half of this declaration, it is important to consider how Jesus' hearers would have understood it. The phrase "the Holy Spirit" (literally, "the spirit the holy") must first be considered.

Too often Christians read into passages of Scripture something that is simply not there or something that wasn't revealed until much later. For example, in this passage, most Christians impose an understanding of the Trinity that Jesus' hearers would not have understood. Since Jesus' hearers could not have understood this to have referred to the third person of the Trinity, we must ask, "In what manner did Jesus intend it to be understood?"

Obviously Jesus was not introducing the doctrine of the Trinity here. In reality what He was doing was emphasizing the two different aspects of His existence, namely, the human and the divine. As was previously noted, up to this point in time, the religious leaders had reproached Jesus solely on the basis of His humanity (cf. Mark 6:3; Luke 4:22; John 1:45; 6:42; 7:41; 9:29). However, with this new accusation of demonic activity and satanic empowerment, they had shifted their attack from His humanity to His divine person. Albert Barnes explains:

> Reflections on his poverty, on his humble birth, and on the lowliness of his human nature might be forgiven; but for those which affected his divine nature, accusing him of being in league with the devil, denying his divinity, and attributing the power which manifestly implied divinity to the prince of fallen spirits, there could be no pardon. This sin was a very different thing from what is now often supposed to be the sin against the Holy Spirit. It was a wanton and blasphemous attack on the divine power and nature of Christ. Such a sin God would not forgive. . . . and the meaning of the whole passage may be: "He that speaks against me as a man of Nazareth—that speaks contemptuously of my humble birth, etc., may be pardoned; but he that reproaches my divine nature, charging me with being in league with Satan, and blaspheming the power of God manifestly displayed "by me," can never obtain forgiveness."[10]

The context makes it quite clear that Jesus was referring to their persistent refusal to accept His claims to divinity. In referring to this passage, Norman Geisler notes: "When it comes to the evidence for the deity of Christ, it would seem that the greater the evidence, the more obstinate is the unbelief of the unwilling. By extrapolation, persistent unbelief in the face of Christ's miracles became at its apex the 'unpardonable sin.'"[11]

Jesus did not state that these hypocrites had committed the unpardonable sin yet, only that a determined mind-set of obstinate unbelief in the face of irrefutable authentication would lead to a condition in which repentance and forgiveness would become unattainable, for failure to accept Jesus' divinity seals one's destiny.

Some Christians fear that during the course of their lives they may have committed the unpardonable sin of blasphemy against the Holy Spirit and therefore have lost their salvation. This is simply not the case, because blasphemy against the Holy Spirit, as represented in this context, is not possible today. This is evident because it was a sin that was *specifically* related to Jesus' earthly ministry as it related to Israel, and as such, the circumstances leading to it are not reproducible today. Lewis Sperry Chafer sums up the matter:

> For want of attention to all that is involved in these and other related Scriptures, there has been a most injurious application on the part of preachers, especially evangelists, of these very Scriptures to the present age. . . . To say that attributing works that men may be doing in the power of the Spirit to Satan is the same offense is to go utterly beyond what is written. The possibility of this particular sin being committed ceased with Christ's removal from the earth.[12]

In summary, the blasphemy against the Holy Spirit referred to a sin that could only be committed by those living at the time of Christ's earthly ministry. It was committed in a historical context and consisted of attributing Christ's ability to cast out demons to an assumed collaboration on His part with Satan. As such, it was a volitional failure to acknowledge the power and presence of God's Spirit as expressed through Jesus' divine nature. Moreover, the sin of blasphemy against the Holy Spirit is not to be equated with the sin of unbelief, as Paul Enns observes:

> The sin of blasphemy against the Spirit is not the same as unbelief. There is no indication in Scripture that if a person has once refused the gospel that he will never again have an opportunity to believe, nor is there a particular sin today that cannot be forgiven. Who has not refused the gospel the first time they heard it but later came to believe in Christ? Of course unbelief will not be forgiven if a person permanently persists in unbelief.[13]

The Servant: Misunderstood by His Family (3:31–35)

(Compare Matthew 46–50; Luke 18:19–21)

Shortly after the encounter in verses 22–30, Jesus' mother and brothers sought Him out (cf. Matt. 12:32–45). Mark records, "And His mother and His brothers arrived, and standing outside they sent word to Him, and called Him."

A great deal has been written concerning the meaning of the phrase, "His brothers." Those holding to an overly high view of Mary insist on her perpetual virginity and therefore deny that this expression is to be taken literally. Although it is true that this expression could be used in a general sense of near relatives such as cousins, it is also true that it referred to literal, physical, siblings (cf. Matthew 13:56; Mark 6:3). If this is the case here, it refers to half brothers and half sisters of the Lord.

The fact that they were standing outside suggests two possibilities: either they were attempting to get inside of a house where Jesus was surrounded by listeners or they were attempting to get His attention as He taught in the open air surrounded by listeners. The fact that, "a multitude was sitting around Him," would seem to indicate the latter.

The purpose of their visit was introduced in verse 21, namely, to get Jesus under control because He had, in the minds of His family, "lost His senses." This is somewhat understandable given the fact that His family did not yet believe in Him, but what of Mary, His mother? Lenski observes:

> It is certainly strange to find the mother of Jesus participating in this affair. Though she is mentioned first as being the nearest relative of Jesus, we cannot think that she was the instigator but prefer to believe that she permitted herself to be drawn into it by the fears and the urgings of the others. Even so, this is a picture of Mary that is far different from the legendary image of "the Mother of God" in medieval and Romish tradition. She is carried along by a mistaken movement. On the other hand, we decline to charge Mary with unbelief (John 7:5) and opposition to her son; she grew in faith like others.[14]

We are not told how long Jesus' brothers were trying to get His attention, but eventually some of those present said to Him, "Behold, Your mother and Your brothers are outside looking for You" (cf. Matt. 12:47). From a comparison of Matthew's and Mark's account, it appears that while Jesus was yet teaching, the message of their presence moved throughout the crowd until it finally reached Jesus.

Matthew adds that Jesus' question, "Who is my mother, and who are My brothers?" (Matt. 12:48) was directed to the person who actually told Him of

His family presence while Luke does not include the question at all. Mark says of Jesus, "And looking about on those who were sitting around Him, He said, 'Behold, My mother and My brothers!'" Again, Matthew is more explicit, indicating that as Jesus made this declaration, He was, "stretching out His hand toward his disciples." No doubt this caused the crowd some concern, so Jesus clarified what He meant, saying, "Whoever does the will of God, he is My brother, and sister, and mother."

> The three terms, brother, sister, mother, used without the articles, are figurative, denoting the spiritual family. All true believers constitute the household of God. Jesus did not add "and father," for in the realm of the spiritual, that term marked a position which no human being could fill. Jesus always used the term Father of the heavenly Father.[15]

Some misunderstand these verses suggesting that Jesus was not respectful of His mother, but this is not the case. The time had come for Jesus to make known to His own family that He belonged to a wider group than any domestic circle, and they must not think that they could make demands upon His life or direct Him in any way. Moreover, in saying this, Jesus revealed that His was a new relationship that included His followers, and this relationship transcended familial ties because it was based upon the "will of God."

Study Questions

1. Under what circumstances is "anger" right and godly? Are Christians today justified to have the same anger as Christ?

2. What was the source of the opposition Christ experienced in this chapter?

3. What counterparts do we have now in the (1) Pharisees, (2) Herodians, and (3) scribes?

4. Why did the Lord not want the demons to tell who He was?

5. On what basis did Christ select His apostles? What would be some of their public tasks?

6. Describe the blaspheming against the Holy Spirit. Can He be blasphemed the same way today? Explain.

7. How is Christ not rejecting His family and His closest kin? What was He saying in 3:33–35?

CHAPTER 4

The Servant Teaches by the Seaside
Mark 4:1-41

Preview:

Four parables and a miracle make up this chapter. From the parable of the sower, we learn that the seed is the word and message of God. From the parable of the candle, we glean the lesson of open witnessing and serving. From the parable of growth, we understand that God's purpose and plan for the age results in great growth and a final harvest. In the parable of the mustard seed, we see the growth of a tiny seed into a tree that houses the birds of the air. From the smallest seed a shade tree flourishes to give blessing. Since Jesus can still the storm, He can help us meet any crisis. For every crisis there is Christ.

The Parable of the Sower, Seed and Soils (4:1-20)

(Compare Matthew 13:1-35; Luke 8:4-15)

At the beginning of chapter 4, Jesus again "got into a boat in the sea and sat down" to address the swelling crowds.

If the Pharisees were at a loss as to what to do about this new teacher who was casting out demons and healing on the Sabbath (1:21-28; 3:1-6), the common people had no such dilemma. They were the ones to whom the message was directed and upon whom the miracles were being performed. Therefore, they were gladly hearing and receiving what Jesus the servant had to say. This however, resulted in large crowds of people seeking Him out, making His prior method of teaching unworkable. The answer was to move away from the more populated areas to the more open areas surrounding the Sea of Galilee. But with the crowds growing daily, even this was not sufficient to keep the people from pressing in on Him as He taught. Therefore, we find Jesus requesting the disciples to provide a boat to "stand ready for Him because of the multitude, in order that they might not crowd Him" (3:9). This method was workable and was often used as He spoke to the crowds.

Verse 2 indicates that Jesus was "teaching them many things in parables." The term parable is first introduced by Mark in 3:23. It comes from the combination of two Greek words, *para*, meaning "alongside;" and *ballō*, meaning "to throw or cast"). Two questions must be asked at this point: (1) What is a parable? and (2) Why did Jesus use parables? The *Theological Dictionary of the New Testament* notes that a parable word is:

> (A)n independent similitude in which an evident or accepted truth from a known field (nature, human life) is designed to establish or illustrate a new truth in the preaching of Jesus (kingdom of God, God's nature and action, piety).[1]

Similarly, *The Bible Exposition Commentary* states:

> A parable is a story or figure placed alongside a teaching to help us understand its meaning. It is much more than "an earthly story with a heavenly meaning," and it certainly is not an "illustration" such as a preacher would use in a sermon. A true parable gets the listener deeply involved and compels that listener to make a personal decision about God's truth and his or her life.[2]

This answers the question concerning what a parable is, but what about the second question? Why did Jesus teach in parables? Interestingly, the disciples themselves asked Jesus this very question in verses 10–12 (see also Matt. 13:10–17). Jesus' replied with a twofold answer. First, this method was used to conceal truth from the hard-hearted, and second, it was used to reveal truth to those earnestly seeking it. James A. Brooks, notes:

> Jesus did not speak in parables for the purpose of withholding truth from anyone; but the result of his parables, the rest of his teaching, and even his miracles was that most did not understand and respond positively. He did speak in parables to provoke thought and invite commitment. Therefore parables are more than mere illustrations. They constitute spiritual tests that separate those who understand and believe from those who do not.[3]

R. Alan Cole shows how Christ was a master teacher by often teaching with parables. These were illustrations designed to sift the worthless chaff from the edible wheat. Many teachers are impressed when the crowds are large, but not Christ. He knew the evil motives of the human heart. When the Lord used parables, He wanted to set forth, as with a test, the motive of the hearer. He was not trying to ascertain intelligence but the spiritual responsiveness of the listener. For those who had spiritual hunger, the meaning in one parable led to deeper understanding in the next. Countrariwise, when the hearer was hardened in the heart the fog of comprehension only increased. In spiritual matters we either hear or we do not hear. To see the spiritual truth (to hear) is the proof that we have received the illumination of that Holy Spirit who alone can open our spiritual eyes, blind by nature, to the truth of God.[4]

Another point of interest in verse 2 is the use of the phrase "His teaching". The common method of teaching used by the scribes primarily involved quoting what other esteemed rabbis had taught. This led to much confusion because, by the time Jesus came on the scene, the people had heard commentary upon commentary and tradition upon tradition. None of the religious teachers would or could dogmatically state that what they were teaching was in fact true. The most they could do was quote a rabbi who supported their position. H.A. Ironside notes, "Jesus spoke as One sent from God. He did not need to bolster His instructions with quotations from human authorities, but preached the Word as the mouthpiece of the Father, whose representative He was."[5]

Jesus did not come to the people commenting upon what others had said. Instead, He taught "his doctrine" as one who was authoritative, performing miracles that served to confirm this fact. He did not receive this doctrine from man but from God (John 7:16), and so "they were amazed at His teaching; for He was teaching them as one having authority, and not as the scribes (1:22; cf. 1:27; 11:18). The use of the phrase "the mystery of the kingdom of God" in verse 11 identifies this parable as a so-called Kingdom parable dealing specifically with Kingdom truths.

This brings us to the content of this parable. It is referred to as the Parable of the sower. Its key components are (1) the sower, (2) the seed sown, and (3) the soil. Briefly we are told that the sower went out to sow his field. As he did so, some of the seed fell beside the road and was devoured by birds; some fell on stony ground without depth and was scorched by the sun and withered away; some fell among thorns and was choked and yielded no fruit; and some fell on good ground, yielding thirty, sixty, and a hundred times what was sowed. Jesus then concluded this parable by declaring, "He who has ears to hear, let him hear."

Verse 10 indicates that the disciples too were somewhat dull of understanding (see also v. 13). "As soon as He was alone, His followers, along with
the twelve, began asking Him about the parables." (Matthew records that they
even questioned Him as to why He used parables [Matt. 13:10]). Jesus
responded to their questions in a tone that was undoubtedly sobering. He
told them "To you has been given the mystery of the kingdom of God." No
doubt this immediately excited their attention. What was this "mystery"?
Simply that, the Father sent Jesus for the purpose of reconciling the world
unto himself (see 2 Cor. 5:19).

The Mystery of the Kingdom

1. The Lord Jesus was rejected when He offered Himself as king to Israel.

2. A period of time would intervene before the kingdom would be literally set up on earth.

*3. During the interim, the kingdom would exist in spiritual form. All who acknowledged
Christ as king would be in the kingdom, even though the king Himself was absent.*

*4. The Word of God would be sown during the interim period with varying degrees of suc-
cess. Some people would actually be converted, but others would be only nominal believers. All professing Christians would be in the kingdom in its outward form, but only genuine ones would enter the kingdom in the inner reality.*[6]

A new spiritual order was being established and this "mystery" was to be
revealed unto them. Theirs was a position of great privilege. It was also a position of great responsibility—something that they would find out soon
enough.

As promised— "To you has been given . . . " —Jesus now reveals to the
disciples the meaning of this parable in verses 14–20.

The context seems to indicate that the sower represents Jesus specifically
but also anyone who proclaims the Word of God ultimately. The seed represents the Word or message of God. The wayside represents those hearers
whose hearts are indifferent to the Word, and so it is immediately stolen from
them by Satan. The stony ground represents those who merely make an intel-
lectual assent to the Word but have no real spiritual change of heart. They initially welcome it for its altruistic and humanitarian advantages, but when they
are required to conform to its message through hardship or open persecution,
they are offended and fall away because they are revealed for who they really
are, merely professors of a disingenuous faith. The remaining group consists
of those who hear the message but are not convinced of its ultimate claim on

their lives. They look good for a while but after time become inattentive to the message and overly concerned with temporal things. They are materially focused, which finally results in their being drawn completely away from the only thing that can deliver them from the world, the Word of God. Each of these types of soil thus represents a different group of nonbelievers.

Finally, Jesus addresses those hearers who are represented by the good soil. They not only hear the message, they accept it fully or "acknowledge it as their own." The idea is that these hearers take the message to heart or as we say nowadays, "make it their own." The result is that these genuine believers consistently produce spiritual fruit in differing measures. The focus is not on, as many teach today, temporal, earthly fruit, but upon spiritual fruit. The final yields (thirty, sixty, and one hundred times as much as was sown) will be determined ultimately at the final harvest (consider Mark 4:24–25; Matt. 25:14–30; and Luke 19:11–27). John D. Grassmick writes:

> Giving out the news of God's kingdom is like sowing seed on various kinds of soil. At Jesus' first coming and in the present age the kingdom is largely veiled in the face of satanic opposition and human unbelief. But despite this, God's rule takes hold in those who accept Jesus' message and His rule manifests itself in spiritual fruitfulness. But God's kingdom will be openly established on earth at Jesus' second coming with a glory yet undisclosed (cf. Mark 13:24–27). Then there will be an abundant harvest. Thus the parable displayed God's kingdom as both *present but veiled* and *future but openly glorious* (cf. 1:14–15).[7]

The Parable of the Lamp (4:21–25)

Whereas verses 10–12 give a demonstration as to how parables camouflage the truth, verses 21–25 emphasize how parables positively bring the truth to light to those who carefully ponder them. In fact, it can be said that these two parables essentially balance one anther.

In these verses, the Lord Jesus utilized a common household lamp composed of a wick placed in a clay bowl filled with oil to point out two important spiritual truths to the disciples. What He has to say at first seems blatantly evident, yet He deems it necessary to communicate it to them. Jesus points out the obvious fact that no one would light a lamp and then immediately conceal it. A lamp so treated could in no way fulfill its purpose. On the contrary, they will place the lamp in a prominent place, in this case, on a lampstand, where all in the house can benefit from its light.

The first point Jesus makes has to do with the disciples' privileged position referred to in the previous parable. They were told, "To you has been given the mystery of the kingdom of God." In the parable of the lamp, Jesus tells them that they are not only privileged but also responsible for that very truth. Jesus tells the disciples to be like that lamp, namely, to shed God's light and thus reveal truth. This is an important message for us today. We must not hoard the truth. We have been entrusted with it not so we can keep it to ourselves, but so that we can share it with others.

Second, this parable also addresses the general issue of why the Lord Jesus was "teaching them many things in parables." He had just told the disciples, "those who are outside get everything in parables " (v. 11). He then proceeded to explain the parable of the sower to them. No doubt the disciples were questioning within themselves whether this truth, just revealed, was to be withheld from the multitudes. Jesus anticipated their question and answered it by using this simple parable. He basically said, "who in their right mind would light a candle and then deliberately hide it?"

The messages contained within the parables were designed to hide the truth from the unbelieving multitudes but not from those earnestly seeking. To the disciples, the truth would certainly be revealed. "The underlying truth was hidden. But the divine intention was that the disciples explain those hidden truths to willing hearts."[8] In other words, Jesus was telling the disciples that the primary purpose of a parable was not to conceal truth, though it did do that, but ultimately to reveal it. Jesus said, "For nothing is hidden, except to be revealed; nor has anything been secret, but that it should come to light" (v. 22). To drive these truths home, He then admonished them, "If any man has ears to hear, let him hear" (v. 23).

Jesus did not give the disciples much time to contemplate what He had just said before He launched into another spiritual admonition. "Take care what you listen to. By your standard of measure it shall be measured to you; and more shall be given you besides. For whoever has, to him shall more be given; and whoever does not have, even what he has shall be taken away from him" (vv. 24–25). Here Jesus introduced the concept of *obligation* along with the double law of spiritual loss and spiritual growth. If one hears and accepts the truth of the gospel and then passes on to others what he or she has learned, God will give that person more truth. However, if one refuses to hear and rejects Christ's Word, that person will lose what truth he or she has learned now and will ultimately suffer loss in the life to come. William Barclay notes:

This may seem a hard saying; but the whole lesson of life is that it is inevitably and profoundly true.

(1) It is true of *knowledge*. The more we know the more we are capable of knowing. We cannot enter into the riches of Greek literature before we have ploughed through Greek grammar. When we have the basic grammar, still more will be given to us. We cannot really get the best out of music without learning something of the structure of a symphony. But possession of that knowledge yields still more and more loveliness. It is equally true that unless we are consistently bent on the task of increasing our knowledge, such knowledge as we have will in the end be taken away from us. Many of us in our youth had a working knowledge of French at school and have now forgotten even the little that we knew because we made no attempt to develop it.

The more knowledge we have, the more we can acquire. And, if we are not always out to increase it, such knowledge as we have will soon slip from our grasp. The Jewish teachers had an oddly expressive saying. They said that the scholar should be treated like a young heifer—because every day a little heavier burden should be laid upon him. In knowledge we cannot stand still; we are gaining or losing it all the time.

(2) It is true of *effort*. The more physical strength we have, the more, within the limits of our bodily frame, we can acquire. The more we train our bodies, the more our bodies will be able to do. On the other hand, if we allow our physical frame to grow slack and flabby and soft we will end by losing even the fitness that we had. We would sometimes do well to remember that our bodies belong to God as much as our souls. Many of us have been hindered from doing the work we might do because we have made ourselves physically unfit to do it.

(3) It is so with *any skill or craft*. The more we develop the skill of hand, or eye, or mind, the more we are able to develop it. If we are content to drift along, never trying anything new, never adopting any new technique, we remain stuck in the one job with no progress. If we neglect our particular skill, we will find in the end that we have lost it altogether.

(4) It is so with the ability to bear responsibility. The more responsibility we take on, the more we are able to bear; the more decisions we compel ourselves to take, the better we are able to take them. But if we shirk our responsibilities, if we evade decisions and waver all the time, in the end we will become flabby, spineless creatures totally unfit for

responsibility and totally unable to come to any decision at all. Again and again in his parables, Jesus goes on the assumption that the reward of good work is still more work to do. It is one of the essential laws of life, a law which we forget at our peril, that the more we have won the more we can win, and that, if we will not make the effort, we will lose even that which once we had won.[9]

The lesson to be learned then is that the more we hear and respond to the Word of God, sharing it with others, the more truth God will entrust to us. However, the reverse is also true. If we fail to respond to truth, we will suffer loss of even what we previously acquired. Ironside states the issue well. "It is a law of that kingdom that to him who uses well what he has, more will be imparted, and he who has nothing but an empty profession will, at the last, be stripped even of that."[10]

The Parable of the Growing Seed (4:26–29)

This parable is unique to Mark. It too is a Kingdom parable and shares several components with the parable of the sower. "It presents a comprehensive picture of the coming of God's kingdom: sowing (v. 26), growing (vv. 27–28), and harvesting (v. 29), with emphasis on the growing phase."[11]

In examining the content of this parable, it is important to remember that there is not always a one to one correspondence between the elements of a parable and actual reality. A parable is designed to teach a *spiritual* truth. The ultimate point of this parable is that there is a spiritual process that leads up to and also includes the harvest.

The sower's job is to sow the seed. This he does. His motivation is not the process of sowing but rather the expectant harvest. He has no control over the seed once it has been sown, so he patiently awaits the reward of his efforts. He sleeps and rises night and day going about his normal activities "The soil produces crops by itself; first the blade, then the head, then the mature grain in the head." He trusts in the fact that the processes of natural law will effect proper growth. The expression "produces crops by itself" suggests that this process of growth is "without visible cause." In other words, once the seed is sown, no human agency is involved. The process of growth and maturity is a work accomplished exclusively by God. Once the fruit has matured, the sower brings out the sickle (an idiom meaning that he sends in the reapers) and gathers the expected harvest.

It seems unlikely that, as some have suggested, the sower represents God, because it is said of the sower that "he himself does not know" how the seed grows. This certainly cannot be true of God. It also seems unlikely that evangelism is the sole focus here because it is also asserted that at the harvest, the sower "puts in the sickle." Although there is a sense in which believers can and do sow God's Word (e.g., by preaching, cf. 1 Cor. 1:21), we know that believers are not responsible for the harvest, nor are they involved in the gathering of it (James 5:18).

There can be little doubt then that the focus of this parable is the coming of God's kingdom by God's sovereign and peculiar work. James Edwards notes:

> Putting forth the sickle for the harvest often symbolizes the arrival of God's kingdom, especially in judgment (Joel 4:13; Rev 14:15; Gospel of Thomas 21). This parable admonishes that alongside and within "business as usual" the kingdom of God is present and growing, even if unobserved. The world may bemoan, "Where is this 'coming' he promised?" (2 Pet 3:4). Such skepticism is the result of awaiting the arrival of God's kingdom as if it were a bolt of lightning, commanding and overwhelming. God does not hurl the kingdom as Poseidon does his thunderbolt. God plants it as a seed, present even now in the ministry of Jesus, hidden and imperceptible, but portending both a harvest and judgment.[12]

The Parable of the Mustard Seed (4:30–34)

(Compare Matthew 13:31–32; Luke 13:18–19)

This parable is introduced by two questions: "How shall we picture the kingdom of God, or by what parable shall we present it?" R. A. Guelich notes that this is a construction that is characteristic of Mark but is also one that is typical of both biblical (Isa. 40:18) and rabbinic style.[13] Why did Jesus question the disciples? The answer lies in the fact that the concept of the reign of God was still not clear to the disciples. They were looking for the institution of the messianic kingdom during their lifetime. Cole notes, "The small beginnings and slow pervasive growth of the kingdom were beyond either the patience or the understanding of the disciples."[14] For this reason, Jesus introduced this prophetic kingdom parable and presented to the disciples the reality of seemingly insignificant beginnings that finally produce inestimable results. It is prophetic in the sense that it reveals that the kingdom of God, initially veiled in Christ, would be gloriously manifested at the end of the age.

After introducing the two questions, Jesus answered them by stating, "It is like a mustard seed, which, when sown upon the soil, though it is smaller than all the seeds that are upon the soil, yet when it is sown, grows up, and becomes larger than all the garden plants, and forms large branches. " Jesus knew that the disciples would immediately get a twofold picture in their minds. First, they would be reminded of the mustard plant that was common in Israel. It was general knowledge that this very large bush, proliferating each spring, sprang from a very tiny seed.[15] Although certainly not the tiniest of seeds, the disciples would have correctly understood Jesus' speech here. John D. Grassmick notes, "In Jewish thinking, its small size was proverbial since it was the smallest of all the seeds sown in the field. It took 725–760 mustard seeds to weigh a gram (28 grams equal one ounce)." Although a tiny seed, it often grew to large size. William Barclay notes, "A traveller in Palestine speaks of seeing a mustard plant which, in its height, was higher than a horse and its rider."[16]

Second, Jesus no doubt intended that the disciples should recall Ezekiel's and Daniel's "tree" illustrations (cf. Ezek. 17:22–24., 31:1–18; Dan. 4:10–26). In both instances the tree figure represented great empires and included the nations that formed them.

Both of these pictures were used by Christ to facilitate the understanding of the disciples. The kingdom of God would be characterized by small, insignificant beginnings initially but would ultimately grow exponentially.

Most commentators agree with this interpretation. However, there are a couple of nuances that some have seen contained within this interpretation. One common interpretive nuance is that this parable also demonstrates the corruption of the early church. Typically, those who take this viewpoint tie the expression "birds of the air" to the parable of the sower, seeing them as representing the forces of Satan. Wilbur M. Smith, quoting Ada Habershon, writes:

> In the first parable the birds of the air represented "the wicked one," according to Matthew, "Satan," in Mark; "the devil," in Luke; and it is more than likely in this thin parable that they have the same significance. In the early centuries of Church history, when persecution had failed to exterminate the light of the gospel, Satan tried by other means to weaken its power and mar its testimony. The Church became mixed with the world and soon strove after political power. It wanted to be like the other kingdoms, and indeed to rule over them.[17]

Although this is a possible interpretation, Edwards argues for a different view. He writes:

> The OT prophets occasionally use the image of birds nesting in branches to allude to the inclusion of the Gentiles in God's chosen people (Ps 104:12; Ezek 17:23; 31:6; Dan 4:9–21). This offers a clue to v. 32, "the birds of the air can perch in its shade." In addition to the surprising growth of the kingdom, the parable of the mustard seed contains a hint

of God's grace to *all* peoples. This may explain its anchor position in chap. 4, for it would have signaled to Mark's Roman Gentile readers that their inclusion in the kingdom was foreordained by the Lord. "Out of the most insignificant beginnings, invisible to human eyes, God creates his mighty Kingdom, which embraces all the peoples of the world."[18]

James Brooks agrees with Edwards, noting:

> Some have questioned, however, whether the growth depicted by the parable is desirable. They have claimed that an abnormally large herb with its branches filled with birds (sometimes symbols of evil) represents an overgrown, apostate, institutional church. Such an interpretation is, however, completely at odds with the meaning of the parables of the soil and the seed and the meaning of the term "kingdom of God."[19]

Grassmick notes that the allusion to birds may merely indicate the end result of the kingdom. That is, it represents the incorporation of the Gentiles into God's kingdom program (cf. Ezek. 17:22–24; 31:6).[20]

What we do know is that this parable introduces a strong contrast between the insignificant and mysterious beginning of the kingdom of God as expressed in the presence of Jesus, with the final greatness of His kingdom that will gloriously outshine all the earth's kingdoms past, present, and future. Brooks correctly states: "That which no one would imagine—or if one did would seem utterly impossible—will in time loom inescapably before us. God's reign will not only be more real than the world can imagine, but it will also be larger and more encompassing."[21]

Verses 33 and 34 close this section of parables by reinforcing that which Jesus had indicated to the disciples previously. He would continue to use parables and did so "And with many such parables He was speaking the word to them, as they were able to hear it.; and He did not speak to them without a parable." But He had also told them "To you has been given the mystery of the kingdom of God " (v. 11). Therefore, "He was explaining everything privately to His own disciples."

The Miracle of Stilling the Storm (4:35–41)

(Compare Matthew 8:18, 23–27; Luke 8:22–25)

This miracle is the first of four (4:35–5:43) possibly placed together for the purpose of validating the preceding words of Jesus or, as some have indicated, "to illustrate the vanquishing of powers hostile to God."[22] In the parables, Jesus spoke of the kingdom of God. Through the working of miracles, He demonstrated that the kingdom of God was "near." Some have seen a parallel between these events and those recorded in the book of Jonah.

The recording of this specific miracle is critical in that it reveals both the human nature and the divine nature of our Lord—the human nature, in that Jesus fell asleep in the boat because He was drained from the day's ministry work, and the divine nature, in that He demonstrated that He not only had power and authority over sickness and demons, but also over nature itself, when He rebuked the waves.

Miracles of Christ in Mark	
Delivering a man in the synagogue from an unclean spirit	Mark 1:21–28
Healing Simon [Peter's] mother-in-law	Mark 1:29–31
Cleansing a leper	Mark 1:40–45
Healing a paralytic	Mark 2:1–12
Healing a man with a withered hand	Mark 3:1–5
Calming the wind and sea	Mark 4:35–41
Healing a man possessed by demons at Gadara	Mark 5:1–20
Healing a woman with an issue of blood	Mark 5:25–34
Raising Jairus' daughter	Mark 5:21–24; 35–43
Feeding the five thousand with five loaves and two fish	Mark 6:32–44
Walking on the Sea	Mark 6:45–52
Healing the daughter of a Syrophoenician woman	Mark 7:24–30
Healing a deaf and dumb man	Mark 7:31–37
Feeding the four thousand with seven loaves and a few fish	Mark 8:1–10
Healing the blind man of Bethsaida	Mark 8:22–26
Casting demons out of a boy	Mark 9:14–29
Healing blind Bartimeaus	Mark 10:46–52
Cursing the fig tree	Mark 11:12–26

The Sea of Galilee was notorious for its storms. William Barclay writes:

A writer describes them like this: "It is not unusual to see terrible squalls hurl themselves, even when the sky is perfectly clear, upon these waters which are ordinarily so calm. The numerous ravines which to the north-east and east debouch [open out] upon the upper part of the lake operate as so many dangerous defiles in which the winds from the heights of Hauran, the plateau of Trachonitis, and the summit of Mount Hermon are caught and compressed in such a way that, rushing with tremendous force through a narrow space and then being suddenly released, they agitate the little Lake of Gennesaret in the most frightful fashion."[23]

The evening had arrived, and Jesus had been teaching from the lake's edge while sitting in a small boat all day. He had had a hard, long day and must have looked forward to some solitude away from the multitudes. He told his disciples, "Let us go over to the other side." At His request, the disciples sent the multitude away and did as Jesus asked. The narrative at this point also indicates that "other boats were with Him." We aren't told the reason for these other boats. They could have been other fishermen or part of the crowd.

Although a trip across the Sea of Galilee could be treacherous, the disciples (a number of whom were experienced fishermen), probably set out across the waters without the slightest concern for their welfare. Jesus was "in the stern, asleep on the cushion." This was the best location for passengers because this portion of the boat experienced the least amount of excessive movement.

The text tells us "there arose a fierce gale of wind, and the waves were breaking over the boat so much that the boat was already filling up." When it became obvious that the disciples were not able to overcome the waves, they awakened Jesus and, in a fit of fear and unbelief, asked, "Teacher, do You not care that we are perishing?" It is interesting to note that Jesus did not respond to their question. The text indicates, "And being aroused, He rebuked the wind and said to the sea, 'Hush, be still.'" The word "rebuked" is in the Greek an aorist active indicative third person singular of the verb *epitimaō*. It is used in Mark 1:25; 3:12; and 9:25 where Jesus rebuked and cast out demons. For this reason, many commentators believe that this storm was a satanic attack upon the Lord Jesus, an attempt to kill him before He could go to the cross. In His rebuke, He demands, "Peace, be still." The Greek verb *siōpaō* actually means *to quiet down, become calm*. The command "Be still" is from *phimoō*, literally meaning "to muzzle." The fact that this verb is in the perfect passive tense suggests a state or being or condition that is to continue indefinitely. At Jesus' command, "The wind died down, and it became perfectly calm."

Having addressed the immediate danger of the storm, Jesus now directed His attention to the disciples, saying, "Why are ye so timid? How is it that you have no faith?" These disciples who earlier that day had sat under the teaching of Jesus and had heard Him tell them of the kingdom and their part in it, these disciple who had witnessed His miraculous power over sickness and demons, had somehow missed the message. They still did not get it. Interestingly, the great fear that had gripped them when the storm was bearing down upon them was now directed toward Jesus. The text says, "And they became very much afraid and said to one another, 'Who then is this, that even the wind and the sea obey Him?'"

They asked the right question. What manner of man indeed! They were just too dull spiritually to answer it correctly at this point. This would not be the last time that Jesus questioned them about their faith (cf. 7:18; 8:17–18; 9:19; 16:14).

Study Questions

1. In how many ways is God's Word like seed?

2. What is the difference between God's Word as seed and what is sown in peoples' minds by human literature and thought?

3. Are we responsible for our responses to the Gospel? Why or why not?

4. Are we ever responsible for the condition of other peoples' hearts? Why or why not?

5. What does the lampstand suggest?

6. How important is it to share God's truth? Explain.

7. What is the harvest in this chapter?

CHAPTER 5

The Servant Manifests His Power
Mark 5:1-43

Preview:

Following Christ's manifesting His power over nature, He demonstrates His power over the devil and demonic forces in this chapter by curing the maniac of Gadara. On His way to the house of Jairus, the ruler of the synagogue, Jesus uses His power over disease by healing a woman who had had a hemorrhage for twelve years. Much to the amusement and later chagrin of the professional mourners outside the house of Jairus, Jesus gently chides them with a touch of humor, then, joined by Peter, James and John, He enters into the room where Jairus's twelve year-old daughter has died. There He reveals His power over death itself, raising the girl to life. Three such cases appear in the Gospels: Jesus raises a child; then the young son of the widow of Nain, and finally Lazarus, who had been dead four days.

The Servant's Power over Demons (5:1-20)

(Compare Matthew 8:28-34; Luke 8:26-39)

The Lord Jesus manifested His power over nature in chapter 4. In this chapter He demonstrates (1) His power over the devil and demonic forces by curing a man with an unclean spirit, 2) His power over disease by healing a woman who had hemorrhaged for twelve years, and finally (3) His power over death by raising Jairus' young daughter from death.

In verses 1-20 we have the record of Jesus' deliverance of a man possessed by a legion of demons. This miracle is important because it not only affirms the power of Jesus over the demonic realm, but it also intimates the not too distant inclusion of the Gentiles in the plan of God. The disciples had just witnessed the Lord Jesus as He calmed the wind and the sea. No doubt they were still reeling from these events as they landed on the shore, but what they were to encounter next would overwhelmed them even more.

According to the text, "they came to the other side of the sea, into the country of the Gerasenes." There has been some debate as to the actual location of the country of the Gerasenes. Various explanations have been given, including Gerasa, Gergesa, and Gadara. William Lane notes:

> The point of arrival is indicated in a general way as the district of the Gerasenes, most probably in reference to a town whose name is preserved in the modern Kersa or Koursi. At the site of Kersa the shore is level, and there are no tombs. But about a mile further south there is a fairly steep slope within forty yards from the shore, and about two miles from there cavern tombs are found which appear to have been used for dwellings.[1]

It should be noted that Mark does not say that the miracle took place in a specific town, but only that it occurred in "the country of the Gerasenes," that is in the general area. One thing we do know for certain is that most of its inhabitants were Gentiles (cf. Mark 5:11, 19).

The text tells us next that "when he had come out of the boat, immediately a man from the tombs with an unclean spirit met Him." Although it is not known for certain, it seems most likely that this man was a Gentile. It is stated that he had an unclean spirit. This may be due in part to the fact that he was living in the tombs and/or because he was living in Gentile territory. According to Jewish law, anyone who had touched a dead body was considered unclean (Num. 19:13). James Edwards writes, "Expanding on this Torah teaching, rabbinic interpretation extended uncleanness from contact with the dead to include contact with anything associated with them, including their bier, mattress, pillow, or tombs."[2] Moreover, among Jews and Gentiles alike, various superstitions about demons had developed. William Barclay comments:

> Out of the tombs there came a demon-possessed man. It was a fitting place for him to be, for demons, so they believed in those days, dwelt in woods and gardens and vineyards and dirty places, in lonely and desolate spots and among the tombs. It was in the night-time and before cock-crow that the demons were specially active. To sleep alone in an empty house at night was dangerous; to greet any person in the dark was perilous, for he might be a demon. To go out at night without a lantern or a torch was to court trouble. It was a perilous place and a perilous hour, and the man was a dangerous man.[3]

We are told next that this man had his dwelling among the tombs. And no one was able to bind him anymore, even with a chain; because he had often been bound with shackles and chains, and the chains had been torn apart by him, and the shackles broken in pieces, and no one was strong enough to subdue him. And constantly, night and day, among the tombs and in the mountains he was crying out, and gashing himself with stones. There are those who wish to dismiss this as a mere psychological malady. This man was, they say, mentally disturbed, but the origin of his problem was clearly demonic, not psychological. John D. Grassmick has correctly noted, "Such behavior shows that demon possession is not mere sickness or insanity but a desperate satanic attempt to distort and destroy God's image in man."[4]

The description given to us by Mark emphasizes the wretched state of this man. We are not told how he came to be in this condition, but it is clear that he was an outcast from society. The local townspeople undoubtedly believed the man mad, for they had apparently endeavored to bind him with both fetters and chains, no doubt to protect both themselves and him. Unsuccessful in their efforts, it seems they finally drove him from them and left him to wander in the mountains and the tombs. It also seems that this man, desiring to put an end to this unbearable way of life, may have sought to kill himself by cutting his flesh with sharp stones, but this was something the demons would not allow. They needed a host to carry out their evil.

Interestingly, the text next states: "And seeing Jesus from a distance, he ran up and bowed down before Him; and crying out with a loud voice, he said, What do I have to do with You, Jesus, Son of the Most High God? I implore You by God, do not torment me!" The English text here is somewhat ambiguous in its translation. The idea here seems to be that the demon-possessed man recognized Jesus for who he was and fell down to worship him. The context of the Greek, however, makes it quite clear that this was not what the demons were doing at all.

It is most interesting that the demons addressed, Jesus by name. Given the tenor of the words that follow, it seems clear that the demons were attempting to control the circumstances. The narrative indicates that the reason for this test of wills was due to the fact that Jesus had commanded the demons, "Come out of the man."

In Jewish tradition, if the exorcist could get the demon to give his name, his power would be broken and he would then be commanded to leave. Here the demon called Jesus by name and then used the strongest possible oath to get Him to leave him alone. Our English word *adjure* translates the Greek word *orkizō*, literally meaning "to cause someone to swear." The *Theological Dictionary of the New Testament* notes:

The sick man sees the superior power of Jesus and tries to keep Him at a distance. But mention of the name of Jesus does not have the expected effect. Jesus, the opponent of demons, is not robbed of His power thereby. Hence the sick man uses the strongest adjuration there is. He calls on God to protect him. But the adjuration is useless. For Jesus is the Son of the Most High God.[5]

A more literal rendering of the Greek text would be, "Why are you confronting me? Jesus, Son of the Most High God, I adjure you by God, do not torment me!" Our English word, *torment* is the Greek word *basanizo*, meaning "to test by the proving stone," that is, "to rub against it," "to test the genuineness of," "to examine or try," then "to apply means of torture to find the truth," "to harry or torture" in a hearing or before a tribunal.[6] The demons were fully aware of Jesus' divine origin. Yet they still attempted to overthrow His authority. William Lane explains:

> The full address is not a confession of Jesus' dignity but a desperate attempt to gain control over him or to render him harmless, in accordance with the common assumption of the period that the use of the precise name of an adversary gave one mastery over him. The very strong adjuration "by God" has a strange, ironic ring in the mouth of the demoniac. He senses that he is to be punished and employs the strongest adjuration that he knows. He invokes God's protection, but the adjuration is without force, for Jesus is the Son of God.[7]

At this point, Jesus turns the tables by asking for the demon's name. The response is, "Legion; for we are many." The Greek term *legion* is a military term borrowed from Latin. It was a term designating the largest unit in the Roman army, comprised of some 5,600 soldiers. Albert Barnes adds:

> The name legion was given to a division in the Roman army. It did not always denote the same number; but, in the time of Christ, it consisted of six thousand—three thousand foot and three thousand horsemen. It came, therefore, to signify a large number, without specifying the exact amount.[8]

What is the importance of the revelation of this name? Perhaps it is as *The Pulpit Commentary* declares, "to teach us how great is the number as well as the malignity of the evil spirits."[9] It could also be to demonstrate the number, power, and objectives of the demons, namely, to overthrow the kingdom of God.

Regardless of the reason why, the demons, realizing the power of Jesus' word over them, "began to entreat Him earnestly not to send them out of the country." Unlike the exorcisms performed by others, Jesus demonstrated true power over them. James Edwards notes:

> The discovery of Greek magical papyri in Egypt informs us of the long and convoluted formulas, spells, conjurations, and catchwords that ancient exorcists employed as they sparred with demonic opponents to gain advantage over them. Likewise, Philostratus describes a long and involved conversation of Apollonius with a demon, including empirical signs that the exorcism had actually been effective.[10]

There is no complex procedure, no special, magical word. It is the power resident within Jesus Himself that brings about the expulsion of the demonic forces within this man.

The narrative then tells us, "Now there was a big herd of swine feeding there on the mountain. And the demons entreated Him, saying 'Send us into the swine so that we may enter them.'" In Matthew's account the demons merely wanted to go into the swine—that is, they wanted to inhabit someone or something. Luke indicates that the demons pleaded not to be sent into the abyss, an apparent reference to their final judgment (Matt. 8:28–34; Luke. 8:26–29). Both ideas are in view in their request.

Jesus made it clear that when a demon is cast out, "it passes through waterless places, seeking rest, and does not find it" (Matt. 12:43–44; Luke 11:24). This suggests that demons are always looking for a host in order to carry out their malevolent desires. They did not want Jesus to render judgment upon them, something they realized He could do, nor did they want to once again become disembodied. They needed a physical body to inhabit.

We are told next, "And He gave them permission." Matthew states, "He said to them, 'Begone!'" (Matt. 8:32). It is clear that the demons would not have left the man had Jesus not given the command to "go." By doing so, He permitted their request to enter into the swine. This resulted in the destruction of the entire herd of swine (v. 13). William Lane makes some excellent observations about this incident:

> The demons made a specific request to enter into the swine, and when Jesus complied, the demons left the man and entered their new hosts. In panic the herd rushed down the slope into the sea and drowned. . . . What must be seen above all else is that the fate of the swine demonstrates the ultimate intention of the demons with respect to the man they had possessed. It is their purpose to destroy the creation of God, and halted in their destruction of a man, they fulfilled their purpose with the swine.[11]

In recent times, this parable has come under undue criticism from those who see themselves as animal rights activists. They ask how Jesus could have been so cruel. William Barclay responds to this question:

> There are some people who will blame Jesus because the healing of the man involved the death of the pigs. Surely it is a singularly blind way to look at things. How could the fate of the pigs possibly be compared with the fate of a man's immortal soul? We do not, presumably, have any objections to eating meat for dinner or refuse pork because it involved the killing of some pig. Surely if we kill animals to avoid going hungry, we can raise no objection if the saving of a man's mind and soul involved the death of a herd of these same animals. There is a cheap sentimentalism which will languish in grief over the pain of an animal and never turn a hair at the wretched state of millions of God's men and women. This is not to say that we need not care what happens to God's animal creation, for God loves every creature whom his hands have made, but it is to say that we must preserve a sense of proportion; and in God's scale of proportions, there is nothing so important as a human soul.[12]

The text next tells us of the reaction of the swine herders and the townspeople. "And their herdsmen ran away and reported it in the city and out in the country. And the people came to see what it was that had happened." There must have been great confusion and turmoil on the part of the townspeople as they tried to calm the swine herders enough in order to get the details of what had happened. Once they had heard them recount the day's events, they hurried out to the "scene of the crime." There can be no doubt that the townspeople were concerned about the financial loss they may have incurred, but it is also likely that their concern transformed into anger as they came out to see who had destroyed their livelihood. Whoever he was, he was going to give an account for this heinous crime. This would be the natural response. However, the text states, "And they came to Jesus and observed the man who had been demon possessed sitting down, clothed and in his right mind, the very man who had had the 'legion'; and they became frightened."

Anger turned to fear. They could not believe their eyes. Here was the demon-possessed man who had terrorized their countryside and whom they had tried on numerous occasions to bind, "sitting down, clothed, and in his right mind." All thoughts of the swine, at least for the moment, disappeared. This scene captivated them, and the townspeople began again asking the swine herders what had happened. The text states, "And those who had seen it described to them how it had happened to the demon-possessed man, and all about the swine. And they began to entreat Him to depart from their region." Once they got all the facts, the response was one of obvious over-whelming fear. This is reminiscent of the storm narrative in 4:35–41. Both narratives end with fear. The disciples, after crossing the Sea of Galilee, were more terrified at Jesus' power to still the storm than at the storm itself, and here the townspeople were more frightened by Jesus' power to expel the demons than they were by the demon-possessed man himself. Similarly, after witnessing an incredible supernatural event, the townspeople, like the disciples, were in awe, but this did not transition into faith.

The narrative continues, "And as He was getting into the boat, the man who had been demon-possessed was entreating Him that he might accompany Him. And He did not let him. " There is a remarkable contrast between the attitude of the townspeople and the attitude of the formerly demon pos-sessed-man. They begged Jesus to go, a request which He granted. The cured man, however, begged to stay with Jesus, a request which He denied.

At first this might seem strange, but, there was wisdom in Jesus' actions. For the time being, it was impracticable for Jesus to continue preaching in the area. The townspeople had not demonstrated faith when confronted with this astounding miracle. Fear had so gripped the people that they would not have heard Him. Moreover, this was a Gentile-dominated area and Jesus' mission was to the Jews. However, by denying the cured man's request to "accompany Him," Jesus guaranteed a powerful witness that could not be overlooked. Jesus told him to, "Go home to your people and report to them what great things the Lord has done for you, and how He had mercy on you. " Jesus gave the cured man the same charge He has given us, namely, "Don't be concerned about telling what you don't know, just tell what you do know!" The cured man's response to Jesus' command was that "he went away and began to pro-claim in Decapolis what great things Jesus had done for him; and everyone marveled." The result of his witness was that when Jesus later returned to the area, the people welcomed Him (7:31–37). It is noteworthy that this man, a cured demoniac, sent out by Jesus, became the first missionary to the Gentiles.

The Servant's Power over Disease (5:21–34)

(Compare Matthew 9:18–26; Luke 8:40–56)

Chapter 4, verses 35–41, display the power of Jesus over nature, while chapter 5, verses 1–20, display his power over demons. This next section calls atten-tion to Jesus' power over sickness and death. The underlying theme here and also in verses 35–43 is healing that leads to salvation by faith. In fact, Mark views each of the physical healings in this chapter as images of spiritual deliverance. Furthermore, there are many common elements in verses 1–20 and 35–43 as James Edwards points out:

Both stories are of females healed by the touch of Jesus; both are called "daughter" by Jesus; and the woman's illness and the girl's age are both given as twelve years. In both stories Jesus is met by rebukes (vv. 17, 40), and both stories bring Jesus into contact with uncleanness (the menstrual hemorrhage of the woman and the corpse of the child). The aspect of uncleanness connects the present sandwich narrative with the previous story (5:1–20). All three characters in Mark 5 transfer their uncleanness to Jesus, and to each Jesus bestows the cleansing wholeness of God.[13]

This section begins with Jesus and His disciples returning to the west side of the Sea of Galilee. The destination was probably their home base in Capernaum. As was becoming the norm, a large crowd, seeing Him as He drew near the shore, began gathering. We are told that, "one of the synagogue officials named Jarius came up, and upon seeing Him, fell at His feet, and entreated Him earnestly, saying, 'My little daughter is at the point of death; please come and lay Your hands on her, that she may get well and live.'"

Jairus is identified as "one of the synagogue officials." Typically, the ruler of the synagogue was a layperson given the responsibility for the physical maintenance of the synagogue and oversight of the worship services. He was always a well respected leader in the local community. William Barclay notes:

The ruler was the administrative head of the synagogue. He was the president of the board of elders responsible for the good management of the synagogue. He was responsible for the conduct of the services. He did not usually take part in them himself, but he was responsible for the allocation of duties and for seeing that they were carried out with all seemliness and good order. The ruler of the synagogue was one of the most important and most respected men in the community.[14]

The fact that Jairus openly came to Jesus for help suggests that (1) at this point in time, apparently not all of the religious leaders had become hostile toward Jesus or (2) Jairus's need overcame his fear of censorship. The fact that he himself came is also noteworthy. He did not send a servant. It was his daughter who was dying, and no one else would understand the magnitude of the situation. Furthermore, the manner in which he came suggests an attitude of (1) selflessness, (2) humility, and (3) belief.

The terminology used by Mark clearly shows Jairus' desperation. He fell (*piptō*, as a present active indicative) at the feet of Jesus, a position of great humility, especially for someone in his position. He earnestly entreated the Lord to come with him. The Greek verb (*parakaleō* as a present active indicative) coupled with the adverb (*polla*) is very strong. The idea conveyed here is that Jairus *repeatedly* and *urgently* called upon Jesus for help. Moreover, Jairus did not refer to his child using the usual word for daughter (*thugatēr*), but instead uses the diminutive form of the word, (*thugatrion*), which denotes endearment and is translated either "little daughter" or "dear daughter."

In describing the girl's condition, Mark noted that she was "at the point of death." Matthew said that she "[had] just died" (Matt. 9:18), Luke, that she "was dying" for the situation was critical, and Jairus's desperation was great, for this was his only daughter and she was only twelve years of age (Luke 8:42). Any parent who has spent time in an emergency room with a sick child can certainly relate to the agony that this man felt.

Jairus's request, "please come and lay Your hands on her, that she may get well and live," is very interesting. This man apparently had heard of Jesus' power to heal and perhaps had witnessed it for himself. In any case, faith had been engendered within him. His desperation caused him to grasp on to that spark of faith. His desperation compelled him to make his way through the crowd. If Jesus could heal others, He could certainly heal his daughter. This is what he believed and this is what he declared.

Mark's record of Jesus' response is both simple and profound, "And He went off with him." In spite of the fact that there were undoubtedly numerous people needing help and ministry, Jesus heard and responded to the desperate need of this man. We are told at this point that "a great multitude was following Him and pressing in on Him." This sets up the scene for the action in the following verses. One can imagine the urgency in Jairus's heart and mind as he and Jesus made their way toward his home. Time was of the utmost importance! It must have seemed like an eternity as they slowly worked their way down the narrow way.

This brings us to the parenthetical and parallel narrative of the woman who was plagued with hemorrhaging for twelve years. For twelve years she had been living a wretched life. She had been in continuous state of ceremonial uncleanness (cf. Lev. 15:25–27). Since physical contact with her or anything she came into contact with rendered others unclean, she was no doubt shunned by people, perhaps even by members of her own family. She apparently was a woman of some means, having had sufficient finances to allow her to consult many different physicians. Nevertheless, their treatments had been ineffective. She was now in desperate straits. Instead of getting better, her condition had steadily grown worse, and the result of so many treatments had left her in financial ruin.

She, like Jairus before her, had heard reports of Jesus' power to heal. She had nothing to lose, so she determined to do whatever it took to get to Jesus.

Making her way through the crowd, she came up behind him, reached out, and touched his garment, for she thought, "If I just touch His garments, I shall get well." James Brooks notes, "The woman's determination to touch Jesus' clothing reflects the ancient idea that the power of a person extended to one's clothing (cf. 3:10; 6:56; Acts 19:11–12) or one's shadow (Acts 5:15)."[15] The result of her faith was that "immediately (*euthus*) the flow of her blood was died up; the flow of her blood was dried up; and she felt in her body that she was healed of her affliction." She was immediately and totally healed!

The text next states, "And immediately Jesus (*euthus*) perceiving in Himself that the power proceeding from Him had gone forth, turned around in the crowd and said, 'Who touched My garments?'" Certainly this must have seemed pointless to the disciples. Hence their question, "You see the multitude pressing in on You, and You say, 'Who touched me'?" Jesus was being pressed upon and touched by a host of individuals. Moreover, the urgent need in their minds was their mission to assist Jairus's daughter. Any delay might be fatal for the child. In spite of their concern, Jesus "looked around to see the woman who had done this."

The woman, realizing that she could not hide her healing (Luke 8:47), "came and fell down before Him, and told Him the whole truth."

Some have questioned why Jesus took the time to stop and deal with this woman in such a personal way. Perhaps the answer lies in the fact that although many touched Jesus, this time was unique in that there was an actual transmission of healing power. Though this may be true, it seems more likely that the answer lies in His response to her: "Daughter, your faith has made you well; go in peace, and be healed of your affliction." Jesus wanted to use her as a witness to what faith can accomplish. He also wanted to bring her to the point of a verbal confession of her faith. Moreover, it was important that He correct any misguided superstitions regarding healing. The woman was not magically healed because she touched His garment, she was healed because of her faith. It was her faith in Jesus' ability to heal that wrought this miracle in her body, not the touching of his garment. R. A. Cole writes: "Such faith on the woman's part was at once rewarded by a healing of which she was instantly conscious. But Jesus makes plain, in His reply, that it was her faith which had healed her, not the mere touching of His robe. Otherwise it would have been either superstition or magic."[16]

The fact that Jesus told her to "go in peace, and be healed of your affliction" suggests complete wholeness and perfect healing. In this manner He sets His stamp of approval upon her act of faith.

The Servant's Power over Death (5:35–43)

What must have been going through Jairus's mind as the previous events were unfolding? Didn't Jesus understand the urgent nature of his request? Here his daughter was at the point of death, yet it seemed that Jesus was more interested in helping some wretched woman who had already been sick for twelve years! Couldn't she wait a little longer! Couldn't He heal her later at a more convenient time? It seems only normal that Jairus would have entertained some such thoughts as he witnessed the woman's healing. But that episode was over, and at least now they could get on their way again.

The text then declares, "While He was still speaking, they came from the house of the synagogue official, saying, 'Your daughter has died; why trouble the Teacher anymore?'" What a cold word. There is no comfort, no thoughtfulness, no concern for Jairus's feelings, just cold hard facts! The worst had happened. Lane notes, "The healing of the woman with a chronic hemorrhage resulted in a delay which was catastrophic for the young girl."[17] Similarly Edwards notes, "The interruption, so profitable to the woman, has cost the life of Jairus' daughter. Hope is now lost, and the inevitable conclusion follows, "'Why bother the teacher any more?'"[18]

Jairus had demonstrated faith when he came to Jesus—before he had witnessed the bleeding woman. What would he do now in the light of the information he had just received? Jesus, knowing always what He Himself would do, now asked Jairus to do something incredible. Ignoring the news from Jairus's home, Jesus said, "Do not be afraid any longer, only believe." In other words, he tells Jairus, "You came to me expecting and believing that I could heal your daughter. Ignore what you have just heard and trust me!" Edwards again provides insightful commentary:

The Lord speaks directly to Jairus. There is still one thing Jairus can do, but he must shift his focus from the circumstances of his daughter's death to Jesus himself. "Don't be afraid; only believe." This is the challenge before Jairus, and before everyone who meets Jesus: to believe only in what circumstances allow, or to believe in the God who makes all things possible? One thing only is necessary—to believe.[19]

At this point in the narrative, Jesus apparently dismisses both the crowd and the other disciples because the text states, "He allowed no one to follow with Him, except Peter and James and John the brother of James." Although it is not clearly stated, it may be that these disciples were permitted to accompany Jesus based upon their openness and responsiveness to previous revelation (4:25), or it could be that they had a more intimate relationship with Jesus than the other disciples. Grassmick suggests, "These three disciples served as legal witnesses here in anticipation of Jesus' resurrection, then at His transfiguration (Mark 9:2), and in Gethsemane (14:33).[20] In any event, they were selected to accompany Him to the house.

When Jesus came to the house, the text states that he, "beheld a commotion, and people loudly weeping and wailing." William Barclay writes concerning the mourning ritual:

> Immediately after death had taken place, a loud wailing was set up so that all might know that death had struck. The wailing was repeated at the graveside. The mourners hung over the dead body, begging for a response from the silent lips. They beat their breasts; they tore their hair; and they rent their garments.
>
> The rending of garments was done according to certain rules and regulations. It was done just before the body was finally hidden from sight. Garments were to be rent to the heart, that is, until the skin was exposed, but were not to be rent beyond the navel. For fathers and mothers the rent was on the left side, over the heart; for others it was on the right side. A woman was to rend her garments in private; she was then to reverse the inner garment so that it was worn back to front; she then rent her outer garment, so that her body was not exposed. The rent garment was worn for thirty days. After seven days the rent might be roughly sewn up, in such a way that it was still clearly visible. After the thirty days the garment was properly repaired.
>
> Flute-players were essential. Throughout most of the ancient world, in Rome, in Greece, in Phoenicia, in Assyria and in Palestine, the wailing of the flute was inseparably connected with death and tragedy. . . . The wail of the flutes, the screams of the mourners, the passionate appeals to the dead, the rent garments and the torn hair must have made a Jewish house a poignant and emotional place on the day of mourning.[21]

This would have been the scene Jesus, Jairus, and the disciples encountered as they entered the house.

In the midst of this confusion, Jesus asked, "Why make a commotion and weep? The child has not died, but is asleep." The response of the mourners is immediate and cold—just as cold as the message delivered to Jairus shortly before. We are told that "they began laughing at Him." On the one hand this is understandable. They knew that the child was dead. But on the other hand, they did not know that the one standing before them was the Prince of Life! To Him the child's death was not final nor irreversible.

The next action Jesus took was to rid the home of distractions. He dismissed the professional mourners and took only "the child's father and mother and His own companions," into the child's room. Then, "taking the child by the hand, He said to her, 'Talitha kum!' (which translated means, 'Little girl, I say to you, arise!'). And immediately the girl rose and began to walk." There is a most significant change of tense here. The verb translated "rose up" indicates an instantaneous act competed, while the verb "walked" (v. 42) implies a continuous walking.

Mark's added comment, "for she was twelve years old," refers to the fact that the girl was not yet of marriageable age.[22] As can be imagined, the result of this miracle was that "they were completely astounded."

At this point, Jesus gave two commands. The first was that no one outside of the five witnesses should be told about what happened (cf. 1:44). Most important to the story is the remarkable disclosure of Jesus' authority witnessed by the parents of the girl and His disciples. These few were given the privilege of a divine revelation which was not to revealed to others. The secret is what some call "a witnessed secret" which is to be kept from others by the Lord. The narrative alternates between disclosure of the messiahship and the veiling of the same. A particular reason for the silence may be found in the open lack of faith of those who had mocked Christ with their blatant ridicule and laughter. All the way through the book of Mark it is obvious that Jesus revealed his messiahship only with reserve. On many occasions Christ was not unwilling to show His messianic power and authority to the jeering, unbelieving crowd that had assembled outside Jairus' house. He did not grant that they should see the stunning miracle by which the girl was restored to her parents, and He commanded that it should continue to remain unknown to those remained doubters.[23]

Jesus' second command was that "something should be given her to eat." Here we see the human side of our Lord in that in the midst of bewilderment and exhilaration on the part of the parents, He reminded them that the girl needed food.

In conclusion, it is interesting to note some of the contrasts apparent in the narratives of verses 21–34 and verses 35–43. On the one hand, there is the woman. She is unnamed and at the point of poverty. On the other hand, there is the male ruler of the synagogue who is named and a respected member of the community. While the woman must carefully and secretly approach Jesus because of her uncleanness, Jairus freely approaches and speaks to Him face to face. In fact, the only thing these two people had in common was the hopelessness of their situations and their willingness to believe that Jesus had the answer to their problems.

Study Questions

1. Is demon possession still possible today? Do you know of any instances of apparent demon possession?

2. Why shouldn't the Jews raise hogs for a business investment? What does the Jewish Law say about eating pork?

3. If Jesus knew that Jairus's daughter would die, why did He not prevent that? What lessons would He be trying to teach?

4. What caused the Lord to turn out the professional mourners? Why did He not mourn with them?

5. What kind of relationship did Jairus have with his young daughter?

6. Why did Christ only take Peter, James, and John with Him when He was going to the house of Jairus to raise up his daughter? What made these three disciples special in His ministry?

7. If Christ could have raised more people from the dead, why did He not do so? Does God raise people from the dead now? Why not?

CHAPTER 6

The Servant in His Great Galilean Ministry Mark 6:1-56

Preview:

Jesus' own townspeople spurned this prophet from Nazareth, which was indicative of what was to become the attitude of most of the Jews. But Jesus sent forth His apostles to herald His kingdom and His work, preparatory to what should have been His genuine and general acceptance as the Messiah. After the death of John the Baptist at the hands of King Herod, the Lord appealed to the nation of Israel alone. Thereafter, Christ fed the five thousand not only because they were hungry, but also because they were "like sheep without a shepherd." The chapter concludes when the disciples see Christ walking on the sea, and with mere words, causing the wind to stop.

Return of Jesus to Nazareth (6:1-6)

(Compare Matthew 13:54-58; Luke 4:16-30)

Chapter 6 is the longest chapter in the book of Mark; nevertheless, his customary use of the term "immediately" (6:25, 45, 27, 50, 54) (Greek, *euthus*) keeps the narrative moving at a rapid pace.

We are told that Jesus, "went out from there, and He came into His home town; and His disciples follow Him." Jesus left Capernaum and traveled some twenty miles to the southwest, returning to his *patris* (homeland), namely, Nazareth. This was where He had been raised, had previously ministered, and had been rejected once before. Although He had allowed only Peter, James, and John to accompany Him to Jairus's home, He now brought the whole group of disciples with Him. Some see in this account a parallel with Luke 4:16–30, but the account in Luke came at the beginning of Jesus' ministry, about one year earlier.

D. Edmond Hiebert explains this story of Jesus' journey to Nazareth has a clear parallel in a shorter account in Matthew 13:54–58. Some believe this is the identical event recorded in Luke 4: 16- 31. It would seem to be almost impossible to have the same such rejection in the same location. Notable differences strongly support the view of two separate visits. Luke's account of the visit seems to come at the beginning of the lengthy Galilean ministry, but in the Mark account it appears to be sometime later. In Luke's version, the Lord appeared alone and proclaimed the beginning of His kingly ministry; in the second visit, He came as a teaching rabbi accompanied by His followers. In the first visit, Jesus evoked their violent, uncontrollable rage; in the second, they responded with cool indifference and personal insult. The violent rejection during the first visit did not keep the yearning heart of Jesus from giving His townsmen another opportunity to receive Him. The difference between the two visits seems established by the fact that Matthew clearly notes two separate visits to Nazareth. The story of Christ's rejection by Luke coincides with the visit mentioned in Matthew 4:13 when Jesus left Nazareth to establish headquarters in Capernaum. Coming later is the visit recorded in Matthew 13:54–58 that agrees with Mark's version. After the second visit to Nazareth, Christ began another tour throughout Galilee. Clearly, this visit seems later than that in Luke 4:16–31.[1]

"And when the Sabbath had come, He began to teach in the synagogue:" The first record of Jesus' having spoken in the synagogue is contained in Luke 4:16–30. There it is noted that he "stood up to read" as was "His custom." It was the common custom of the day for the ruler of the synagogue to ask someone to speak if he wished. This provides us with a valuable lesson. If Jesus found it necessary to faithfully attend the local synagogue, should we not also be faithful in our participation in our local church?

Surely Jesus' reputation and acclaim had preceded Him, and yet we are told that He did not begin teaching until the Sabbath. This seems to suggest that unlike the multitudes in the surrounding areas who continually thronged Jesus and eagerly hung on His words, the residents of His hometown did not see any reason to esteem Him, nor were they overly excited at His return.

When Jesus began to speak, He was interrupted by their reaction. It was that "many listeners were astonished." At first glance this seems a normal response but closer examination indicates otherwise. The verb "were astonished" has the idea "to strike with panic, to be struck with terror, to be struck with a sudden and startling alarm."[2] The root of this compound verb (*ekplēssō*) means to strike or smite with the idea of flattening out. The imperfect or past tense indicates that their reaction was a process, they were "being" astonished at Jesus' teaching.

Jesus' words did not lead them to faith, but rather revealed their unbelief. Their narrow-minded presumptions spawned doubt and confusion, which led to sarcastic and cynical questionings among themselves. An examination of these questions reveals that they first attacked Jesus' ministry. They began asking, "Where did this man get these things? and what is this wisdom given to Him, and such miracles as these performed by His hands? The use of the Greek *touto*, this "one/man," can only signify contempt in this context, as is apparent from the following verses. They knew Jesus. He was one of them, and yet they referred to him in a most derogatory manner. It is remarkably sad that the townspeople recognized both His wisdom (expressed in their midst) and His mighty works (no doubt reported to them), and yet they were oblivious to what those things revealed.

As this process of "being astonished" continued, they realized that they could not refute Jesus' words or deeds so they then attacked Him personally. "Is not this the carpenter . . ?" It is only here that Jesus is explicitly referred to as a carpenter and the purpose of their question is clear, as D. Edmond Hiebert explains, "Their designation of Him by trade placed Him on a level with themselves. They rejected any thought that He was better than they."[3]

"Is not this . . . the son of Mary . . . ?" Here was perhaps the most biting attack of all. By referring to Jesus as the son of Mary, they were insinuating that He was illegitimate. Louis Barbieri notes, "They acknowledged that He was 'the son of Mary,' but this was actually a derogatory comment, for a Jewish man was never identified with his mother, even if his father had died.[4]

As if this were not enough, they finally removed any possibility in their own minds that Jesus could be anything other than a mere man by listing his family members. "Is not this . . . the brother of James, and Joses, and Judas, and Simon? Are not His sisters here with us? Their familiarity with Jesus' immediate family was for them the blind spot that they could not remove. Jesus was one of them. How could He be anything else?

The fact that Jesus' siblings are mentioned is significant. Although four brothers are named, James and Judas are apparently the only ones actively involved in the early church, James functioning as the spokesman at the Jerusalem assembly in Acts 15, and Judas (Jude) writing the book named for him. The use of the plural "sisters" indicates that He had at least two, and the fact that they are unnamed suggests, according to Jewish custom, that there were more than likely unmarried. This clearly disproves the false teachings that Mary was a perpetual virgin and that Jesus was an only child.

The final outcome of their "being astonished" is that "they took offense at." The Greek word *scandalizō* means "to give offense, cause to stumble." Our English word scandal is derived from this. The *Theological Dictionary of the New Testament* states, "The original stem has the sense of 'springing forward and back, 'slamming to,' 'closing on something,' or 'trapping,' but later the meaning 'offense,' or 'reason for punishment,' occurs in the papyri."[5]

Also contained within the meaning of this word is the idea of "being offended and repelled to the point of abandoning."[6] These people were trapped by their prejudices and narrow-mindedness. They were repelled by "this one" because of their external familiarity with Him. This rejection of Jesus by His unbelieving neighbors is incredible when contrasted with his successes in the preceding narratives.

Jesus' proverbial response, "A prophet is not without honor, except in his home town, and among his own relatives, and in his own household," is not uncommon, and one can find many parallels in both Jewish and Greek literature. In making this comment, Jesus compares Himself and His experience to that of the Old Testament prophets. Like them, He too is dishonored and speaking in what may be considered a prophetic manner, He intimates that He will be rejected by His immediate family, His extended family, and finally by Israel—something He had already begun to experience (cf. 3:20–21,31–35).

We are next told, "He could do no miracle there except that He laid His hands upon a few sick people and healed them." The statement that Jesus, "could do no miracle there", has been taken in a couple of ways. One explanation is that, it was the people's unbelief that prevented them from bringing sick folk to Jesus, thus limiting His exposure to the needs of the people. Lenski writes: "The reason this unbelief prevented his working more than a few miracles is the fact that so few came to him for help. Even when the people living in other localities did not believe in Jesus they at least brought all their sick to him."[7]

Another view set forth is that the people's unbelief somehow "tied" Jesus' hands, limiting His ability to perform miracles and rendering Him virtually powerless. These same teachers indicate that there must be an "atmosphere of faith and expectancy" if God is going to be able to do all He wants to do. Such a view reveals a lack of comprehension of the sovereignty of God and also reveals an insufficient understanding of who Jesus is. This mind-set ultimately puts man in control of God.

If before becoming new creatures in Christ we are truly dead in trespasses and sin and are enemies of the cross, how is it then that we are ever saved?

If our nature is depraved and we are bound by unbelief, then our unbelief has "tied" God's hands and there is no hope for us.

This cannot be the reason for Jesus' failure to do "miracles". If the people's unbelief tied Jesus' hands, how is it that "He laid His hands upon a few sick people, and healed them?"

The better answer to this question has to do with the outcome of performing miracles in the midst of unbelief. Clearly, "He felt it morally impossible to exercise His beneficent power in their behalf in the face of their unbelief (Matt. 13:58). . . . He refused to force Himself upon those who did not want Him."[8] William Lane explains why it would have been problematic to do so:

> It is not Mark's intention to stress Jesus' *inability* when he states that he could perform no miracles at Nazareth. His purpose is rather to indicate that Jesus was not free to exercise his power *in these circumstances*. The performance of miracles in the absence of faith could have resulted only in the aggravation of human guilt and the hardening of men's hearts against God. The power of God which Jesus possessed could be materialized in a genuinely salutary fashion only when there was the receptivity of faith.[9]

The fact that Jesus performed any healings in the midst of the people's unbelief was indicative of the fact that, as the God-man, He could do so at will. The *KJV Bible Commentary* is correct when it asserts, "By definition God's omnipotence cannot be limited. When Mark said the God-man could there do no mighty work, the repression was self-imposed, based upon His own principles and volition."[10]

Clearly, Jesus could have performed any miracle He wanted to even in that environment of unbelief. God's manifested power is not dependent upon our faith, but only upon His purposes. Moreover, contrary to what many teach, faith is not always a necessary requirement for miracles, for many occurred in the face of unbelief (3:1–6; 4:35–41; 6:35–44).

Upon witnessing the reaction of His neighbors, it is said of Jesus that, "He wondered at their unbelief." There are only two occasions where it is said that Jesus "*wondered*" (see Matt. 8:10; Luke 7:9). In this instance, Jesus marvels at His neighbors' unwillingness to believe what they had heard about Him and their unwillingness to believe what they were seeing Him do. Surely in His hometown He had a right to expect to find some faith.

The phrase, "And He was going around the villages, teaching" introduces a new paragraph. D. Edmond Hiebert notes that this was a transitional statement and was actually set off as a distinct paragraph. It specifically focused on the outcome of the visit to Nazareth but also set the background for the future mission of the Twelve. Mark literally said, "He was going round the villages in a circle," indicating that the tour of Galilee started at Nazareth and ended near the place where He began. Christ's main purpose and mission here was teaching. Matthew 9:35 gives a more complete and comprehensive picture of this tour.[11]

Repentance, the Message of the Twelve (6:7–13)

(Compare Matthew 10:5–15; Luke 9:1–6)

Many theologians divide Jesus' wider Galilean ministry into three parts: 1:14—3:6; 3:7—7:23; and 7:24—9:50.

This section is part of the second phase of Jesus' Galilean ministry and deals with His sending forth of the Twelve. "And He summoned the twelve, and began to send them out in pairs;" David Hewitt remarks:

> Jesus' initial call to his disciples in Mark 1:17 was "Come, follow me . . . and I will make you fishers of men." Mark 3:14 tells us that Jesus chose them with two purposes in mind. Firstly "that they might be with him" and secondly "that he might send them out to preach." This is the pattern of discipleship. We are called to him, equipped by him and then sent out as his representatives.[12]

Dr. A. B. Bruce notes that this sending out of the disciples was Jesus' original plan and purpose for them. By calling (*proskaleitai*) the Twelve He *began* at length to do what He had proposed from the beginning, i.e., to send them forth as missionaries (*apostellein*).[13]

The fact that Jesus "began to send them out"(*ēpxatō*, aorist middle deponent) indicates that they were not sent out all at once but were individually commissioned. This suggests that after they had collectively received their empowerment, they individually received instruction as to where they were to go.

There are a number of reasons for sending the disciples out in pairs (see Eccl. 4:9-12). They would have protection, encouragement, and companionship, but most important they would be able to spread out in six different directions and thus cover more area. This method (sending out in pairs) had been used by John the Baptist (Luke 7:19; John 1:37) and would continue to be used by the early Church (Acts 11:30; 12:25; 13:2; 15:22; 15:39-40; 17:14-15; 18:5; 19:22). Perhaps this was also done to satisfy the 'witness' requirements contained in the Law of Moses (Num. 35:30; Deut. 17:6; 19:15; 2 Cor. 13:1; 1 Tim. 5:19). It was a good ministry plan then and is a good plan today. Concerning how the pairs were made up is suggested in Matthew 10:2-4 where their names are listed together–Simon and Andrew, James and John, Philip and Bartholomew, Thomas and Matthew, James the son of Alphaeus and Thaddaeus, and Simon the Canaanite and Judas Iscariot.

Jesus, "was giving them authority over the unclean spirits." The use of the imperfect tense in Greek, "(He) was giving authority to them," indicates that Jesus continually gave them "authority" over unclean spirits throughout the time of their mission. This authority and power over demons would serve to authenticate their message to the people. Lenski notes that authority (*exousia*)

> is both the right to do a thing and the power to exercise that right. The genitive is objective: "authority over the unclean spirits," the adjective "unclean" being emphatic since it is added by a second article in the Greek. . . . The fact is that Jesus fitted the apostles out with powers that were like his own, only their powers were a gift to them from Jesus, those of Jesus were inherent in himself.[14]

And He instructed them that they should take nothing for their journey, except a mere staff; no bread, no bag, no money in their belt; but to wear sandals; and He added, "Do not put on two tunics." The disciples had walked with Jesus and seen His many miracles but they had not truly been tested with regard to their personal reliance upon Him. This mission would require absolute dependence upon their Lord if it was to be successful. D. Edmond Hiebert comments:

> The major point in these instructions is that they were to go forth without elaborate preparations. Jesus intended the mission to be a lesson in trust to His disciples. They were to learn that in His service their needs would be supplied (Matthew 10:10). When during Passion Week Jesus asked them about their experience, they testified that they had lacked nothing (Luke 22:35).[15]

This first set of instructions was not designed to force adversity upon the disciples. Rather, it was in fact designed to focus their attention and concern on His ability to supply their needs. This was an important lesson if they were to succeed once Jesus was no longer with them physically.

At this point Matthew provides details that are not included in Mark's account. He records Jesus' command that they, "Do not go in the way of the Gentiles, and do not enter any city of the Samaritans; but rather go to the lost sheep of the house of Israel. And as you go, preach, saying 'the kingdom of heaven is at hand. Heal the sick, raise the dead, cleanse the lepers, cast out demons; freely you received, freely give'" (Matt. 10:5–8).

Included in the endowment of power over unclean spirits is the power to "heal the sick, raise the dead, cleanse the lepers." In other words, the disciples were to mirror the works of their Master. As they did this, they were to preach [*kērussō, to preach to a public and official proclamation designed to persuade, urge, warn to comply*] saying, 'The kingdom of heaven is at hand'".[16] Verse 12 tells us that included in this proclamation was the warning to repent (*metanoeō,*"to change one's life, based on complete change of attitude and thought concerning sin and righteousness").[17] The disciples were to first preach, then under the guidance of the Holy Spirit, the works were to follow. The focus of their message was repentance because "the kingdom of heaven is at hand" (Matt. 10:7).

The order of events here is critically important. It cannot be stated strongly enough that the works were designed solely to authenticate the message and the messenger. They were never designed to draw attention to the disciples themselves. Moreover, once the message had been authenticated and the canon closed, this was no longer necessary. This method of ministry was transitory in nature and, in spite of what some would teach, is no longer extant today.

In verses 10–11 Mark provides the second set of instructions in the form of direct discourse. This deals with the conduct of the disciples while on their ministry tour. They were told, "Wherever you enter a house, stay there until you leave town." The disciples were not to go from house to house, because this might cause undue competition or envy among neighbors. Like their Master, they were not to please themselves, nor were they to compromise their mission effort by endeavoring to provide for their own needs.

Matthew notes that when the disciples entered into a city they were to "inquire who is worthy in it" (10:11). Their message was not to be hindered in any way. It would not do to align themselves with those who could bring disgrace upon their ministry. They were to look for a worthy host who believed their message and accepted them as representatives of the Lord.

Jesus next told His disciples, "Any place that does not receive you or listen to you, as you go out from there, shake off the dust from the soles of your feet for a testimony against them." This is a clear declaration that the disciples can expect to suffer rejection. Upon encountering unbelief among their hearers, they were to shake the dust from their feet. It was a common practice among devout Jews that after passing through a pagan country they would shake the dust off of their clothes and shoes. In this way they demonstrated their uniqueness as God's people and God's coming judgment upon the pagan. By so doing, the disciples made it clear that they had fulfilled their ministry responsibility and that those who had rejected it would answer to God.

R. Alan Cole accurately and clearly sums up this situation. "Those who reject the message of Jesus, brought by His servants, are not 'God's people,' but have similarly made themselves 'Gentiles' as far as the kingdom of God is concerned, in front of the 'two witnesses' demanded by the Law (Dt. 17:6)."[18]

This is understandable because the message delivered and the works performed were sufficient to convince the hearts of those who would believe. The reason for this judgment is clear. William Lane explains:

Jesus authorized the disciples to be his delegates with respect to both word and power. Their message and deeds were to be an extension of his own. The commissioning of the Twelve has a rich background in the juridical practice of Judaism, which recognized the official character of actions performed by authorized individuals. Reduced to its simplest form, the law acknowledged that "the sent one is as the man who commissioned him."[19]

Again, it should be noted that Jesus affirmed that the disciples would encounter rejection (Matt. 10:16–42). They had seen the rejection of their Master recently both by the Gadarenes and by His own hometown. Jesus prepared them for this certainty. The result of such unbelief was that it would be "more tolerable for the land of Sodom and Gomorrah in the day of judgment, than for that city" (Matt. 10:15). The expression, "more tolerable" suggests degrees of punishment. Moreover, in His condemnation of Capernaum, Jesus said that "if the miracles had occurred in Sodom which occurred in you, it would have remained to this day" (Matt. 11:23). This does not preclude the sinfulness of Sodom and Gomorrah but does suggest that there would have been some who would have believed the message! Not receiving Jesus and His message, given the continual demonstration of His wisdom and power, was the ultimate degree of unbelief.

Verses 12–13 tell of the obedience of the disciples and of their successful campaign. Interestingly, there is no evidence that Jesus anointed with oil as part of His healing ministry. Why the disciples did so is somewhat of a mystery. Lenski explains that the use of oil here was an exception in relation to healings, and that it was used only in the early tour of the apostles. Christ did not use oil in this way, nor did the apostles after that initial trip. Christ may have first called for the oil; it is doubtful that the apostles themselves thought of employing it in healing. The oil was only an adjunct to the miracles because the true healing power came through the word as spoken by the apostles under the authority of Jesus. The use of the oil may have been only for psychological purposes as an aid in the faith of those who were sick. While believing patients were healed there were other instances in which faith preceded the miraculous healing (Matt. 8:6; Mark 3:1; John 9:1). To bring about faith was the purpose of the miracles and to kindle it where it did not exist, or to justify and strengthen it where it was not before. The apostles were beginners in the work of the Lord and they needed this help to minister. After Pentecost the sick to whom the oil was applied understood the apostles were now taking in hand to do what their Master had done before. They understood the anointing was in connection with Jesus. In many cases the faith was already there and in many other cases followed when the great words of healing were spoken in the name of Jesus.[20]

We do know that in biblical times olive oil was often used as a medicine (cf. Luke 10:34; James 5:14). It is significant to note that there is a distinction made between the casting out of devils and the healing of the sick. This clearly reveals that sickness is not always related to demonic activity as some teach.

Record of John's Martyrdom (6:14–29)

(Compare Matthew 14:1–12; Luke 9:7–9)

Verses 14–29 introduce a parenthetical section designed to fill in important information that Mark felt was relevant to the narrative. It is likely that these events took place two or three months earlier. It is also interesting to note that this passage and Mark 1:2–8 are the only two passages in the book of Mark that do not directly talk about Jesus.

Most commentators divide this narrative into two parts, but it is easier to see it as being made up of three parts. The first tells of Herod's having heard of Jesus, no doubt in part due to the ministry of the Twelve (vv. 14–16). This suggests that the disciples were careful to exalt Jesus in all that they did. It begins with a brief declaration of Herod Antipas's fears about Jesus and reveals some of the common opinions concerning Him. Herod was apprehensive that Jesus might really be John the Baptist risen from the dead. Some thought Jesus might be the fulfillment of the Elijah prophecy of Malachi 4:5–6 or that He might be "one of the prophets." Terrified, Herod tended to believe that Jesus was John, for his conscience tormented him because he knew that John indeed was a prophet.

The second part tells of the reason for John's death (vv. 17–20). The story is simple but sad. Evidently Herod had gone to hear John preach, possibly out of curiosity or some degree of concern. John spoke out against Herod's sinful relationship with Herodias, the wife of his half brother Phillip. "For John had been saying to Herod, 'It is not lawful for you to have your brother's wife,'" based on Leviticus 18:16 and 20:21. Herod then had John imprisoned. In the expression "for John had been saying" (v. 18), the verb, "had been saying"(*elegen*) is in the imperfect, indicating that this rebuke had been made on more than one occasion. This seems to hint at the fact that either (1) Herod had met with John occasionally, perhaps while he was yet in prison, or (2) before his imprisonment, John had sent this rebuke to Herod by the hands of his disciples.

The text says, "Herod was afraid of John, knowing that he was a righteous and holy man, and kept him safe." Herod's fear was ongoing (*ephobeito*, imperfect passive deponent); nevertheless, he continued to protect John from his wife's evil intent for him. "He used to enjoy listening to him" seems a strange statement until we take into account that even evil men can appreciate the goodness of the righteous without repenting of their wickedness. David Hewitt correctly notes:

> "Herod was a man caught in two minds. Fascinated by John and his message and yet afraid of the consequences of that message for his own life. The Apostle Paul meets a similar man in authority–Felix (see Acts 24:24–26). Felix, like Herod, was fascinated but afraid."[21]

The third part tells the actual manner in which John's death occurred (6:21–29). Herodias sought an opportunity to have John the Baptist eliminated (her jealousy and anger and guilt pressed in upon her). When her daughter, Salome, danced before the king on a festive occasion, the monarch made a rash promise, offering to give her anything possible in his kingdom. Coached by her mother, she asked for John the Baptist's head.

Why did Mark insert this parenthetical passage? Just before this, Jesus commissioned, empowered, and warned His disciples about the rejection that lay ahead. Mark uses this narrative about John the Baptist to drive home Jesus' warning more fully expressed in the parallel account in Matthew 10:16–42. No doubt it was designed to focus the reader upon the cost of righteous service in a depraved world. James Edwards correctly writes:

> The sandwich structure draws mission and martyrdom, discipleship and death, into an inseparable relationship. This is precisely what Jesus will teach in 8:34, "If anyone would come after me, he must deny himself and take up his cross and follow me." There, as here, both words are addressed to disciples. Whoever would follow Jesus must first reckon with the fate of John. John's martyrdom not only prefigures Jesus' death, but it also prefigures the death of anyone who would follow him.[22]

Similarly, James Brooks sees this account as a foreshadowing of the death of Jesus. He provides the following insightful observations.

> John, like Jesus, was executed by a secular ruler. Herod, like Pilate, did not want to execute his prisoner but caved in to pressure from others. Herodias, like the chief priests, schemed to bring about the execution. John's disciples, like Joseph of Arimathea, tenderly buried the body of their leader.[23]

Report of the Apostles to Jesus (6:30–32)

(Compare Luke 9:10–11)

This represents one of four systematic withdrawals that Jesus made from Galilee, one to the eastern coast of the Sea of Galilee (6:31–56), one to the region of Tyre and Sidon (7:24–30), one to Decapolis (7:31–8:9), and finally one to Caesarea Philippi (8:10–9:1). These withdrawals seem to have served two purposes, namely, as an opportunity for Jesus to provide further in-depth training of the Twelve and as an opportunity for them to secure needed rest.

"And the apostles gathered together with Jesus". This is the only place where Mark calls the Twelve "apostles"(*apostoloi*). Hiebert notes regarding the use of this title:

> It is fitting here, because they were returning from their first official mission as His commissioned representatives. Perhaps Mark intended the term here not as an official title but in the general sense of missionary; yet he probably did have in mind also the official connotation of the word, which it certainly had by the time he was writing.[24]

This marked the termination of their first ministry tour. The Gospels do not indicate how long they were gone but it seems likely that Jesus would have set a fixed time and place for their return. Many believe that they met back at the city of Capernaum. They returned just as they had been sent out, namely in pairs. This is suggested by the present passive verb *sunagontai* (historical present–"they *continually* gathered together").

As they returned, they "reported to Him all that they had done and taught." Without question, the disciples would have been filled with enthusiasm as they reported back to Jesus.

Interestingly, Mark notes that the disciples told Jesus first "all that they had done" and then what they had "taught". The order of their report suggests that the disciples were perhaps more excited about the "power" they had been given to do miracles than the message. Perhaps Jesus saw that they were preoccupied with their accomplishments or that they were emotionally and physically weary. Ray Stedman correctly notes Jesus' concern for His weary disciples. He adds that it is clear from this that our Lord recognized this as a period of danger to these disciples. Christ made provision for their needed rest so they could think through what all had taken place. From the accounts of Matthew and Luke it is clear that these men were very excited about their new ministry. They were greatly encouraged by the results and like boys released from school, they were anxious to report to Christ all that had taken place. They were so "turned on" Christ had to caution them, "Don't rejoice over the fact that the demons are subject to you, but rejoice rather that your names are written in heaven." The Lord observed that they were in danger of being overcome by pride and exaltation at the work they had done.[25]

There was perhaps another reason for this withdrawal. Matthew indicates that John's disciples came to Jesus with the report of John's death. It appears that this may have happened at about the same time that the Twelve were returning (Matt. 14:12–13). This sad news coupled with the successful ministry of the Twelve no doubt would have stirred up the crowd, already eager to force Jesus to become their political leader, to move against Herod. For these reasons, Jesus purposely removed Himself and His disciples from the area.

Regardless of the reasons, the disciples needed to be refreshed (*anapausasthe*) (literally "rest up")[26] so He called upon them to "come away by yourselves to a lonely place and rest a while. (For there were many people coming and going, and they did not even have time to eat.) And they went away in the boat to a lonely place by themselves." Notice the situation that the weary disciples encountered: "there were many people coming and going, and they did not even have time to eat." They had just come back from an exhausting mission, yet the people continued to make demands upon them. It is important to remember that no matter how much good one does, there will always be more to do. People have many needs and are often oblivious to the fact that ministers have needs too. Therefore, budgeting one's time is essential.

It has been said that if we do not "come apart" occasionally, we may "come apart" for a long time. It is wiser to burn on than to burn out! Knowing this, Jesus emphatically called the Twelve aside, "You yourselves come and no one else!" No other disciples were invited. No family members were invited. The disciples were to find their refreshment alone with their Lord!

Reasons for Feeding the Five Thousand (6:33–44)
(Compare Matthew 14:13–21; Luke 9:10–17; John 6:1–13)

The feeding of the five thousand is the only miracle recorded by all four evangelists. Those who deny its factual historicity go against four witnesses.

The Lord's intent had been to pull the disciples away from the crowds to an isolated location where they could rest and share the events of their recent missionary tour (vv. 31–32). But this was not to be. No doubt, Jesus' reputation, and now that of His disciples, was at its highest Galilean and the needy and the curious among the people were determined to get to them one way or another.

"And the people saw them going, and many recognized them, and they ran there together on foot from all the cities, and got there ahead of them." Apparently, a large number of the people present deduced where it was that they were headed and, on foot, outran them. It must have been similar to the experience of many of our movie stars and musicians today, yet much more intense. As these people made their way around the shore, the local townspeople no doubt became curious about the goings on and joined them so that by the time they arrived at their destination, the crowd was very large. Needy people are determined people, and the fact that Jesus and the disciples were back in their local area meant that they would have an opportunity to have their needs met.

It must have been a sight to see. Jesus and the disciples would have been able to see the people running and gathering ahead of them. It is likely that these tired disciples began to wonder if they would ever have time alone with Jesus again. These pesky people were never satisfied! If this was the disciples' attitude, it certainly was not Jesus' attitude. Jesus did not view this as an inconvenience, but rather as another opportunity to minister truth to the people. Lenski notes that the word "compassion" here means:

> In spite of all the unbelief that Jesus encountered, and in spite of His desire to withdraw from His great public activity and to be alone with His disciples, His heart was moved at the sight of all this crowd that had so rapidly and eagerly followed Him. . . . The eyes of Jesus saw more than a mass of people, they saw the spiritual condition of those people. He saw the fate of these people unless they were shepherded.[27]

The English phrase "He felt compassion" is an aorist passive deponent from the Greek verb *splagchnizomai*. This verb is used only in reference to Jesus in the New Testament (e.g., Matt. 9:36; 14:14; 15:32; 18:27; 20:34; Mark 1:41; 6:34; 8:2; 9:22; Luke 7:13; 10:33; 15:20) and indicates much more than mere emotion on the part of Jesus. In the Synoptic Gospels it is used with a theological meaning expressing the divine mercy present within Jesus. The *Theological Dictionary of the New Testament* notes that the use of this verb signifies "a Messianic characterization of Jesus rather than the mere depiction of an emotion."[28] "It suggests something more than mere pity; it suggests actual help. Here the compassion is not just for physical need but for lostness."[29]

The expression "they were like sheep without a shepherd" is often seen in a pastoral context; however, Edwards notes:

> Although this image elicits pictures of Jesus helping weak and helpless sheep (Matt 9:36), a pastoral connotation is not its primary connotation in Jewish tradition. As a metaphor, the shepherd of sheep was a common figure of speech in Israel for a leader of Israel like Moses (Isa 63:11), or more often of a Joshua-like military hero who would muster Israel's forces for war (Num 27:17; 1 Kgs 22:17; 2 Chr 18:16; Jer 10:21; Ezek 34:5; 37:24; Nah 3:18; Zech 13:7; Jdt 11:19). It is, in other words, a metaphor of hegemony, including military leadership and victory.[30]

Israel is here portrayed as a people without direction, purpose, or leadership. They, like sheep, were helpless, exposed, and lost. This prompted within Jesus a desire "to teach them many things." It is interesting to note that Jesus' compassion is expressed first and foremost in that He saw their need for sound doctrine and supplied it. We know from Luke's account that the content of His teaching was "the kingdom of God." We find there also that Jesus healed "those who had need of healing" (Luke 9:11). Jesus and the disciples had come for a rest, but the ministry had just picked up where it had left off on the other shore!

The text tells us that Jesus continued teaching and ministering to the needs of the people until, "it was already quite late." At this point, the disciples approached Jesus with the suggestion that Jesus "send them away, so that they may go into the surrounding countryside and villages and buy themselves something to eat." It may well be that the disciples were sincere in their concern for the crowd. It may also be that there were tired and desirous of that long awaited rest for which they had been looking. But the Lord had something else in mind.

"He answered and said to them, 'You give them something to eat!'" Here they were in a solitary desert location with no special resources. One can only imagine what must have gone through the minds of the disciples at this point. It reminds us of Moses' experience with the children of Israel in Numbers 11. The people became weary of the manna and cried out for meat. Moses' complaint was, "Where am I to get meat to give to all this people? . . . Should flocks and herds be slaughtered for them, to be sufficient for them? Or should all the fish of the sea be gathered together for them, to be sufficient for them?" (vv. 13, 22).

With a note of some frustration, the disciples ask Jesus, "Shall we go and spend two hundred denarii on bread and give them something to eat?" The denarius was the primary silver coin of the Roman empire and was the ordinary pay for a day's work. This amount was equivalent to about eight months' wages, a significant sum of money! Even if they had the money, it just wasn't feasible for them to run to town, buy the bread, and come back.

These same disciples had just come back from a successful missionary tour and had witnessed numerous miracles during their time with the Lord. Perhaps it was their fatigue or perhaps it was their dullness of spirit, but in any case, they should have realized that if Jesus was commanding them to feed the people, He was going to provide the resources to do so. God's answer to Moses is applicable here, "Is the Lord's power limited?" Feeding this group was something that was beyond their ability—the very thing Jesus wanted them to understand in the first place.

To more fully set the stage for what He was about to do, Jesus sent the disciples out on a reconnaissance mission to see what the crowd itself had to contribute. "And when they found out, they said, 'Five loaves and two fish.'" This Jesus did, not for His own benefit, but for the benefit of the disciples. Jesus wanted the disciples to know that what He was about to do was not based in any way upon human ability or provision. William Lane thoughtfully summarizes the situation.

> They were utterly unprepared for Jesus' instruction to provide for the needs of the multitude. This is evident from the astonishment expressed in their question about purchasing bread, which is disrespectful in tone, but points unmistakably to the impossibility of complying with Jesus' order. . . . Jesus' refusal to let the issue rest by insisting that they count their reserves of bread forces the recognition that the situation was beyond human resourcefulness.[31]

"And he commanded them all to recline by groups on the green grass. And they reclined in companies of hundreds and of fifties." What a test of faith! The disciples, without knowing what Jesus was about to do, were commanded to organize the people. With nothing more than the word of Jesus to go on, they obeyed. The stage was now fully set. Louis Barbieri, quoting Henry Barclay Swete, comments:

> The purpose of the arrangement was probably to prevent a dangerous scramble for the food, or at any rate, confusion and disorder (cf. I Cor. xiv. 33, 40), and to secure an easy and rapid distribution: twelve men could serve fifty to one hundred companies in a comparatively short time. Incidentally the division into companies made the counting of the multitude a simple matter, and accounts for the same number being given by the four evangelists.[32]

Once order was established among the crowd, Jesus took the five loaves and the two fishes in His hands and looking toward heaven, "blessed the food, and broke the loaves." We do not know what Jesus said but it is likely that He offered up the common Jewish prayer offered before meals, "Blessed art Thou, O Lord our God, King of the world, who bringest forth bread from the earth". According to custom, this would have been answered by the people responding, "Amen!"

Finishing the prayer of blessing for the provisions, the text tells us that Jesus "kept giving them to the disciples to set before them; and He divided up the two fish among them all." The English word "gave" is from the Greek root word *didōmi* (as an imperfect active indicative). This indicates the continual action of giving. Miraculously, the loaves and the fishes were multiplied in Jesus' hands. What an incredible picture! Just as God had given manna to their ancestors in the wilderness, so Jesus provided food for them. The parallel would not have been overlooked by the people.

The magnitude of this miracle is fantastic. Some have tried to force a sacramental meaning to the feeding of the five thousand. This is nonsense! The people were not given some small morsel of food, for "they all ate and were satisfied." The verb *chortazō* suggests entire satisfaction. They all ate until there was no more desire for food. But the miracle did not stop there for "they picked up twelve full baskets of the broken pieces, and also of the fish." Jesus went beyond their highest expectations. After collecting what remained, the Twelve discovered that Jesus had made provision for them, providing one basket per disciple!

Mark closes the account by noting that "there were five thousand men who ate the loaves." The plural form of the Greek word *anēr* is used. This word refers to "males" only. If women and children were present, the crowd would have been significantly larger.

Though Mark does not indicate the reaction of the crowd to this miracle, John does, writing, "When therefore the people saw the sign which He had performed, they said, 'This is of a truth the Prophet who is to come into the world" (John 6:14).

Rescue of the Twelve Apostles in the Storm (6:45–52)

(Compare Matthew 14:22–32; John 6:15–21)

"And immediately He made His disciples get into the boat and go ahead of Him to the other side to Bethsaida, while He Himself was sending the multitude away." It is clear that neither the crowd nor the disciples had understood the purpose of the miracle they had just witnessed and as John writes, Jesus perceived "that they were intending to come and take Him by force, to make Him king" (John 6:15). Because of this impending threat, Jesus urgently commanded the disciples to set sail without Him to cross the Sea of Galilee for Bethsaida. The command was urgent because the disciples were susceptible to the desires of the crowd. We are not told how Jesus handled this problem, but we are told that he "was sending the multitude away." The ability to repress the misguided desires of the excited crowd was no less miraculous!

After dismissing the crowd, Jesus "departed to the mountain to pray." Mark speaks of Jesus' leaving the people for solitary prayer on more that one occasion (see 1:35–39; 6:45–46; and 14:26–42). In each of these cases it is nighttime and Jesus is confronted with a possible crisis. Hiebert comments on this event and says that His actions show His consciousness that that He is now facing an important turn of events. The Lord needed counsel and strengthening to face what was coming. The offer of the crown was a repeat of what happened in the wilderness temptation to bypass the pain of the cross. Christ needed the fellowship and communion with His heavenly Father for facing each day and the consequences of His decisions. He also shared His petitions with the Twelve disciples so they would not surrender to misleading and false messianic expectations. Prayer clearly played a vital place in the life and ministry of Christ.[33]

After Jesus finished His prayer and communion with the Father, we are told that evening had come. Specifically, it was at the "fourth watch of the night" or between 3:00 and 6:00 in the morning. Jesus, alone on the land, watched them as they labored at rowing the ship now in the midst of the sea. Mark writes that Jesus took note of the fact that "the wind was against them." These disciples who had been hoping for rest and relaxation now found themselves in another difficult and stressful situation. How they had managed to row that boat to the middle of the sea is impressive. They had had little or no rest! The word rendered "toiling" is translated "vexed" in 2 Peter 2:8 and implies more than physical strain. The disciples were under severe mental and emotional distress. For all they knew, the boat might capsize and they themselves might be drowned in the violent waters.

In the midst of this horrifying experience, we are told that "He came to them, walking on the sea; and He intended to pass by them." Louis Barbieri, again quoting Henry Barclay Swete, notes:

> The reader is left to complete the picture; the Lord must be imagined as walking on a seething sea, not upon a smooth surface . . . now on the crest of a wave, now hidden out of sight It was the darkest hour of the night, and the moon probably had set; only the outline of a human form could be seen appearing from time to time, and approaching the boat.[34]

This is an interesting picture, and one that does not adequately give a sense of authority and control on the part of Jesus. Lenski's explanation more likely better suits the actual events:

> The wind howled, the waves dashed high, but they affected him not at all. He was not pitched about or tossed up and down; he was not soaked with waves or spray striking him. Before him, as he moved his feet, a smooth, apparently solid path lay, on which he walked as on ordinary ground. He did not move or float in the air as a specter is supposed to do. No unearthly light played around him as painters generally imagine. It was simply Jesus just as they had seen and left him the evening before—but now walking on the storm-tossed sea.[35]

Of three authors, Mark is the only one who indicates that Jesus "intended to pass by them." The emphasis here is on the language Mark chooses to explain this event. It is likely that the terminology used would have been understood by Mark's readers as expressing a theophany, because the very same Greek wording is used in the Septuagint to do just that (see Ex. 33:19, 22; 1 Kgs. 19:11). Another consideration is that the Greek verb used here could be understood to mean "to come alongside." Jesus did not plan to pass by, leaving them to the storm, but actually headed toward them and paralleled their course. His purpose in doing so was simply to reassure them of His presence. He had sent them out in the boat, and He was aware of their circumstances.

We are told that when the disciples saw Jesus walking on the sea, their first response was one of great fear and trepidation, for "they supposed that it was a ghost." Jesus did not rebuke them but immediately spoke to their fear, saying "Take courage; it is I, do not be afraid." He then entered into the boat, and suddenly "the wind stopped." John notes also that upon entering the boat, "immediately the boat was at the land to which they were going" (John 6:21).

The disciples' emotions were already frazzled with fatigue and fear, but the text tells us that with this event, they became "greatly astonished." This is a very emphatic statement, literally reading "and exceedingly, extraordinarily beyond measure, within themselves, they were confused, astounded, and amazed!"

One can certainly understand their reaction. But notice Mark's very next comment: "For they had not gained any insight from the incident of the loaves, but their heart was hardened." Unlike you and me, these disciples had directly witnessed many mighty miracles and works of power at the hands of Jesus. They had even been used themselves to heal the sick and cast out demons. Mark's comment causes us to reflect upon the fact that had they considered what they already knew about Jesus, their reaction would have been one of faith rather than fear.

The disciples still were not spiritually in tune with the Master and it is clear that "a natural man does not accept the things of the Spirit of God; for they are foolishness to him, and he cannot understand them, because they are spiritually appraised" (1 Cor. 2:14). How often we miss out on what the Master is doing in our midst and what He desires to do through us because we are too addicted to our own fleshly desires!

Reception of Jesus at Gennesaret (6:53–56)

(Compare Matthew 14:34–36)

Finally, these bedraggled disciples made it to the other side of the lake. What would be the response of the people this time? Incredibly, in contrast to His first visit, it is said of the townspeople, "immediately the people recognized Him, and ran about that whole country and began to carry about on their pallets those who were sick, to the place they heard He was." What was it that caused such a tremendous change in the attitude of the people? Although there were many contributing factors (no doubt His ministry at Capernaum and the many reports of his healing power had come to their knowledge), the one that must have caused the greatest change in the people was the living testimony of the demon-possessed man healed by Jesus on his first visit to their shores. This speaks to the great need for us all to be a living testament to what God has done in our lives. As has so often been said, "Your living example may be the only Bible that your neighbor ever reads!"

Being so welcomed by the people, Jesus was now in a position to reach out to a broader group, as is suggested by the words "And wherever He entered villages, or cities, or countryside," because the door was now fully opened to Him and His message.

As was the norm whenever Jesus ministered, it wasn't long before the common people began to come to Him for healings of all kinds. In this instance, as in others, "they were laying the sick in the market places, and entreating Him that they might just touch the fringe of His cloak; and as many as touched it were being cured." We are never told whether the disciples were afforded an opportunity to find rest, but it is clear that even if they had, it would not have been for long. It is important to note that, as was the case with the woman with the hemorrhage, the touching of the border of Jesus' garment was not merely physical contact with His clothing, but an actual, vital touch of faith!

Study Questions

1. With the disciples as examples, show how the Lord moves men and women from vocational occupations into the ministry.

2. Is it good for ministers to have a trade or other ability? Why or why not?

3. Should God's ministers and missionaries at this time do exactly as the apostles did on their preaching mission? Why or why not?

4. How does the world tend to reward people of God who preach the truth?

5. Is it important for believers to cease work from time to time and seek spiritual solitude and rest? When would such practices be appropriate?

6. Are God's servants necessarily to expect great earthly rewards? Why or why not?

7. What is the difference between the questions Jesus asked the disciples and the questions they asked Him? At what level were they often operating from when they asked questions?

8. How does this chapter show Christ is greater than a mere man?

CHAPTER 7

The Servant Looks at the Heart
Mark 7:1-37

Preview:
Christ had contempt and little patience with the Pharisees who had an outward show of religion but lacked inner spirituality. He used stern and strong language with these hypocrites, whose speech was full of false piety, but lacked the requirements for understanding God's Word. Their obsession with externals masked the reality of their internal and wicked state. Jesus used this occasion to unveil what sin really is and how it springs from the depraved human heart (cf. Jer. 17:9). Vicarious faith can be seen in Jesus' miracles this chapter. In the first, a mother intercedes for her absent daughter, and in the second, others bring a deaf and mute man to Jesus. In the first miracle, Jesus performs the healing in absentia; in the second, He uses His spittle and direct contact.

The Hypocrisy of the Pharisees (7:1-16)

(Compare Matthew 15:1-20)

This section is not directly linked to the preceding narrative. At the conclusion of chapter 6 and also Matthew 14, Jesus was actively healing the sick. It appears, when one compares this account with the other Gospels, that He and the disciples continued on to Capernaum. There He gave His message concerning the Bread of Life (see John 6:22–71). The events described in Mark 7:1–23 likely occurred shortly after that.

"And the Pharisees and some of the scribes gathered together around Him when they had come from Jerusalem." The scribes were a professional group generally associated with the Pharisees. They were a sect made up of men who thought it their responsibility to study and defend the scriptural and traditional law. As such, they were the law specialists or lawyers of their day. Regarding these Pharisees, E. Stanley Jones writes:

> They came all the way from Jerusalem to meet Him, and their life attitudes were so negative and faultfinding that all they saw was unwashed hands. They couldn't see the greatest movement of redemption that had ever touched our planet—a movement that was cleansing the minds and souls and bodies of men. . . . Their big eyes were opened wide to the little and marginal, and blind to the big. So history forgets them, the negative—forgets them except as a background for this impact of the positive Christ. They left a criticism; He left a conversion. They picked flaws, He picked followers.[1]

This gathering of Pharisees occurred because word had spread that Jesus' teaching was emphatically different from theirs. This had been demonstrated in His dealings with outcasts (2:15–17), His approach to fasting (2:18–22) and His attitude toward Sabbath observance (2:23–28). What follows shows His mind-set regarding ritual defilement.

The crux of the matter is defined in the statement, "The Pharisees and some of the scribes had seen that some of His disciples were eating their bread with impure hands, that is, unwashed . . . and . . . asked Him, Why do Your disciples not walk according to the tradition of the elders, but eat their bread with impure hands?" (vv. 1–2, 5). In verses 3–4 Mark explains the background of the problem in the minds of the Pharisees. William Lane addresses this issue of washing:

> The biblical mandate that the priests had to wash their hands and feet prior to entering the Tabernacle (Ex. 30:19; 40:13) provided the foundation for the widespread practice of ritual washings in Palestinian and diaspora Judaism. . . . The Pharisees surpassed the priests in their zeal to safeguard themselves from ritual defilement and were strong proponents of "the priesthood of all believers" in the sense that they considered the priestly regulations to be obligatory for all men.[2]

In response to their question, Jesus sternly attacked their hypocrisy even calling the Word of God as witness against them: "Rightly did Isaiah prophesy of you hypocrites, as it is written, This people honors Me with their lips, but their heart is far away from Me. But in vain do they worship Me, teaching as doctrines the precepts of men." He then added His own indictment against these religious hypocrites: "Neglecting the commandment of God, you hold to the tradition of men . . . You nicely set aside the commandment of God in order to keep your tradition." These men, who knew the law so very well, could not miss Jesus' poignant remarks. Full well they knew Isaiah's prophecy—the people of Israel alleged great loyalty and commitment to the Lord, but inwardly were two-faced.

These Pharisees, with their highly structured and sophisticated ceremony, feigned worship of God, exchanging and elevating their traditions for the principles and guidelines contained in the Law they claimed to know so much about. Like the Romish church that would come later, instead of recognizing the Word of God as the sole authority in all matters of faith and practice, they elevated their tradition above the clear revelation of the Scripture.

These scribes and Pharisees came to attack Jesus, but He turned the tables on them and returned the attack, supporting His claims with Scripture and also with a clear example they could not defend. Moses said, "Honor your father and your mother"; and, "He who speaks evil of father or mother, let him be put to death"; but you say, "If a man says to his father or his mother, anything of mine you might have been helped by is Corban (that is to say, given to God)," you no longer permit him to do anything for his father or his mother; thus invalidating the word of God by your tradition which you have handed down; and you do many things such as that. Here, Jesus quotes the fourth commandment (Ex. 20:12). Unlike the scribes and Pharisees, who looked to the rabbinical schools for their interpretations, Jesus went to the heart of the matter and quoted the Law to them. "This is not a deduction or a speculation of old rabbis, this is the plainest kind of commandment from God himself, which is recorded in the Torah by Moses."[3]

Moreover, Jesus openly attacked their hypocrisy by exposing their inner motivations. William Kelly remarks:

> The leaders had devised the scheme to secure property for religious purposes and to quiet persons from all trouble of conscience about the Word of God. . . . It was God Who called on man to honour his parents, and Who denounced all slight done to them. Yet here were men violating, under cloak of religion, both these commandments of God! This tradition of saying "Corban," the Lord treats not only as a wrong done to parents, but as a rebellious act against the express commandment of God.[4]

This rebuke from the Lord is so well framed that these religious hypocrites have no response. Lenski points out that the case of the Fourth Commandment is only a single illustration Jesus declares by adding that the Pharisees and scribes keep doing . . . many such like things, i.e., things that in like manner rob the divine Word of its authority for the conscience. These critics of the Lord who thought that they might a case against Him not only have their answer, a complete vindication of Jesus and his followers, but have an indictment turned against themselves, one that that they could not possibly give an answer to. The heaviness of this indictment and charge shows clearly that Christ is finished with them. They not only now have nothing to say, they are actually overwhelmed.[5]

This contest raised an important question concerning the nature and source of genuine defilement. H. A. Ironside writes:

> Hitherto the more conscientious an Israelite was, the more anxious and concerned he was about what he ate or drank, lest he even inadvertently take in something that was ceremonially unclean. If he did eat something considered unclean, he would be defiled and unfit to join with the congregation of the Lord when gathered together for worship in the temple.[6]

God Looks at the Heart	
The intent of man's heart is evil from his youth	Gen. 6:6
Out of the heart are the issues of life	Prov. 4:23
"Wash your heart from evil"	Jer. 4:14
The heart is more deceitful than all	Jer. 17:9
Make your heart like the heart of God	Ezek. 28:2
Love the Lord your God with all your heart	Luke 10:27
God knows the heart	Acts 15:8
Doing the will of God from the heart	Eph. 6:6

Since this matter was of such primary importance, Jesus did not leave it without setting the record straight. Having silenced His opposition, Jesus took the opportunity, as was His custom, to teach the common people. Without hesitation Jesus called again to the people (who no doubt had backed off to see what would happen). The English word "called" is actually an aorist middle participle of the verb *proskaleomai*. It is a compound form made up of the preposition *pros* and the verb *kaleō*. The significance therefore is of a face-to-face meeting.

Once Jesus had their attention, and knowing that questions about ceremonial defilement were now pressing upon their minds, Jesus declared, "Listen to Me, all of you, and understand: there is nothing outside the man which going into him can defile him; but the things which proceed out of the man are what defile the man."

Clearly and succinctly, Jesus said that it is what comes out of a man that defiles him and not what he takes in. This is a profound statement. By so saying, Jesus set Himself against the letter of the law (Leviticus 11; Deuteronomy 14) and demonstrated the higher spiritual fulfillment of it. Louis Barbieri correctly summarizes Jesus' teaching and points out that the issue of clean and unclean meats what not fully understood even by the apostles until long after the ministry of Christ (Acts 10:14-on). Barbieri adds:

> The issue of defilement had nothing to do with external materials that might come into contact with a person's body. It was the religious leaders' contention that unwashed hands will defile the food and then the partaker's body. But Jesus said that nothing entering from the outside defiles a person. Although the logical effect of what the Savior has just said would abrogate all the Levitical distinctions between clean and unclean meats. . . . Defilement starts from within a person and proceeds outward. Whereas Jesus contradicted the rabbinic view of His time, He certainly presented a biblical view of defilement (cf. Jer. 17:9–10; Eccl. 9:3).[7]

Understand that Jesus' intention here was not to invalidate the Mosaic laws, but rather to confront the fallacy that depraved men can in any way achieve genuine holiness through legalistic observances. Jesus wanted his hearers to know that religiosity is powerless to cleanse the heart, something that even the disciples had missed. Jesus would make this truth clearer in the events that were to follow.

To conclude His teaching, Jesus gave His oft-repeated command to the people, "If any man has ears to hear, let him hear."

The Heart of Humankind (7:17–23)

(Compare Matthew 15:12–20)

Evidently Jesus' words in verse 15 took the disciples by surprise, for the text tells us, "when leaving the multitude, He had entered the house, His disciples questioned Him about the parable." Like the people to whom Jesus had addressed His remarks, the disciples too were fettered with a legalistic way of thinking. Jesus' apparent dissatisfaction at their failure to comprehend truth was captured in His response, "Are you so lacking in understanding also? Do you not understand, . . . ?" In spite of their dullness, Jesus makes clear to them that, "whatever goes into the man from outside cannot defile him; because it does not go into his heart, but into his stomach, and is eliminated[.] (Thus He declared all foods clean.)" The disciples had a hard time casting off their legalism. Jesus told them that outward things such as food and drink are merely physical and temporal and therefore cannot affect the heart and spirit of man.

On the other hand, He explained, "That which proceeds out of the man, that is what defiles the man. For from within, out of the heart of men, proceed the evil thoughts, fornications, thefts, murders, adulteries, deeds of coveting and wickedness, as well as deceit, sensuality, envy, slander, pride and foolishness. All these evil things proceed from within and defile the man." In the simplest of terms, the Lord shows them that it is the defilement of spirit that matters most.

Keeping the context in mind here, one realizes that although the scribes and the Pharisees were adept at keeping the outside of the cup clean, their twisting of the law (in this case the law of Corban), demonstrated an inward defilement (a willingness to disregard their parents needs) that exposed their evil hearts. Theologically, Jesus' comments foreshadowed the end of the dispensation of law and the soon to be inaugurated dispensation of grace.

An important lesson to be gleaned from this passage is that like the Bereans, we must search the Scriptures daily. William MacDonald writes:

> One of the great lessons in this passage is that we must constantly test all teaching and all tradition by the Word of God, obeying what is of God and rejecting what is of men. At first a man may teach and preach a clear, scriptural message, gaining acceptance among Bible believing people. Having gained this acceptance, he begins to add some human teaching. His devoted followers who have come to feel that he can do no wrong follow him blindly, even if his message blunts the sharp edge of the Word or waters down its clear meaning.
>
> It was thus that the scribes and Pharisees had gained authority as teachers of the Word. But they were now nullifying the intent of the Word. The Lord Jesus had to warn the people that it is the Word that accredits men, not men who accredit the Word. *The great touchstone must always be, "What does the Word say?"* (emphasis added)[8]

The Healing of the Syrophoenician Woman (7:24–30)
(Compare Matthew 15:21–28)

Interestingly, the narrative now moves from ritual defilement to ethnic defilement. We are told, "And from there He arose and went away to the region of Tyre." William Lane makes the following insightful observations:

Mark's placement of the incident in the district'" of Tyre immediately following the discussion of clean and unclean provides a concrete example of Jesus' disregard for the scribal concept of defilement. It invites comparison with Acts 10:9ff. where Peter, after being instructed in a trance not to regard as defiled what God has cleansed, ministered to the household of Cornelius in Caesarea.[9]

There can be little doubt that the purpose of this withdrawal to "the region of Tyre," was to obtain the sought-after rest that had been so thoroughly interrupted in the wilderness (6:30–34) and at Gennesaret (6:53–56). We are told that "when He had entered a house, He wanted no one to know of it; yet He could not escape notice." Same story, second verse! Many from this area had been ministered to by Jesus previously (see 3:8), so it wasn't long until the news got out that the great prophet was in town.

Jesus sought rest but would not find it here either because "a woman whose little daughter had an unclean spirit, immediately came and fell at His feet." Mark then gives a brief description of this woman, noting that the woman was "a Gentile, of the Syrophoenician race." The double reference used here, "region of Tyre" and "Syrophoenician race," reveal in no uncertain terms that Jesus, a Jew, was acting contrary to the law, associating with Gentiles. A. T. Robertson quoting F. F. Bruce, notes that the designation here indicates that this woman is "A Greek in religion, a Syrian in tongue, a Phoenician in race."[10] There is no mistaking she is a Gentile!

This woman was greatly distressed and came begging (imperfect active indicative of *erōtaō*, indicating continuous action) Jesus to "cast the demon out of her daughter." At first look, Jesus' response—"Let the children [Israelites] be satisfied first, for it is not good to take the children's [Israelites'] bread and throw it to the dogs [Gentiles]"—seems calloused, but this is not the case at all. Lane notes:

> It seems appropriate to interpret Jesus' statement on the background provided by the OT and later Judaism where the people of Israel are designated as the children of God. Understood in this light, Jesus acknowledges the privileges of Israel and affirms that the time has not yet come for blessings to be extended to the Gentiles. "Let the children first be fed" has reference to God's election of Israel and his appointment that the gospel be proclaimed "to the Jew first and (then) to the Greek" (Rom. 1:16; 2:9f.; Acts 3:26; 13:46).[11]

Jesus' answer was in no way a refusal of her request but was instead a test of her faith. Jesus' ministry was first and foremost to the Jews. She had no claim on Israel's Messiah, nor did she merit a place of benefit as a Gentile (the

Gentiles were as yet aliens from the commonwealth of Israel, strangers from the covenants of promise, without Christ, without hope, and without God in the world; see Eph. 2:11–12). It was important then, that she understand and acknowledge this vital truth. She demonstrated that she indeed understood this fact when she exclaimed, " Yes, Lord, but even the dogs [Gentiles] under the table feed on the children's [Israelites] crumbs."

Having elicited the necessary response and seeing the Gentile woman's faith and humility, Jesus replied, "Because of this answer go your way; the demon has gone out of your daughter." Given Jesus' recent teaching in 7:15, His response is both compassionate and appropriate. We are next told that when the woman came to her house, "she found the child lying on the bed, the demon having departed."

The Healing of a Deaf Man (7:31–37)

(Compare Matthew 15:29–31)

In this section we find the second of three miracles performed by Jesus while traversing through the Gentile regions. This account is found only in the book of Mark.

We are told, "He went out from the region of Tyre, and came through Sidon to the Sea of Galilee, within the region of Decapolis." The route that Jesus and the disciples took led them from Tyre, north to Sidon, then southeast to the northern part of the Sea of Galilee. There they would have entered into a boat and passed over the Sea of Galilee, finally arriving once more in the vicinity of Decapolis (ten cities).

The reader will remember that it was in this region that Jesus confronted and healed the demoniac of Gadara. After delivering the man, Jesus told him to go home and tell what great things the Lord had done for him. This he did, and the news spread throughout all Decapolis.

Soon after Jesus arrived, we are told that some of the people brought to Him "one who was deaf and spoke with difficulty, and they entreated Him to lay His hand upon him." This is an interesting commentary by Mark. Apparently these people had seen Jesus heal before or at least had heard about His ministry. They not only brought the deaf man to Jesus, they attempted to tell Jesus how to go about healing him!

The text tells us that Jesus "took him aside from the multitude." Jesus did this in order to deal with him on a personal and private level. We are not told the reason for this, but it is likely that Jesus did this either to protect the man from public spectacle or to head off any possible attempt to forcibly make Him king. It is also quite possible that Jesus did this for a more practical reason, namely, so that the man might not be distracted. Whatever the reason, it is obvious that Jesus wanted to deal with this man one on one.

Once isolated from the crowd, we are told that Jesus "put His fingers into [the man's] ears, and after spitting, He touched his tongue." Then we are told that "looking up to heaven with a deep sigh, [Jesus] said to him, 'Ephphatha!' that is, 'Be opened!' And his ears were opened, and the impediment of his tongue was removed, and he began speaking plainly."

There can be no question that Jesus could have merely spoken the word and the deaf man would have left hearing and speaking plainly. What then is the significance of Jesus' actions here? Let us consider the actions themselves. First, Jesus put his fingers into the man's ears; second, He spit; third, He touched his tongue; fourth, He looked up to heaven; fifth, He sighed; and sixth, He said, "Be opened." Even a cursory review of these actions makes it quite clear that before Jesus actually healed this man, He instructed Him using a rough form of sign language.

All of the physical actions described were done to prepare the deaf man for what was about to happen. We are not told if this man was aware of who Jesus was or even if he believed that Jesus could heal him. The fact that this man could neither hear nor speak suggests a situation in which it would have been important to first establish trust and security. This is exactly what each physical action accomplished.

It is important to note here that in this instance there is no suggestion that this man had any faith at all in what Jesus was about to do. This was a miracle of sovereign will! Jesus determined to heal this man, and so he was healed. Praise the Lord!

After Jesus healed this man He "gave them orders not to tell anyone; but the more He ordered them, the more widely they continued to proclaim it. And they were utterly astonished, saying, 'He has done all things well; He makes even the deaf to hear, and the dumb to speak.'" Notice here that Jesus charged "them" to tell no man. Matthew reports (15:30–31) that Jesus healed many more on this occasion, and so the command to silence is to the whole multitude.

James Edwards shows that the commandment to silence in verse 36 is quite clear but it is blunt; it is not a suggestion or simply advice and it is not ambiguous. However, just like the Jewish people, the Gentiles also break it. In this way, both the Jewish and Gentile response to Jesus is remarkably similar. Edwards points out that "The great differences between Jews and Gentiles on points of law, purity, and ethnicity fade before the truly *human* question and most significant issue of all, which is the question of faith in Jesus."[12]

Kenneth Wuest provides the following insightful comments that the clause "He gave them orders," from the verb *diastellomai*, means "first 'to separate; then 'to define or distinguish,' and as that which is separated or distinguished is emphasized, 'to command or straightly charge.' It is in the middle voice, showing the charge was given with the personal interest of Jesus in view. It was for His sake and the future welfare of His ministry, that the command was given."[13]

Similarly, A. T. Robertson remarks:

Human nature is a peculiar thing. The command not to tell provoked these people to tell just as the leper had done (Mark 1:44f.). The more Jesus commanded . . . them not to tell the more they told. It was a continuous performance. Prohibitions always affect some people that way, especially superficial and light-headed folks.[14]

In the end, the multitude's assessment of Jesus was correct, "He has done all things well." Unfortunately, their emotion and excitement over the miracles He performed, blinded them to the authority behind those very miracles. If they thought about where the miracles originated, they would have heeded His command. It is even so today. Many seek after signs and wonders but fail to hear and heed the Master's commands.

Study Questions

1. Is it possible for people who claim to be "religious" to ever turn against Christ and the gospel? Explain.

2. What drives people to be continually fault-finding in the relations with others? What is the difference between fault-finding and being discerning about people's real problems?

3. How important are external matters and outward appearances?

4. What are some instances of "teaching for doctrines the commandments of men"?

5. Does being a person who is faithful at tithing nullify one's obligations to care of and provide for the family?

6. Which is more important—outward observances or inner attitudes? Why?

7. Was Jesus rude to the Syrophoenician woman, or did He have something He wanted to bring out in His discussion with her? What would that have been?

CHAPTER 8

The Servant Announces His Rejection and Death
Mark 8:1–38

Preview:

Jesus and His disciples had been in north Galilee, traveling up into the regions of Tyre and Sidon where many Gentiles lived. Then they headed back toward Galilee through Decapolis, ten cities built by the Romans and populated largely by Gentiles. These cities were located north and east of Galilee. In this chapter Jesus is near the Sea of Galilee for a while then again goes north and east toward Philippi. He feeds the four thousand miraculously, responds to the Pharisees' delegation by refusing to offer a "sign," heals a blind man, and then predicts His coming death and resurrection. The chapter closes with Jesus' emphasis on the value of the soul.

The Servant Feeding the Four Thousand (8:1–9)

(Compare Matthew 15:32–39)

The circumstances surrounding the feeding of the four thousand are similar to the occasion of some months before (cf. 6:34–44), and for this reason, some have imagined that the gospel writers, compiling oral traditions, were confused about the number fed. This is nothing but a flawed attempt on the part of liberals to discredit biblical authority. The apostle Matthew, who was an eyewitness to the events, and Mark, who worked closely with Peter, another eyewitness, describe both events.

In the feeding of the five thousand, the people were Jews, chiefly from the Jewish towns of Capernaum, Tiberius, and Bethsaida. In the record of this second miraculous multiplication of food, the location was east of the Sea of Galilee toward Decapolis, and Gentiles were the recipients. James Brooks writes:

> Given that Jesus did feed two multitudes . . . why did Mark record both. . . ? The answer must be the different symbolic significance of the two. For Mark the feeding of the five thousand seems to symbolize Jesus' provision for the Jews; the feeding of the four thousand, his provision for the Gentiles.[1]

The *Expositor's Bible Commentary* also supports the view of two separate feedings.

> There are strong reasons to support the view that 6:34–44 and 8:1–9 are indeed accounts of two separate events. 1. The language in the two accounts though similar also has significant differences (see commentary for details). 2. Jesus himself clearly refers to two feedings (8:18–21). 3. Verse 4 does not seem to be an insurmountable problem since it would be presumptuous to assume that the disciples always expected Jesus to meet a crisis situation by performing a miracle (cf. commentary for additional interpretations of 8:4). . . . The accounts certainly are similar. Yet their differences suggest that on two different occasions Jesus fed a multitude. There can be little doubt that Mark thought them to be two separate events.[2]

As has been seen previously, wherever Jesus went He attracted large crowds. The expression "In those days" suggests a connection with the immediately preceding narrative and explains why there was a "great" multitude (see 7:31–37). Given Jesus' recent teaching concerning defilement, it is correct to note, as does William Lane, that "there can be no doubt of the Gentile associations of the Decapolis and of Mark's interest in the apostolic mission to the Gentiles."

The text reveals to us the compassion of the Lord for this multitude, for He realized they had "remained with [Him] now three days, and [had] nothing to eat" and He knew that they would "faint on the way; [for] some of them [had] come from a distance." Note that the reference to "three days" is unique to Mark's account and differentiates it from the feeding of the five thousand in 6:33–44. There the crossing, the meal, and the return all take place in one day.

Although it cannot be denied that many of the people were there to see and experience the miracles that Jesus performed, it is also true that others were there sitting under His teaching ministry. The importance of this fact is that along with the physical hunger that all of the multitude was feeling, there was also a spiritual hunger within that same multitude. There were those present who had clearly demonstrated their awareness of spiritual values, eagerly taking in the Word of the Lord.

Another important aspect of this miracle is that we see the love of the Lord exhibited. Obviously the heart of the Lord was touched by the need of the multitude. He was aware of their need, and because of His love for them, He would not leave them to fend for themselves. R. Alan Cole expresses this well.

> There is a tendency today to spiritualize the miracles so much that we lose sight of their primary meaning, which is that, when Jesus saw anyone cold, hungry, ill or in distress, His heart went out to them in love and pity (verse 2). In other words, although the miracles of Jesus were certainly used as "signs" to point to a spiritual message, the recipient was not made merely a spiritual "stalking-horse." The root of all ministry, whether physical or spiritual, is this genuine inner constraint, which the New Testament writers unanimously see as the love of Christ, at work in us (2 Cor. 5:14).[3]

Jesus always knew what He would do. He was never caught off guard. Therefore, He made this information known to His disciples. What would their response be? Would they remember the earlier feeding and exhibit faith? Jesus revealed His heart to them, offering them an opportunity to initiate and participate by faith in what He would do next.

Alas, their response revealed their continued spiritual dullness, as they asked, "Where will anyone be able to find enough to satisfy these men with bread here in a desolate place?" Louis Barbieri correctly observes:

> Their answer to Him seems somewhat surprising when one considers that they had already been through an experience where Jesus had fed 5,000 men, plus the women and children. . . . Surely the disciples remembered that the Master had fed a large group on a previous occasion, but it seems that they were slow of hearing and slow to learn.[4]

Similarly, James Brooks writes:

> The statement in v. 4 may not indicate they had forgotten the first feeding or that they had no idea Jesus *could* feed the crowd but that they did not know what he would do. It could even be thought to reflect an unwillingness to be presumptuous. However, v. 4 more likely exemplifies the incredible dullness of the disciples, which is not out of line with the way Mark described them elsewhere.[5]

It is noteworthy that Jesus did not immediately reprove them but instead proceeded to meet the multitude's need. He asked the disciples, "How many loaves do you have?" He had asked the very same question in 6:38. If the disciples had been spiritually astute, they would have remembered this and realized what it was that Jesus was about to do. It should be pointed out here that the question had nothing to do with Jesus' ability to multiply the food. It was asked for perhaps two reasons: first, to bring to remembrance the feeding of the five thousand, and second, to demonstrate for everyone present the hopelessness of a human answer. It is also interesting to note that on this occasion "the disciples were to have the privilege of sharing with others the provision they had made for their own need. This time they did not procure the food from someone else."[6]

Then Jesus "directed the multitude to sit down on the ground," and "taking the seven loaves, He gave thanks, and broke them." Next He "started giving them to His disciples to serve them." A comparison of this miracle with the feeding of the five thousand shows the same procedure.

The outcome as before was that "they ate and were satisfied." Moreover, Jesus again demonstrated His ability to superabundantly supply their need in that they "picked up seven large baskets full of what was left over of the broken pieces." It is clear in this instance that the Lord was demonstrating His divinity and His ability to abundantly meet every need.

The Servant Responding to the Pharisees (8:10–13)

(Compare Matthew 16:1–4)

No doubt Jesus was again concerned about the possibility of the multitude getting out of control and attempting to force His hand. Therefore, "immediately He entered the boat with His disciples, and came to the district of Dalmanutha." Here is another instance where the two accounts of the miraculous feedings differ. In this account, Jesus got into the boat with his disciples, while in chapter 6 He stayed back to dismiss the crowd and had the disciples get into the boat and go to Bethsaida ahead of Him.

Biblical scholars are unsure as to the identity of Dalmanutha. The parallel passage (Matt. 15:39) says that Jesus went into the "region of Magadan." It is quite possible that the district of Dalmanutha and the region of Magadan, being located on the western shore of the Lake of Galilee, referred to the same general location.

The text tells us that upon arriving in Dalmanutha, "the Pharisees came out and began to argue with Him, seeking from Him a sign from heaven, to test Him." In Matthew's account the Pharisees come along with the Sadducees to tempt the Lord. It is common knowledge that the Pharisees and Sadducees were deeply alienated from one another on both religious (see Acts 23:6–8) and political grounds.

R. C. H. Lenski makes an excellent point that the banding together of the Pharisees and the Sadducees marked the progress of the joint hostility. Nevertheless, the two parties had their differences. Lenski shows how the Pharisees stood for stern holiness and carried along the thinking of the common people with them. The Sadducees were the skeptics and the high brows and represented the aristocracy in the land. Their leader was the high priest and he was the representative of the priestly-political nobility that was wealthy, influential, and powerful. One of the wives of Herod the Great was Mariamne, the daughter of Simon, the high priest. The Sadducees must be considered with the same class as the Herodians who sought the support of the Herodian family (8:6; 8:15). Mark does not deal with all of the details of this clash and shortens it considerably and uses it only as an introduction to what is about to come. Thus, he omits any reference here of the Sadducees.[7]

Due to their dislike for each other, it seems obvious that these religious and political leaders sought to put Jesus off with a feigned loyalty and concern. They came deceitfully, desiring only that He should present to them conclusive proof of His God-given power. It must be remembered, however, that these same parties had attributed His works to the devil previously and by so doing had openly implied that the signs and wonders He did were not only insufficient evidence of His messiahship, but were indeed demonically produced (cf. 3:22; Matt. 10:25; 12:24–27; Luke 11:15–20).

In their pretense, what they wanted was something beyond dispute, "a sign from heaven" (cf. 1 Cor. 1:22). But the truth of their intent is revealed in that they came to Him "to test Him." In reality, they did not believe that Jesus could do what they asked, and they could therefore discredit him before the people. "Though religious leaders had seen so many signs and display of Divine goodness and power, they still asked for a sign from heaven. Unbelief ever looks for something new and is never satisfied. Their request may be looked upon as a temptation. He could have shown a sign from heaven, but with that He would have left the humble path of the Servant."[8] The *Expositor's Bible Commentary* notes:

> Here the temptation was for Jesus to produce a "sign from heaven." Two interpretations commend themselves. First, since the word *sēmeion* is used, a word by which the Synoptists denote an outward compelling proof of divine authority, what the Pharisees were asking was for more proof than Jesus' miracles *dunameis* afforded. Jesus resolutely refused the request for such a sign because it arose out of unbelief. Second, since the

word *dunameis* ("mighty acts") is regularly used for Jesus' miracles in the Synoptics, and since the Pharisees ask for *sēmeia* ("signs"), what they are requesting is evidence of Jesus' trustworthiness, not of his supernatural power. . . . The former interpretation seems more likely. . . . They want a higher level of sign—from heaven, i.e., clearly from God.[9]

Jesus of course perceived what these hypocrites were up to, and "sighed deeply in His spirit." D. Edmond Hiebert notes concerning this expression:

Sighed deeply is an intensive compound form occurring only here in the New Testament; in 7:34 Mark used the simple verb. This intensive form literally means "groaned upwardly," indicating that the groan welled up from the very depths of His inner being. Jesus was deeply distressed by the moral perversity of these Jewish leaders. He groaned sympathetically in the presence of physical suffering (7:34), but obstinate sin evoked a deeper reaction from Him. This reference to the emotional reaction of Jesus is peculiar to Mark, apparently derived from Peter's vivid memory.[10]

Similarly, James Edwards notes:

The original Greek reads that Jesus "groaned in his spirit." The word for "groaned" (Gk. *anastenazein*) is a rare word, occurring only here in the NT, and fewer than thirty times in all of Greek literature. A survey of its uses reveals that it is not an expression of anger or indignation so much as of dismay or despair. *Anastenazein* is used to describe persons who find themselves in situations where they are pushed to the limit of faithfulness. The antagonism of the Pharisees parallels the antagonism of the Israelites to Moses in the wilderness—and Jesus' groaning in dismay seems to reflect God's disgust with the bent and recalcitrant Israelites (Exod 33:5).[11]

Jesus' expressive reaction to their questionings and unbelief is telling. Speaking as if to Himself, but in their hearing, He shoots a question back to them, "Why does this generation seek for a sign?" Of course Jesus knew why they were asking for a sign, but by returning this question to them, He reveals to them that He knows their hearts and motives. It is their hardness of heart and unbelief that prevents them from accepting the signs already given and so Jesus responds, "Truly I say to you, no sign shall be given to this generation." Grammatically speaking, this expression in Greek is a conditional clause with an unexpressed conclusion. It is used here to make an emphatic assertion and should be understood to mean that under no circumstances would a unique, special sign of the kind they were seeking be given. James Brooks notes:

The Greek involves an elliptical sentence with only a protasis ("if a sign shall be given to this generation"). The apodosis that must be supplied is probably "may I die" or "may I be cursed." The result then is an emphatic denial of the request for a sign.[12]

Interestingly, the parallel account in Matthew includes the statement, "and a sign will not be given it, except the sign of Jonah" (Matt.16:4). This sign of course refers to His death, burial, and resurrection. This addition is perhaps due to the fact that Matthew is addressing his gospel specifically to the Jews.

Realizing that no good could come from further dialogue with them, Jesus left them and "again embarked and went away to the other side."

The Servant Warning about "the Leaven" (8:14–21)

(Compare Matthew 16:1–12)

Verse 14 tells us, "And they had forgotten to take bread; and did not have more than one loaf in the boat with them." This is an interesting way to begin this section, yet it sets up the scene that follows. The fact that the disciples were concerned that they had only "one loaf" of bread with them for the journey reveals their spiritual dullness. When they should have been contemplating what had transpired between Jesus and the Pharisees and Sadducees, they were instead concerned about their bellies.

The Lord knew what they were thinking and decided to use their concern as an opportunity for instruction, "He was giving orders to them, saying, 'Watch out! Beware of the leaven of the Pharisees and the leaven of Herod.'" It is clear that uniformly in the New Testament, as in the Old, leaven symbolizes evil (cf. Ex. 12:15; Lev. 2:11; Matt. 13:33; 16:12; 1 Cor. 5:6). Moreover, leaven is never the gospel, nor is it ever related to anything good. Though this reference should have been plain to the disciples, they missed the point entirely and the Lord then rebuked them. "Why do you discuss the fact that you have no bread? Do you not yet see or understand? Do you have a hardened heart? Having eyes, do you not see? And having ears, do you not hear? And do you not remember?" The wording of the Lord's rebuke surely took them back to chapter 4 where He had said, "those who are outside get everything in parables, in order that while seeing, they may see and not perceive; and while hearing, they may hear and not understand" (Mark 4:11–12).

The Lord then reminded them of the previous miracles of the loaves and fishes and added one more rebuke: "Do you not yet understand?"

What was it exactly that they should have understood? When Jesus referred to the "leaven of the Pharisees" He obviously was referring to their hypocrisy and the fact that they exalted human traditions above the commandments of God. Furthermore, their religiosity was based only on externals without regard for the weightier matters, such as judgment, mercy, and faith. By referring to the "leaven of Herod," Jesus was warning them against worldliness and the seduction of religious power.

As for the anxiety and slowness of heart of the apostles, who had seen miracles of divine provision but still thought Jesus was talking about their one loaf of bread on board, we must be careful not to be too critical. How often have we too misunderstood or fretted, forgetting that Jesus is the Great Provider!

The Servant Healing a Blind Man (8:22–26)

Upon arriving in the city of Bethsaida, once again Jesus encountered many in need. However, because of the lack of repentance among the citizens, He had pronounced condemnation upon the city (cf. Matt. 11:21). Since this judgment was in effect, He elected to restrict His healing ministry there.

Mark records that some unnamed persons, "brought a blind man to Him, and entreated Him to touch him." The similarity of events in this account and the one in 7:31–37 is interesting. In both accounts, it appears that there were some who were actually looking for the infirmed in order to bring them to Jesus. Perhaps it was out of a real sense of compassion or perhaps it was just to see what Jesus would do—we do not know.

The interesting thing, however, is that on both occasions Jesus did basically the same thing. As in the case of the deaf-mute, Jesus left the immediate location. "Taking the blind man by the hand, He brought him out of the village." There was also a physical application involved—"spitting on his eyes" and "laying His hands upon him." And finally, Jesus charged the formerly blind man, "Do not even enter the village." This miracle and the miracle of healing of the deaf-mute in 7:31–37 have no parallels in any of the other gospels but are unique to Mark.

As noted above, only Mark records this healing in Bethsaida. In this case, the healing came progressively, for the blind man first saw men "like trees, walking about," which could mean that he saw men carrying branches on their backs, thus resembling walking trees. This is insightful in that this man most certainly must have been sighted at some point in his life. If not, he would have had no concept of what a tree looked like, nor of what men looked like when they walked.[13] Furthermore, the command "Do not even enter the village" could not have included the ones who had brought the blind man to Jesus initially, because they would have had to assist the newly healed man in finding his way home.

It should also be pointed out that the fact that this man's healing was progressive in no way supports the teaching of so-called faith healers for progressive healings today. It must be acknowledged that although this healing took some amount of time, the man walked away with his sight "restored," and he "began to see everything clearly." He was not admonished to go home and continually make positive confessions so that God could complete the healing! No! He walked away totally restored! Moreover, just as in the healing of the deaf-mute, nothing is said regarding this man's faith or behavior. Neither is there any suggestion that his faith was progressively growing to the point that his healing could be realized. On the contrary, his healing came from the sovereign touch of Jesus regardless of the measure of his faith.

The Servant Acknowledging His Messiahship (8:27–30)

(Compare Matthew 16:13–16; Luke 9:18–20)

Caesarea Philippi is not the same Caesarea encountered previously on the Mediterranean coast, but rather a beautiful city near Mount Hermon. Here a marble temple stood, built by Herod the Great to honor the Roman emperor Augustus. While in this region, far from Jerusalem and amid many Gentiles, Jesus asked His disciples, "Who do people say that I am?"

Jesus didn't put this question to the disciples because He needed the information, but because He wanted them to contemplate the many opinions they had heard concerning Him. This reflection would serve as a backdrop for their own profession of faith and would move them toward an understanding of the divine plan of the ages. Furthermore, their full devotion to the reality of Jesus' messiahship was essential before He could tell them about His forthcoming death, burial, and resurrection.

During this time there was a general expectancy among the Jews that before the Messiah prophesied in the Old Testament would appear, He would be preceded by the some great Old Testament prophet. Most held that this would be Elijah, based on Malachi 3:1 and 4:5. The disciples' answer to Jesus' question reflects this expectation.

While the disciples were contemplating these things, Jesus compelled them to move beyond a mere parroting of what others had said about Him to formulating a personal judgment. He did this by asking them, "But who do you say that I am?" The fact that the second person plural personal pronoun comes at the beginning of the sentence, emphasizes the contrast, "Others have said this about me, but what do you say?" James Edwards makes the following insightful comments regarding this situation:

> Jesus asks for a judgment about him in the midst of the journey, not at the end of it when all questions are answered and proof is finally in hand. Faith is a judgment about Jesus, and a willingness to act on the judgment in the face of other possible judgments. Indeed, for the disciples at this point in the Gospel, faith will necessitate a choice *contrary* to the prevailing consensus of crowds and religious leaders. Faith means actively following Jesus *on the way*, not demanding signs (8:11–13) or turning to go one's own way (10:22).[14]

The Messiahship of Christ	
The scepter shall not depart from Judah … until Shiloh (Peacemaker) Comes	Gen. 49:10
God will install His King upon Zion "My holy mountain"	Psa. 2:6
The LORD says to my Lord: Sit at My right hand	Psa. 110:1
The LORD will stretch forth the scepter (of the Messiah) from Zion	Psa. 110:2
The Messiah is a priest after the order of Melchizedek	Psa. 110:4
A virgin shall conceive and bear a Son whose name is Immanuel	Isa. 7:14; Matt. 1:23
The Messiah will sit on David's throne and over his kingdom	Isa. 9:7
The Spirit of the Lord will rest on the Branch, the son of Jesse	Isa. 11:1–2
From Bethlehem will come the Ruler who will shepherd God's people Israel	Micah 5:2; Matt. 2:6
Israel's Leader and Ruler shall come forth from their midst	Jer. 30:21
Mary's Son will reign over the house of Jacob forever; His kingdom will have no end	Luke 1:33
The Holy offspring [of Mary] shall be called the Son of God	Luke 1:35

Before anyone else can answer, Peter responds, "Thou art the Christ." Peter's response is revealing because it demonstrates that he had transitioned from a personal judgment to a heartfelt confession. Christ or *Christos* is the Greek form of the Hebrew *Maschioch* or Messiah, meaning the anointed Prophet, Priest, and King of Scripture. In making this declaration, Peter revealed what only the Holy Spirit could have shown him, what only the Father and demons had previously known about Jesus, namely, that He is the Anointed One.

This was a critical point for the disciples, for until now, they had been mostly onlookers. However, the Twelve could no longer remain uncommitted, for along with revelation comes responsibility. The path of sorrow and suffering lay ahead, and only a solid commitment and a close fellowship founded upon the faith expressed here would keep them on track. The revelation that Jesus was the Christ was not for all, and so the Lord charged them to, "tell no one about Him." Lenski notes two reason for this charge of silence.

> In the first place, they were not yet ready to [proclaim His messiahship] properly. The fullness of what "the Christ" meant was not yet revealed to them. In the second place, to proclaim Jesus as the Christ would arouse the false hopes of the multitude who were looking for an earthly Christ, one who would fulfill their grand political hopes.[15]

The concerns about the false hopes and political agendas of the multitudes were legitimate, as is demonstrated in the verses that immediately follow.

The Servant Prophesying His Coming Death (8:31–33)

(Compare Matthew 16:21–23; Luke 9:22)

In these verses we are told that, "He began to teach them that the Son of Man must suffer many things and be rejected by the elders and the chief priests and the scribes, and be killed, and after three days rise again. And He was stating the matter plainly." What a shock this was! But they had been brought to this point after careful planning. Alfred Plummer writes:

> It was indeed a new beginning. Slowly, fitfully, and still very defectively, the Twelve had been brought by Him to see that He was the promised Messiah; and now He began to teach them that the King and Conqueror whom they had been expecting must suffer shame and death.[16]

The Lord knew what was in store for Him and told the disciples in plain language. There were no parables with hidden meanings now. Jesus carefully and boldly laid out the sequence of events that would be forthcoming. This was a revelation to the disciples that did not line up with their understanding of the Messiah and what he would do. Therefore, "Peter took Him aside and began to rebuke Him." The actual rebuke is given in Matthew's account, where Peter says, "God forbid it, Lord! This shall never happen to You" (Matt. 16:22).

What prompted Peter to utter these words is conjecture. Perhaps he felt that Jesus was disappointed by recent events and it was his place to encourage the Lord. After all, the Lord had just made a great pronouncement about him. More than likely the reason for Peter's action had to do with the fact that this talk of the Messiah's death in no way fit the disciples' beliefs and hopes for a theocratic kingdom and peace for Israel.

In spite of Peter's sincerity, Jesus saw it for what it was, namely a desire motivated by Satan. Unwittingly, he was tempting Jesus as Satan had done in the wilderness. Peter, the rock, had unconsciously aligned himself with the adversary. His desire for the kingdom and authority was not the Father's will at that time. There was one path for the Savior, the path of the cross. That Jesus should not go to the cross, was what Satan wanted for he knew it would mean his own defeat.

At Peter's rebuke, the Lord turned about and looked at His disciples. Realizing the potential of Peter's influence on the group the Lord quickly "rebuked Peter, and said, Get behind Me, Satan; for you are not setting your mind on God's interests, but man's." This was harsh but necessary, for Peter had taken it upon himself to speak for the group. It should be pointed out here that Jesus' reference to Peter as Satan was not meant to suggest that Peter and Satan were one and the same. Nor was it meant to suggest that Peter was suddenly possessed by Satan. It merely implies that Peter was unwittingly acting as Satan's spokesman at this point.

This is the first announcement by Christ of His approaching sufferings. The disciples, like the Old Testament writers, did not yet understand the difference between "the sufferings of Christ and the glories to follow" (1 Peter 1:11). This teaching of the cross and death was difficult to grasp.

The Servant Teaching the Way of Discipleship (8:34–38)

(Compare Matthew 16:24–28; Luke 9:23–27)

Still reeling from the announcement of Jesus' forthcoming suffering and death, the disciples are now confronted with the issue of commitment. This makes perfectly good sense. Jesus had informed them of what lie ahead. He now informed them of the cost of discipleship.

Jesus "summoned the multitude with His disciples." Mark is the only writer who notes the presence of other people on this occasion, but it is not hard to imagine they were there. They were always there. It was always difficult for Jesus and the disciples to get away from the crowd for any prolonged period of time.

It is significant that Jesus called the people to Him to hear this message. It is not only the Twelve who must count the cost, but all those who desire to be His disciples. There is no missing the point here when Jesus says, "If anyone wishes to come after Me, let him deny himself, and take up his cross, and follow Me." Louis Barbieri remarks:

> Taking up one's cross was not a Jewish metaphor, but it was a figure that would have been common to Mark's readers. Every condemned criminal was required to carry his cross or his crosspiece to his place of execution. By making a criminal carry his cross, the Roman government was showing that they had authority over that individual. When Jesus Christ said a disciple must take up his cross in a decisive act, He was teaching that one must come to the realization of who is the authority in one's life.[17]

Taking up one's cross was a frightful symbol and coupled with the exhortation, that "whoever wishes to save his life shall lose it," added to the force of the message. Happily, Jesus went on to tell his hearers that there is also a reward for those who so commit themselves to His cause—"whoever loses his life for My sake and the gospel's shall save it."

To reinforce the impact of this analogy in the strongest possible manner, Jesus added, "For what does it profit a man, to gain the whole world, and forfeit his soul? For what shall a man give in exchange for his soul?" No man can gain the whole world and no man can exchange his soul, for it is not his to give. What then is Jesus saying here? Hiebert captures the idea.

> The paradoxical statement (verse 35) derives its force from the two meanings of the word *life* (*psuchē*), often translated" soul," the self-conscious life. The term here has a lower and higher meaning. In both statements it first means the outward, earthly life with its pleasures and aims and then the inward, spiritual life which begins here and reaches into eternity. The one who refuses to become a disciple to preserve the lower thereby destroys the higher; the present self-sacrifice of the interests of the lower life will result in true and ultimate self-preservation.

In verse 36, *for* elucidates by contrasting the higher life with the world, all that it stands for as estranged from God. The thought is presented under a commercial metaphor, and the question implies that there is not profit in the suggested transaction. The present gain is pictured in its highest form, "gain the whole world," a clear impossibility for any individual. But granting the impossible, if a man should accomplish it and thereby forfeit his life, what is the profit in it? The argument is valid whether *life* be taken in its lower or higher meaning.[18]

Jesus summarily explained the seriousness of this commitment by telling His audience, "Whoever is ashamed of Me and My words in this adulterous and sinful generation, the Son of Man will also be ashamed of him when He comes in the glory of His Father with the holy angels." This is the first place Mark gives an explicit reference to the future glorious return of Christ. Hugh Anderson remarks, "The supreme paradox is that this lowly One, who confronts men with the choice between the authentic life of discipleship and the inauthentic existence of self-concern, will occupy the place of power and glory with God in God's final judgment of the world."[19]

Self-denial, symbolized by "taking up one's cross and following Christ" is not a popular subject. Yet a true believer must say no to the old nature, to great worldly success, to the enticements of selfish prosperity and to the pleasures of sin because "All that is in the world, the lust of the flesh, and the lust of the eyes and the boastful pride of life, is not from the Father, but is from the world" (1 John 2:16). We all naturally shrink from the thought of suffering, yet we know that following God's will in this fallen world will eventually result in it.

Many have lost their lives for the gospel's sake in past ages. Many are doing so today. This may not be required of us at the present time, but regardless, *let us deny ourselves!"* This we must always practice, enabled by God's grace.

Those who want to preserve and keep their lives in this world without regard to eternity will lose their souls forever. This is no profit at all.

Study Questions

1. In terms of getting to the important spiritual issues, what are the differences between Jesus' questions and the disciples' questions?

2. What is the difference in the disciples' attitude and Jesus' attitude about the hungry multitude? How should believers today react to those who are starving and living without the basic needs?

3. Besides looking for a healing, what are some of the reasons that the blind man may have come to Christ?

4. Did the friends of the blind man really believe Christ could heal him?

5. Why did some say Jesus was Elijah? Why did they not think immediately that Jesus was the promised Messiah?

6. How can believers today sometimes oppose the Lord and need His rebuke?

7. For Christians today who are living two thousand years beyond the time of Christ, what does it mean to "take up His cross?"

CHAPTER 9

The Servant Reveals His Divine Glory
Mark 9:1-50

Preview:

The transfiguration, during which Christ shows forth His divine splendor and the Father speaks audibly in the hearing of three apostles is a true high point in the book of Mark. The Servant of the Father and of humans is glorified. After giving an account of the powerlessness of the disciples to work miracles apart from Christ, Jesus speaks of His crucifixion for the second time. Amazingly, the apostles do not grasp that concept and argue about which of them would be the greatest in the kingdom age. Then Jesus speaks of rewards for service and retribution in hell for the wicked.

The Servant Showing His Innate Glory (9:1-13)

(Compare Matthew 17:1-13; Luke 9:28-36)

At the end of chapter 8, the Lord imposed a heavy charge upon the disciples and all those who would choose to follow Him. He spoke of laying down one's life for the sake of the kingdom. Here, at the conclusion of this section (8:34-9:1) Jesus continues this kingdom theme and presents the Twelve with a positive aspect of faithful discipleship, namely, that "some . . . shall not taste of death until they see the kingdom of God after it has come with power." The expression "who shall not taste death" is emphatic, being introduced by the

Greek *ou mē,* and more literally means "who shall absolutely by no means taste
of death." The verb is the aorist middle deponent subjunctive form of *guomai*
and in context here means "to experience something cognitively or emotionally."[1] D. Edmond Hiebert, commenting on the expression "shall not taste
death," notes that it is "a Hebrew idiom for physical death. The figure regards
death as a bitter poison which all, sooner or later, must taste. The emphatic not
stresses that those in view will assuredly not drink the potion until after the
indicated event."[2]

These words must have excited the hearts of the disciples yet also must
have generated questions in their minds as to what they meant. In fact, this
declaration must have come as quite a surprise to the disciples. What could
this authoritative and prophetic statement by Jesus mean?

Several suggestions have been given as to what "see[ing] the kingdom of
God after it has come with power" means. These include Jesus' resurrection
and ascension, the pouring out of the Holy Spirit at Pentecost, the destruction
of Jerusalem in A.D. 70, the second coming of Jesus, and the transfiguration.
The fact that each of the Synoptic writers immediately follows this statement
with an account of the transfiguration strongly suggest that this is what was in
view. Additionally, the transfiguration clearly provided a foretaste of the glory
of the Lord (see v. 38).

Six days after Jesus made this startling announcement, He headed off
toward a high mountain with Peter, James, and John. When they had reached
some predetermined area, "[Jesus] was transfigured before them." Luke notes
that this transfiguration took place while Jesus was in prayer, also mentioning
that the three disciples were "overcome with sleep" (Luke 9:29, 32). It is quite
possible that Jesus was praying for His disciples who had misunderstood the
announcement of His death. It is also likely that Jesus was praying for strength
to bear what lie ahead namely, the cross.

The English word *transfigured* is the Greek verb *metamorphoō* meaning "to
change in a manner visible to others" or "to change inwardly in fundamental
character or condition."[3] Here it refers not merely to a change in outward
appearance, but to a change in inherent form (cf. Rom. 12:2; 2 Cor. 3:18). R.
A. Cole comments on this event:

> In a sense, we are wrong to call this "the transfiguration," as though it was
> unique: the true great transfiguration, the metamorphosis, had already
> taken place at Bethlehem when God took human form, as Philippians
> shows (Phil. 2:6–7). On the mount of transfiguration Jesus was but reas-
> suming His own true form, even if only temporarily: faith had momen-
> tarily passed into sight for the three disciples.[4]

The result of this glorious transformation is that "His garments became radiant and exceedingly white, as no launderer on earth can whiten them."

Next we are told, "Elijah appeared to them along with Moses; and they were talking with Jesus." Understandingly, the question is often raised as to why Moses and Elijah appeared with Jesus. The best answer is that Moses was present because he was the indirect agent in the giving of the Law while Elijah was present as the official representative of all Old Testament prophets. It has also been observed that their presence with Jesus was to serve as an assurance for the disciples that Jesus' death, proclaimed in the Law and the Prophets, was to be accepted as God's will.

R. A. Cole again provides insight and points out that we sometimes take too quickly the appearance of Elijah with Moses with Christ on the mountain as the witness of Law and Prophets to Christ. While this is true, it is more. The prophet Moses had himself mentioned the coming of Christ prophetically (John. 1:45; Luke 24:27), and both the scribe and Pharisee also was waiting for Elijah to come as Messiah's forerunner (9:11), on the authority of Malachi (Mal. 4:5). This was clearly part of orthodox Jewish theology. As the Lord hinted, there had already been a fulfillment of this prophecy at one level in the coming of John the Baptist (9:13), but nevertheless there was still the truth of the arrival and coming presence of Elijah in person here.[5]

In the parallel accounts in Matthew (17:3) and Luke (9:30), the order is reversed, listing Moses first. The reason for this difference in Mark may be due to the fact that the disciples had recently been discussing Elijah (cf. 8:28). Mark tells us that Elijah and Moses "were talking with Jesus." In Greek this is what is called a periphrastic construction indicating a lengthy conversation. Luke adds that they were discussing Jesus' forthcoming death (Luke 9:31).

The magnitude of this event was so powerful that the three disciples were awestruck. Being the spokesman for the group, Peter said, "Rabbi, it is good for us to be here; and let us make three tabernacles, one for You, and one for Moses, and one for Elijah." Luke records that Peter spoke up as Moses and Elijah were about to depart. How he knew this is not revealed.

Mark provides his own insight here, noting that Peter "did not know what to answer; for they became terrified." Unfortunately, neither Peter nor the other disciples understood the will and plan of God. H. A. Ironside writes:

[Peter] did not realize the incongruity involved in putting even the greatest of God's servants on a level, as it were, with the Lord Jesus Himself. Moreover, he did not recognize the transitory character of the scene that enthralled him. He wanted to erect three tabernacles in order to give some permanent place of dwelling to each of the three who conversed together.

How many since Peter's day have thought to honor Christ by giving special prominence to His servants—whether prophets, apostles, saints, or angels—and have never realized that in thus recognizing them as worthy of such homage they have actually dishonored the Master Himself![6]

It would appear that Peter desired to prolong this experience, revealing that He misunderstood the importance of this meeting. He was about to be divinely corrected.

Mark next records that, "a cloud formed, overshadowing them, and a voice came out of the cloud, 'This is My beloved Son, listen to Him!'" So that there could be no mistake as to the exalted nature of the Son, God the Father spoke. Matthew notes that the cloud appeared while Peter was yet speaking (Matt. 17:5). Before the thoughts had been formulated in Peter's mind, God knew what he was going to say and intervened! Why did the Father speak? Because the focus of the disciples must not be on the event they were experiencing, but on the person of Christ. Warren Wiersbe explains:

> The Father interrupted Peter's speech and focused their attention, not on the vision, but on the Word of God: "Hear Him!" The memory of visions will fade, but the unchanging Word abides forever. The glorious vision was not an end in itself; it was God's way of confirming the Word (see 2 Peter 1:12–21). Discipleship is not built on spectacular visions but on the inspired, unchanging Word of God.[7]

In other words, the disciples were not to hear Moses or Elijah; they were to hear Jesus and Jesus alone! Hiebert remarks:

> "'Hear him'—the present imperative sets forth the continuing duty. *Hear*, in the sense of hear and obey, indicates that the person of Jesus must be obediently heard. He, rather than Moses or Elijah, is now God's authorized spokesman."[8]

The mention of the cloud here is reminiscent of the cloud of God's presence in the book of Exodus, representing the Shekinah glory of God (cf. Ex. 13:21; 16:10; 19:9, 16; 24:15–16; 33:9). R. Kent Hughes makes an insightful observation at this point.

> It had been six hundred years since anyone in Israel had seen the shekinah glory. But as Jesus and his inner circle stood in silence in the night air, "a [luminous] cloud appeared and enveloped them" (v. 7a). It was the shekinah! It is fair to imagine that from below any who happened to look up at Hermon saw it—the mountain was capped with the divine incandescence. Peter, James, and John were in the cloud which Moses was not

even permitted to directly behold. Jesus was with them, and thus they could stand radiant in the shekinah glory![9]

Matthew notes that at the sound of the voice from heaven the disciples, "fell on their faces, and were much afraid" (Matt. 17:6). When they finally dared to look up, they "saw no one with them anymore, except Jesus alone." Mark's account here is a summary. Matthew adds that "Jesus came to them and touched them and said, Arise, and do not be afraid" (Matt. 17:7).

When Moses and Elijah vanished, Jesus Christ alone remained to be worshiped and adored. No doubt confused and amazed, the disciples were not left alone to fend for themselves. James R. Edwards correctly notes:

In the depths of their bewilderment, Jesus is with the disciples. The disciples—then as now—are not expected to go it alone in this hard and joyous thing of discipleship. Precisely where they hear the gospel, where they see both its glory and their own inadequacy, there Jesus is with them. The one who calls disciples to follow him does not abandon them for glory, but turns from glory to accompany them "on the way" to Jerusalem and the cross.[10]

The text tells us next that on their way down the mountain, Jesus "gave them orders not to relate to anyone what they had seen, until the Son of Man should rise from the dead." This is the final command to silence in Mark's gospel. Up to this point the requirement of silence had been unqualified, but now the disciples were told that this command was to continue in effect until "the Son of man should rise from the dead." Of course the disciples had no way of knowing that the time frame of this command of silence would be a very short time.

The fact that they continued "discussing with one another what rising from the dead might mean" indicates that they still did not get the big picture, nor had they understood the significance of the transfiguration. It was probably this very thing that prompted Jesus to command them to silence. This messianic secret would have to be kept until after the resurrection.

With the appearance of Elijah at the transfiguration and this command to silence fresh upon their minds, the three began to question the common belief that Elijah's return must precede that of the Messiah. On the mountain they had been given undisputable confirmation of Jesus' valid claim to the office of Messiah. They now sought to reconcile their understanding of this teaching. They approached Jesus and asked Him, "Why is it that the scribes say that Elijah must come first?" Louis Barbieri summarizes the confusion in the minds of the disciples concerning this issue.

How was Elijah's appearance at the Transfiguration to be reconciled with the official doctrine of his return? They were also wrestling with the concept of Elijah's coming. And if indeed Jesus was the Messiah, where was Elijah? Did Elijah's presence on the Mount of Transfiguration satisfy the Old Testament prophecies?[11]

In this instance Jesus affirms the teaching of the scribes, stating "Elijah does first come and restore all things." While Jesus, to a point, confirms the teaching of the scribes, He also expands upon it while at the same time, redirecting its focus away from the scribes, ill-conceived notion of the kingdom. He does this by asking, "How is it written of the Son of Man that He should suffer many things and be treated with contempt?" In so many words, Jesus was saying, yes, Elijah must come, but what will you do with the Scriptures indicating that Messiah must suffer and die? He was calling upon the disciples to reflect upon what the Scripture itself teaches as opposed to what the scribes said it taught.

Hiebert explains that Christ now brings up a similar problem. How, introduces a question, but how far does the question extend? The ASV puts the question mark at the end of the verse. Then Jesus asked the question: "What about the scriptural teaching concerning the suffering Messiah?" Some have surmised that the question mark should come at the close of the first clause, "And how is it written of the Son of man?" If this is true then Christ asked the disciples to think about the scriptural record concerning Himself, the Messiah and the Son of man. By this He filled out the essentials of the teaching, namely, "That he must suffer many things, and be set at nought." This was the important to the point of the discussion. What He was about to face explained His assertion concerning His coming resurrection. The great trials of suffering He would undergo would result in His being considered as worthless, ignored, and certainly treated with contempt as though He were nothing. That opinion the leadership would have of Him would bring about His death. With this, the Old Testament prophecies of His suffering (Isa. 53; Psa. 22) would be fulfilled.[12]

Jesus continued declaring, "But I say to you, that Elijah has indeed come, and they did to him whatever they wished, just as it is written of him." The force of this statement is that if Elijah had already come and had not been recognized by the religious institution, and if the Jewish leaders had mistreated him (according to the Scriptures), how could the current scribal teaching concerning Messiah's coming and reigning be correct?

William Lane shows how the allusion to Isaiah 53, where the Servant of God is rejected and treated as a horrible object of hatred, reinforces the Lord's insistence about His Sonship. The unexpressed question in regard to the necessity of Christ's suffering lies hidden in the question of verse 11. In verse 9 Christ had referred to His resurrection from the dead, and His suffering and rejection as introduced in verse 12b by way of explanation. This is misunderstood unless it is considered together with His exaltation as it is inseparably bound up with His death and humiliation. How Christ answered the question of the disciples about Elijah has a deep meaning. Basic to the question is what is the function of Elijah in his coming to earth. It is the restore the nation of Israel through repentance as promised in Malachi 4:6, and fulfilled in the prophetic ministry of John the Baptist.[13]

How marvelously the Father authenticated the ministry of His Son. He now bids all to *"hear Him"*. Had the Jews accepted and received Jesus as their Messiah, John the Baptist would have fully fulfilled Malachi 4:5–6, but since Jesus was rejected, the final fulfillment remains future (Revelation 11).

The Servant Restating the Primacy of Prayer and Fasting (9:14–29)

(Compare Matthew 17:14–20; Luke 9:37–42)

Once Jesus and the three disciples reached the foot of the mountain, they encountered the remaining disciples along with "a large crown around them." This was not unusual. There were always multitudes looking for Jesus. What made this occasion unique was the fact that "some scribes [were] arguing with them." The text does not tell us directly the topic of the confrontation, but as the narrative continues it seems likely that it dealt with the failure of the remaining nine disciples to exorcise a demon from a young boy. No doubt their questions were designed to discredit the disciples and ultimately Jesus himself.

The nine were unable to deliver the boy, and more than likely they were unable to answer the scribes. Confusion was beginning to grow among the multitude, influenced by the scribes, so Jesus drew near to deal with the situation. When the multitude saw Jesus, they "immediately . . . began running up to greet Him." The text also tells us that "when the entire crowd saw Him, they were amazed." No doubt this was due to His sudden appearance in their midst and the fact that their questionings were directly related to Him.

Jesus asked the scribes, "What are you discussing with them?" This question served two purposes. First, it shifted any hostilities away from the disciples, and second, it rebuked the scribes for their failure to come to Him with their questions. One can only speculate at the relief these disciples felt upon seeing Jesus and having Him step up to the plate on their behalf. On the other hand, the scribes who were having their way now had to deal with

Jesus, and that immediately moved them from an offensive posture to a defensive posture.

It is interesting that the scribes did not answer Jesus' question. Perhaps they were waiting to see what Jesus would do. In any case, "one of the crowd answered Him, 'Teacher, I brought You my son, possessed with a spirit which makes him mute; and whenever it seizes him, it dashes him to the ground and he foams at the mouth, and grinds his teeth, and stiffens out. And I told Your disciples to cast it out, and they could not do it.'"

Now the scene was set. This father had been wise to bring his poor son to be healed, but Jesus was not available because He was on the mountaintop. Disappointed that Jesus was not present, he nevertheless went to the nine remaining disciples. After all, had they not also been given power over demons?

Though they had indeed been given power over demons, it soon became evident that in this instance they lacked the faith to heal the boy. Realizing this, the scribes saw an opportunity to go on the attack and did so, either not caring or ignoring the fact that this father was now distraught.

Jesus' response is interesting. "O unbelieving generation, how long shall I be with you? How long shall I put up with you?" Although he addresses the man, it is obvious that this question is directed not merely to the man but to all present and especially to the nine disciples.

Lenski explains how the three synoptic Gospel writers record this pained exclamation, however, only Matthew and Luke add the comment about the generation that it has been perverted. Here is one of those times in the Gospels where Christ allows His most inner feelings to be expressed in words. His heart is expressing the pain and disappointment over the failure of the nine disciples to drive out the evil spirit. The crowds and the multitudes are not charged with unbelief in this matter. It is likewise wrong to charge the father with unbelief because it is he who brought his son to the disciples with the urgent request for mercy. In the story the father certainly shows forth his faith (9:24). The Lord actually rebukes his disciples for their lack of trust in the matter. They were helpless and impotent in their attempt to cast out this spirit. Though the disciples had walked with Him for so long, yet the old unbelief, which marked their entire generation, again cropped out; because of it they had failed to heal this child (see Matt. 17:19, 20). It was only right that Christ could have expected them to have greater faith then that present generation.[14]

Having rebuked His disciples, Jesus nonetheless did not leave them to fend for themselves. He continued to express His desire to use them by commanding them, "Bring him to Me!" Although they had failed, He will not fail them. Jesus will continue to use them! In obedience the Nine brought the boy to Jesus. When the demon saw Jesus, "immediately the spirit threw him into a convulsion, and falling to the ground, he began rolling about and foaming at the mouth." Regarding this event, Lane writes:

> The description of the destructive energy released at unexpected intervals by the demonic spirit indicates the seriousness of the boy's condition. Violent convulsions, foaming at the mouth, involuntary gnashing of the teeth, rigidness followed by utter exhaustion, resemble the symptoms of the major form of epilepsy. . . . What was involved, however, was not simply a chronic nervous disorder but demonic possession. The violence of the seizures, and the reference to repeated attempts to destroy the youth by hurling him into a fire or water (Ch. 9:20, 22, 26), indicate that the purpose of demonic possession is to distort and destroy the image of God in man. That this destruction should be heaped upon a child only serves to indicate how radical the issue is between demonic power and Jesus, the bestower of life (Ch. 9:27).[15]

Jesus, seeing this, asked the boy's father, "'How long has this been happening to him?' And he said, 'From childhood.'" The man then elaborated, "It has often thrown him both into the fire and into the water to destroy him." This questioning was not for Jesus but for the man. Jesus wanted him to reflect on the fact that no one had been able to deliver the child and that by coming to Jesus for help, the man must understand that another element was needed, namely, faith in Jesus' ability to do what he asked.

At this point the man revealed the level of his faith. "If You can do anything, take pity on us and help us!" We must not be too hard on this man. He had just experienced the failure of nine of Jesus' disciples to deliver his son. He had also had to endure the scribes who cared nothing for his son but were only interested in besmirching Jesus and His disciples.

Jesus responded to the desperate man, "If You can! All things are possible to him who believes." The spiritual perception of Jesus overwhelmed the man. In that instant the man realized that Jesus knew what was in his heart. The text tells us, "Immediately the boy's father cried out and began saying, 'I do believe; help my unbelief!'" In so many words the man said, "I have faith, but my faith is not as strong as it should be." These words demonstrated his exasperation because of the powerlessness of Jesus' disciples. He had initially come with faith to see Jesus, but some doubt in Jesus' ability to deliver his son had crept in due to the immediate circumstances.

Lenski makes an astute observation that miracles are not dependent on faith but only on the will of Jesus. This is clear where Jesus heals without faith, when after the healing, the one cured then sought to respond in faith to what had happened. For example, with the story of the impotent man at the pool of Bethesda (John 5:1), he did not even know the name of Christ, and yet he was healed! The man who was given sight in John 9 gradually came to faith in the Lord. And how many demoniacs trusted Christ before the demons were driven out of their bodies? Did the widow at Nain or her dead son believe before the miracle? However Jesus worked but few or no miracles where the crowds were unbelieving and hostile (6: 5), but this was done for the simple reason that miracles would be wasted on such people.[16]

In this exchange we see the Lord Jesus' wisdom and compassion. Instead of immediately delivering the boy, He dealt with the father's spiritual need. He was not only concerned with delivering the boy from the demon, but He was also concerned for the spiritual soundness of the father who would shortly see a miracle take place.

We are told next, "When Jesus saw that a crowd was rapidly gathering, He rebuked the unclean spirit, saying to it, 'You deaf and dumb spirit, I command you, come out of him and do not enter him again.'" As usual, Jesus avoided unnecessary publicity. He would not let the crowd dictate the path before Him!

At Jesus' command, "after crying out and throwing him into terrible convulsions, it came out; and the boy became so much like a corpse that most of them said, 'He is dead!'" This deliverance came about through the spoken, authoritative word of the Lord Jesus. The use of a double rebuke makes it clear that this demon was to leave and never return! The fact that the demon made one more attempt at destroying the boy may be indicative of the contempt that it had for Jesus Himself.

So violent was this departing attack that many believed the boy to be dead. No doubt hearing the comments of the people, and to abolish any concerns the father may have had, Jesus, "took him by the hand, and raised him; and he got up." Matthew explains the permanence of the healing, noting that the boy "was cured at once." While Luke adds that Jesus "healed the boy, and gave him back to his father" (Luke 9:42).

With the boy now healed and the scribes silenced by the miracle, Jesus and the disciples entered into a house. While there, "his disciples began questioning Him privately, Why could we not cast it out?" This of course does not refer to the Twelve, but to the nine disciples who were unsuccessful in their efforts. This was a legitimate question given that they had on other occasions been empowered to do so.

Jesus' response is telling. "This kind cannot come out by anything but prayer." This reply seems to suggest that a spiritual element, namely, a committed prayer life, was lacking in the disciples in general but especially in these nine. Perhaps the disciples had taken their spiritual power for granted. After all, it had always been available before.

What these nine disciples had failed to grasp was the importance of their ultimate dependence upon God. They had failed to cultivate this dependence through persistent, prayerful communion. Moreover, their inability to cast out the demon was due to their failure to pray for power for the task at hand. Lane suggests:

> The disciples had been tempted to believe that the gift they had received from Jesus (Ch. 6:7) was in their control and could be exercised at their disposal. This was a subtle form of unbelief, for it encouraged them to trust in themselves rather than in God. They had to learn that their previous success in expelling demons provided no guarantee of continued power. Rather the power of God must be asked for on each occasion in radical reliance upon his ability alone. When faith confronts the demonic, God's omnipotence is its sole assurance, and God's sovereignty is its only restriction. This is the faith which experiences the miracle of deliverance.[17]

Jesus made it clear that some spiritual battles (we wrestle not against flesh and blood) are not easily won. Satanic forces and evil powers cannot be overcome and cast out without genuine, prevailing, earnest, sustained prayer . . . and fasting, abstaining from food or other things that might distract us from the battle.

The Servant Repeating the Prediction of His Death (9:30–32)

(Compare Matthew 17:22–23; Luke 9:43–45)

After the deliverance of the demon-possessed boy, Jesus and the disciples "went out and began to go through Galilee." Leaving the region of Caesarea Philippi, it was necessary that they pass through Galilee. But this was the last phase of Jesus' earthly ministry, and it was important that He not be encumbered with the continual needs of the multitudes. Therefore, Mark records that, "He was unwilling for anyone to know about it." This would be Jesus' last visit to Galilee, for betrayal and death ultimately awaited Him in Jerusalem.

The next verse clearly tells us Jesus' reason for this separation from external distractions. It was so He could continue uninterrupted to develop His teaching regarding His forthcoming betrayal and death, something the disciples had not yet fully grasped.

"For He was teaching His disciples and telling them, 'The Son of Man is to be delivered into the hands of men, and they will kill Him; and when He has been killed, He will rise three days later.'" The verb "taught" is an imperfect stressing both the continual nature of Jesus' act of teaching and the content of His teaching. It was imperative that the disciples open their minds to the reality of Jesus' revelation to them.

The fact that Jesus would be delivered into the hands of men is a new component not seen in His previous teaching in 8:31. The expression, "is to be delivered" in Greek is a prophetic present passive indicative. The present tense implies certainty while the use of the passive voice hints at an agent in this betrayal. This same verb *paradidōmi* is used in Matthew 26:25 regarding Judas's betrayal (cf. Matt. 27:3; John 12:4; 13:2; 18:2, 5), in Acts 3:13 regarding the delivering up of Jesus to death by the people, and finally in Romans 8:32 regarding God's delivering up Jesus for our salvation. Hiebert comments on this idea: "By a conscious act of will, man may perpetrate betrayal, but only as the will of God permits it in order to fulfill the divine purpose. Scripture clearly teaches that the Passion of Christ had its ultimate ground in God's initiative and plan for our salvation."[18]

Once again Mark demonstrates the spiritual dullness of the disciples, saying that "they did not understand this statement." It should be noted that it was not the words themselves that the disciples failed to understand, but the theology behind them. Their deep-seated traditional misunderstanding regarding who the Messiah was and what He would do, blinded them to the truth of Jesus' words. They simply could not reconcile what He was saying.

Mark goes on to say that they, "were afraid to ask Him." Certainly they must have remembered the recent rebuke that Peter experienced when he attempted to challenge Jesus about this issue (8:33). Perhaps they feared that their questions would be seen in a negative light, only to bring another sharp rebuke. Matthew's account notes that this teaching caused them to be "deeply grieved" (17:23). Apparently they understood Jesus' comments enough to realize that the path they were on did not lead to earthly glory and fame, but rather to suffering and possibly death. In our assessment of the disciples here, we should not be too harsh, because as Lenski correctly notes:

we are too familiar with the crucifixion and resurrection of Jesus properly to place ourselves into the position of the disciples when Jesus foretold these things. His words concerning his resurrection seemed as strange and incredible to them as those about his death. To the last their minds struggled against the plain meaning of what was dinned into their ears, what they were afraid to know, they actually did not know or grasp.[19]

Although the disciples feared to ask Jesus about these things, their fear was not of such a degree that it controlled their thinking. It wasn't long, as the following passage indicates, until their minds became occupied not with questions concerning Jesus' teaching, but with questions concerning authority and personal honor.

The Servant Redefining True Greatness (9:33–37)

(Compare Matthew 18:1–5; Luke 9:46–48)

Finally arriving at their destination in Capernaum, Jesus and the Twelve entered into a house. The text makes it very clear that while they were traveling, the Twelve began to argue about "which of them was the greatest." It is quite possible that this disputing arose because of the recent experience on the Mount of Transfiguration. Matthew informs the reader that this disputing actually dealt with who would be, "greatest in the kingdom of heaven." Whatever led to their disputing, it showed that the Twelve did not understand or accept Jesus' predicted passion.

Being the God-Man, Jesus knew what the disciples were thinking, because He knew what was in every man. He asked them, "What were you discussing on the way?" Again, the question was not for His own knowledge but was put to the disciples to cause them to reflect upon their shameful attitudes and behavior. Like a child caught with his hand in the proverbial cookie jar, the disciples "kept silent." What could they say?

"And sitting down," Jesus, ever the teacher, "called the twelve." In the Middle East it was customary to sit down and gather one's disciples around when a formal teaching session was in process. This clearly suggested to the disciples that Jesus was about to say something of great importance.

Intriguingly, Jesus did not directly rebuke them but instead, endeavored to bring them to some spiritual sense. First, Jesus clearly revealed His knowledge of their disputing, saying to them, "If anyone wants to be first, he shall be last of all, and servant of all." Second, He gave them an object lesson. The text indicates that "taking a child, He set him before them, and taking him in His arms, He said to them, 'Whoever receives one child like this in My name receives Me; and whoever receives Me does not receive Me, but Him who sent Me.'"

Jesus' dramatic use of a child to further illustrate His teaching is significant when one considers the position children held in ancient society. This point is driven home when one considers that both the words *child* and *servant* are the same in Aramaic.

We are mistaken if we imagine that Greek and Jewish society extolled the virtues of childhood as do modern societies in general. Societies with high infant mortality rates and great demand for human labor cannot afford to be sentimental about infants and youth. In Judaism, children and women were largely auxiliary members of society whose connection to the social mainstream depended on men (either as fathers or husbands). Children, in particular, were thought of as "not having arrived." They were good illustrations of "the very last" (v. 35).[20]

Given this cultural background, Jesus' use of a child here well suited the point He was trying to make. This is true because "the child is representative of his class, a type of the simple, trusting, unassuming disciple"[21] and therefore encompasses the idea of humility among Christians. But this fact in and of itself did not accommodate all that Jesus wanted the disciples to understand.

Jesus also wanted the disciples to reflect upon His attitude and actions toward this child. He Himself served as an example of how the disciples were to receive the seemingly insignificant follower. Jesus here demonstrates what it means to be the servant of all in that He is willing to lower Himself to minister to the needs of this culturally insignificant child; therefore they could do no less!

The lesson Jesus was intent on teaching them was in essence this: lowliness is the path to greatness and service is the way to sovereignty; pride is not conducive to preeminence in the kingdom of God. He who would be chief must be prepared to go down, for in humbling himself, he shall be exalted.

The great law of humility in the kingdom of God is not "Use thyself for thy self alone"; nor "Use others for thyself"; but rather "Use thyself for others." This is a profound lesson in the principle and spirit of greatness. Christ is the great example of humility (cf. Phil. 2:5–8).

The Servant Reassuring about Rewards (9:38–41)

(Compare Luke 9:49–50)

After this poignant illustration, as if he had heard nothing the Lord had just said, John tells Jesus, "Teacher, we saw someone casting out demons in Your name, and we tried to hinder him because he was not following us." Barbieri insightfully remarks:

> "It is interesting that in the immediate context the disciples were unable to cast out a demon, but they were working against someone, probably a true believer, who in the name of Jesus was actually being victorious over the demonic realm."[22]

It is obvious from the manner in which he disregarded what Jesus had just said that John was convinced that the call to discipleship was not a call to service but a call to privilege. It may be that he desired to avoid the Lord's teaching concerning true greatness because he yet aspired to sit either at the right hand or left hand of Christ in the kingdom age (Mark 10:37).

John's words revealed a sense of self-gratification and self-exaltation. One would expect John to indicate that his disapproval was due to the fact that the man was not following Jesus, but instead, he indicated that his concern was due to the fact that the man was not following "us," a likely reference to John and his brother, James.

Instead of congratulating John, the Lord put forth a twofold correction. This is easily and often missed. John had rebuked the man for not following "us," namely, John and his brother, indicating John's failure to honor the Lord as he should have. Jesus, on the other hand, said, "He who is not against us is for us." By so doing, Jesus rebuked John's exclusive use of "us" and at the same time demonstrated grace and love toward John by His inclusive use of "us."

Jesus continued, "Do not hinder him, for there is no one who shall perform a miracle in My name, and be able soon afterward to speak evil of Me." Jesus insisted that the man was not an enemy, but a friend. If he was for Christ, he could not be against Him.

Finally, Jesus said, "For whoever gives you a cup of water to drink because of your name as followers of Christ, truly I say to you, he shall not lose his reward."

The issue here is what is done in Jesus' name! No matter what the deed, whether exorcisms, healings, miracles, or even the simple act of giving a cup of water to a fellow believer, if it is done in Jesus' name, it will be rewarded.

Even the smallest kindness done in Christ's name will be rewarded. A cup of water given to a disciple be cause he belongs to Christ will not go unnoticed. Casting out a demon in His name is rather spectacular. Giving a glass of water is commonplace. But both are precious to Him when done for His glory. "Because you belong to Christ" is the cord that should bind believers together. These words, if kept before us, would deliver us from party spirit, petty bickerings and jealousy in Christian service.[23]

The lesson is clear here. Just because someone who is serving God in another realm is not with our crowd does not mean we are to try to stop him. No one is to be forbidden to serve Christ because he is operating in a different place or a different realm or under a different name. Each must stand or fall before his own Master.

The Servant Reminding about Hell (9:42–50)

(Compare Matthew 18:6–9)

More than likely, with the child still in His arms and the disciples focused on him, Jesus made a powerful declaration: "Whoever causes one of these little ones who believe to stumble, it would be better for him if, with a heavy millstone hung around his neck, he had been cast into the sea." It is clear from this statement that John's brazen attitude held the most serious of consequences. This is a warning to all who would cause another to stumble and leave serving the Lord!

As seen previously, the term "little ones" refers to humble disciples who are perhaps immature in faith, but also certainly includes children who believe in Christ. Therefore this issue of causing a fellow believer to stumble is grave—so much so that Jesus indicates that it would be better for that person to drown himself before allowing it to occur.

Now that He is on the topic of sin, Jesus shifts His focus from offending or sinning against others to the danger of being led into temptation and offense (sin) personally and individually. To stress the importance of this teaching, Jesus uses hyperbole to make His point, saying, "If your hand causes you to stumble, cut it off . . . And if your foot causes you to stumble, cut it off . . . And if your eye causes you to stumble, cast it out." The point is that it is imperative that we should take swift and earnest action against anything that might seduce us away from our commitment to Christ. The threefold command is given to emphasize the critical nature of this issue and also to point out that temptations come from many and various means!

Jesus next enters into an affirmation concerning the reality of hell and its characteristics. This is an issue of great emotion for many. In fact, many today try to bypass the Bible's clear teaching concerning hell, declaring that if God is a God of love, He would never allow such a place as hell to exist! With so many words, they dismiss the doctrine of hell entirely or spiritualize all references to it.

This is a very dangerous thing to do when one considers that the Lord spoke more about hell than all the other writers of Scripture combined. If we are willing to believe, accept, and teach what He said regarding the Father, heaven, and prayer, and concerning loving one another, how is it that we feel we have the authority to declare what Jesus says here about hell as wrong?

The issue of sin and its effects is so critical that Jesus states, "It is better for you to enter life crippled, than having your two hands, to go into hell . . . it is better for you to enter life lame, than having your two feet, to be cast into hell . . . it is better for you to enter the kingdom of God with one eye, than having two eyes, to be cast into hell." Obviously Jesus was not literally suggesting self-mutilation. Even if someone cut off his hand or foot or plucked out an eye, he would still remain a sinner. Sin does not originate in the physical body, but in the heart (cf. 7:18–23). Henry Barclay Swete sums up Jesus' point Jesus, saying "Better to live under a *sense* of partial mutilation and incompleteness than to perish in the enjoyment of *all* one's senses (italics mine)."[24]

Lane makes the observation that Jesus was not calling for physical self-mutilation, but instead He was making the point about the most costly of sacrifices. The sinful member of the body must be placed under control in order that the whole body be not cast into hell. And likewise, concern for what a hand, a leg or a foot does must not lead to a denial of the sovereignty of God or one's loyalty to Christ. This was exemplified in the story of Jewish martyrdom (2 Macc. 7:2–41), where the sacrifice of bodily members and life itself was accepted in order to be true to God and to receive life from His hand. This is an example for martyrdom in the church as well. Whenever there is something in the Christian walk that would cause one to be unfaithful to the Lord must be removed and discarded promptly, just when a doctor must amputate a limb for the survival of the patient.[25]

In this discussion about hell, Jesus describes what it is like, comparing it to a fire that "is not quenched" and a place where "their worm does not die"! These phrases are repeated four and three times respectively indicating the certainty of the characteristics of hell. The use of these terms pictures both an external torment (the fire) and an internal torment (the worms) that never end. Jesus' comments most likely refer back to Isaiah 66:24.

The fire of hell is real, though it may not be the kind of fire we presently have in this world; the worm not dying speaks of the everlasting continuity of the lost soul in a state of suffering. Worms in the grave devour the decaying body, then die. Not so in hell. Surely no one would deliberately choose the penitentiary of the universe instead of the blessings of paradise! But, of course, the majority do, for the road to destruction is broad and the gate is wide.

To conclude this teaching, Jesus then states, "For every one will be salted with fire. Salt is good; but if the salt becomes unsalty, with what will you make it salty again?" The closing statements in this pericope are unusual. John D. Grassmick suggests the following three possibilities:

> Everyone may be explained in one of three ways: (1) It could refer to every unbeliever who enters hell. They will be salted with fire in the sense that as salt preserves food so they will be preserved throughout an eternity of fiery judgment. (2) "Everyone" could refer to every disciple living in this hostile world. They will be "salted with fire" in the sense that Old Testament sacrifices were seasoned with salt (Lev. 2:13; Ezek. 43:24).

Disciples, living sacrifices (cf. Rom. 12:1), will be seasoned with purifying fiery trials (cf. Prov. 27:21; Isa. 48:10; 1 Peter 1:7; 4:12). The trials will purge out what is contrary to God's will and preserve what is consistent with it. (3) "Everyone" could refer to every person in general. All will be "salted with fire" in a time and manner appropriate to their relationship with Jesus—for nonbelievers, the preserving fire of final judgment; for disciples, the refining fire of present trials and suffering. This last view seems preferable.[26]

Perhaps the best explanation is that here fire and salt speak to the issue of trials and the costs of discipleship. Discipleship must be totally consuming. Trials will come, and it is the disciple who willingly takes up the cross and forsakes the sinful pleasures of this life for a life of faith who will enjoy life eternal.

Finally, Jesus commands the disciples, "Have salt in yourselves, and be at peace with one another." They had been striving for places of honor and disputing over who would be the greatest. Now Jesus laid down the law as it were, telling them that peace must reign in their hearts toward one another! Peace would be greatly needed if they were to survive the difficult days ahead.

Study Questions

1. How would you explain the superiority and greatness of Christ to someone who was lost and did not know Him as Savior?

2. How does the confirming words of God the Father from the cloud impact you in regard to the person of Christ? How would you use these words in witnessing to the lost?

3. What do we learn from the father who brought to Christ his demon possessed son? Are most believers this honest about about their faith?

4. What in this chapter touches on Christ's coming experience of rejection by the crowds when He arrives in Jerusalem?

5. How can we sometimes hinder the simple faith in the Lord expressed by a little child?

6. What should be our response to those with those whom we differ on doctrine but are still preaching the clear message of salvation in Christ? What then should be our attitude?

CHAPTER 10

The Servant on His Way to Jerusalem
Mark 10:1-52

Preview:

Five people or groups of people come to Jesus in this chapter, each with a need, problem, or question. First, the Pharisees approach Christ, raising the issue of marriage and divorce in a foolish attempt to discredit Christ and His teachings if possible. Second, the disciples try to turn away a group of children brought to Christ by their parents, that He might touch them. The third incident is that of the rich young ruler, who, though outwardly righteous, clings covetously and selfishly to his riches. The fourth group includes James and John, who are aspiring to achieve the highest rank in the kingdom age. Last, blind Bartimaeus cries out for a blessing and is healed. These events transpire as Jesus travels from Perea, east of the Jordan River, to Jericho, en route to Jerusalem.

Divorce and Remarriage (10:1-12)

(Compare Matthew 19:1-9)

Having completed His ministry in Capernaum, Jesus rose up and once again headed toward Jerusalem. Matthew notes that Jesus departed from Galilee. Both are correct as Capernaum is located in Galilee. This signaled the close of Jesus' ministry in the area that had been His center of operation. He would never again return.

Jesus, along with His disciples, "went from there to the region of Judea, and beyond the Jordan." It is likely that Jesus traveled south across the mountains of Samaria into Judea and at some point crossed the Jordan and entered into the region of Perea, which was controlled by Herod.

Upon arriving there, the "crowds gathered around Him again." As this was toward the end of Jesus' public ministry, He would have been recognized by the locals. Matthew says that while there, Jesus healed the sick. Mark, on the other hand, focuses on the fact that "according to His custom, He once more began to teach them." The double use of the word "again" suggests that whereas His recent focus had been on training the disciples, He now turned His focus back to the teaching of the people.

At every turn, Jesus' enemies sought an occasion to harass Him, and so here too, the Pharisees "came up to Him, testing Him, and began to question Him whether it was lawful for a man to divorce a wife." Mark is careful to point out that they were not interested in truth but asked solely for the purpose of "testing Him." To understand the significance of the Pharisees' questions, it is necessary to reflect upon the topic of divorce as it was taught and believed in Jesus' day.

William Lane notes that divorce was considered lawful to both the Pharisees and the scribes, and probably among the majority of the Jewish population. With provisions, divorce was allowed and permitted by Moses in Deuteronomy 24:1. The point of contention in that passage was the phrase "something shameful." By the time of the first century opinions were split among two camps. The students of the rabbi Shammai argued that this referred to something morally shameful, probably adultery. The followers of rabbi Hillel contended that in addition to any moral fault, that which became an annoyance or embarrassment to the husband was a legal ground for divorce.[1]

R. C. H. Lenski comments on the wide divergence of belief between these two schools.

> Before the time of Jesus the schools of Shammai and of Hillel differed on the interpretation of Deut. 24:1. The former said: "The man is not to release his wife except he have found something indecent in her." . . . Hillel allowed as a charge that in cooking the wife had burned her husband's food; and Rabbi Akiba, using from Deut. 24:1 the words, "that she find no favor in his eyes," allowed her to be released whenever the husband found a better-looking woman. Shammai was stricter, Hillel utterly lax.[2]

That the Pharisees supported Hillel's teaching is clear when Matthew's account is brought to bear. In Matthew 19:3 the Pharisees ask, "Is it lawful for a man to divorce his wife for any cause at all?" By posing their question in this way to Jesus, they sought to make Him commit Himself. Depending upon His answer, they could find those who would oppose Him, thereby weakening His influence with the common people.

No matter what Jesus said, in their minds it would require a choice that would entangle Him in Jewish partisanship. On the one hand, it was a question of His orthodoxy, but on the other hand, it may be that the Pharisees hoped Jesus would offend Herod and meet the same fate that John had. In any case, it was a subtle maneuver to get Jesus to ensnare Himself.

Jesus was not going to be caught up in their petty arguments, and so, instead of answering them immediately, Jesus turned the tables and asked them, "What did Moses command you?" Jesus was not afraid to deal with the problem, but before doing so, He would first establish the appropriate parameters for the discussion. It was important that the people understand that it was not the schools of Shammai and Hillel but the divine law that must resolve the issue.

The response of the Pharisees, "Moses permitted a man to write a certificate of divorce and send her away," demonstrated that they were not there for the purpose of truth but, as previously indicated, merely to "test Him." Jesus asked them what Moses had commanded. Ignoring His direct question, they did not answer, but instead tried to shift the discussion in their favor by declaring the *procedure* for divorce. D. Edmond Hiebert explains the reason for this tactic:

> In saying "Moses suffered"—that is, "allowed, permitted" they implied that he had "turned over to" them the right of divorce. They pointed out the law's procedure for divorce: that if they wanted to put away a wife, repudiate her, and terminate the marriage, they were to write a bill of divorcement, prepare a written divorce certificate as the formal instrument for her dismissal. Their statement emphasized the privilege of divorce but did not mention the legal restrictions Moses had stipulated. They were interested in the legal aspect of the issue the law's provision for the practice of divorce—but not in its deeper moral aspect. They were more concerned with their own rights within the limits of the law than with the matter of God's will when facing the problem of divorce.[3]

In response to their attempt to skirt the issue, Jesus set forth the correct understanding of marriage and at the same time rebuked them, saying, "Because of your hardness of heart he wrote you this commandment." In this declaration Jesus made it clear that this concession in the law did not institute or authorize divorce. It simply permitted, under strict guidelines, the husband's right to divorce his wife. The intention was to restrain the ultimate outcome of "[their] hardness of heart," namely, unbridled and uncontrolled divorce.

As teachers of the law, the Pharisees should have known and understood God's will in this matter, but since they chose to hide behind a supposed loophole, Jesus took them back to the institution of marriage, stating, "But from the beginning of creation, God made them male and female. For this cause a man shall leave his father and mother, and the two shall become one flesh; consequently they are no longer two, but one flesh. What therefore God has joined together, let no man separate." James Brooks indicates the significance of this.

> Jesus moved the discussion to a higher plane by going beyond interpreting Moses' legislation to God's original intention for marriage as seen in the creation. The quotation is from Gen 1:27. The entire verse reads: "God created man in his own image, in the image of God he created him; male and female he created them." Just as God is inseparably one being, so he intended for a male and a female in marriage to become one being who would not be divided. . . . The divine ideal as seen in creation is the permanent union of a man and a woman in marriage and no divorce whatsoever.[4]

Lenski agrees and comments on the phrase "What therefore God hath joined together, let no man separate": "The plain implication is that any man who divides what God has thus by his own creation united into one flies in the face of God and his will—a serious opposition, indeed. How indissoluble marriage is according to God's own creation is thus made clear."[5]

Here was another instance where Jesus revealed the Father's heart intention. He had also done this when the Pharisees approached Him about the Sabbath. The legitimacy and orthodoxy of Jesus' argument and wisdom could not be defeated, settling the question once and for all. It was now up to the Pharisees to acknowledge this and do what was right, something they would not do.

Jesus left the Pharisees to ponder this revelation and with the disciples entered into the home of one of the locals. In the safety and seclusion of the house, "the disciples began questioning Him about this again." The disciples' request for further clarification on this issue and their response (cf. Matt. 19:7–10) suggests that they too subscribed to the more liberal view of divorce.

In the private house setting, Jesus continued His teaching, adding to it the element of remarriage. This expanded revelation revealed the compounded error of the Pharisees' teaching concerning divorce, for "whoever divorces his wife and marries another woman commits adultery against her; and if she herself divorces her husband and marries another man, she is committing adultery." Jesus did not intend to imply that adultery is the result of remarriage but rather the result of a frivolous divorce. In other words, if the divorce is not legal according to Jewish law, a second marriage becomes adulterous.

There was great carelessness among the Jews of Jesus' day in regard to the sanctity of marriage. His critics remind Him that Moses allowed divorce (Deuteronomy 24:1-4). Jesus' reply indicates that this legislation was only intended to be permissive and provisional, enacted to meet the special exigency of the times. Moses found himself confronted by evils which he saw as impossible to extirpate, for dissolution of marriage had become common among the Jews, who had freely adopted the manner and customs of surrounding nations. But our Lord showed that such legislation (under the Law) could not be final. The ideal relation of the sexes was established at the beginning, when God made them male and female, "one wife for one husband, to be united so closely that they should become not only one in heart and soul but actually 'one flesh.' It was a union designed for perpetuity (in life) and thus our Lord clearly taught when He said 'What therefore God hath joined together, let not man put asunder.'"[6]

Marriage was the first divine institution, and divorce has never been the perfect will of God (cf. 1 Cor. 7:10-16). Nevertheless, it occurs. It is not an unpardonable sin. Christ accepts us at salvation as we are but by making us new "creatures." The new birth, causes "old things to pass away and all things to become new." People must be reached for Christ not where they should have been, but where they are.

Christians who have been married and divorced and then remarry cannot be eliminated from serving Christ if their hearts are right with God. The ideal, a lifelong unbroken marriage, must be taught as God's perfect will, but real-life situations must be dealt with in the total context of Scripture (see, e.g., John 4:1-29), and He who forgave the woman taken in adultery (John 8:1-11) can meet the needs of any person or couple who comes to Him.

Disciples and Children (10:13-16)

(Compare Matthew 19:13-15; Luke 18:15-17)

Jesus' concern for the powerless continues in this pericope. Having discussed the issue of marriage, it is appropriate at this point for Mark to introduce children. Like women, children under first-century Jewish law also had few legal rights. C. S. Keener notes that in the Jewish culture of the day, "Children were loved but were socially powerless; the high infant mortality rate meant that they were physically powerless as well, many dying before attaining maturity."[7]

As this scene developed, Jesus apparently was still in the house and at least some of the disciples were outside. Once parents and other family members realized where Jesus was, "they were bringing children to Him so that He might touch them." It seems only natural that parents would want to bring their children to Jesus. In their eyes He was a respected rabbi and teacher, and His blessing would be important to them. Warren Wiersbe explains that "it was customary for parents to bring their children to the rabbis for a blessing, and so it was reasonable that they would bring the little ones to Jesus."[8]

As the numbers outside the house began to grow, emotions among the crowd also began to grow. One can easily understand how the parents in the crowd would have begun to maneuver and push their children to the fore-front. The disciples, however, were used to handling large crowds and began to rebuke these parents and their children. Louis Barbieri correctly notes:

> This act does not imply that the disciples were mean to or angry with these people. They probably sensed that Jesus was occupied with other things. He was moving with purpose toward Jerusalem (cf. Luke 9:51), where He was going to be delivered into the hands of wicked men and crucified. Since He was spending a great deal of time with His disciples to instruct them, perhaps they felt His time could be better spent minister-ing to adults.[9]

The fact that the disciples rebuked these interested parents reveals that they still did not perceive the total love of Christ for all, regardless of age, sex, background, or any other factor. It is also clear that they did not yet under-stand or remember His teaching concerning children in Capernaum (Mark 9:36–37; Matt. 18:2–14).

As soon as their actions became known to Jesus, "He was indignant [much displeased]." Hiebert comments:

> The verb much displeased, used only here of Jesus, is a term of strong emotion and denotes His pained, angry reaction to what was going on. He was deeply displeased that the very men whom He had so explicitly taught misunderstood so grievously the basic principles of His ministry.[10]

Jesus' immediate response was to issue a double command: "Permit the children to come to Me; do not hinder them; for the kingdom of God belongs to such as these. Truly I say to you, whoever does not receive the kingdom of God like a child shall not enter it at all." The inference is that children will want to come to Jesus. Lenski, quoting Pank, writes:

> As the flower in the garden stretches toward the light of the sun, so there is in the child a mysterious inclination toward the eternal light. Have you never noticed this mysterious thing, that when you tell the smallest child about God, it never asks with strangeness and wonder: "What or who is God? I have never seen him!"—but listens with shining face to the words as if they were soft, loving sounds from the land of home? or

when you teach a child to fold its little hands in prayer, that it does this as if it were a matter of course, as if there were opening for it that world of which it has been dreaming with longing and anticipation? or tell them, these little ones, the stories of the Savior, show them the pictures with scenes and personages of the Bible—how their pure eyes shine, how the little hearts beat![11]

Lane agrees with Lenski and adds:

Unlike adults, who do not want anything to be given to them, children are comparatively modest and unspoiled. The Kingdom belongs to such as these because they receive it as a gift. The ground of Jesus' surprising statement is not to be found in any subjective quality possessed by children but rather in their objective humbleness and in the startling character of the grace of God who wills to give the Kingdom to those who have no claim upon it.[12]

Christ's words "for the kingdom of God belongs to such as these" should be taken as denoting those who have certain definite qualities or characteristics. He is not thinking merely of children here, but of those characterized by a spirit of openness, reliance, and trustfulness.

Having resolved the issue, Jesus turned to the children. "He took them in His arms and began blessing them, laying His hands upon them." After having cleared up any misunderstandings with regard to His wishes, Jesus responds to the desire of the parents and blesses the children. By so doing, Jesus makes it clear that even children, that part of society thought to be of less value, were to be given access to Him. This act along with Jesus' teaching forever changed the cultural view of children.

Deceit of Riches (10:17–22)

(Compare Matthew 19:16–26; Luke 18:18–27)

Jesus once again took up His journey toward Jerusalem and the cross. While on the way, "a man ran up to Him and knelt before Him, and began asking Him, 'Good Teacher, what shall I do to inherit eternal life?'" The first thing that stands out in this verse is the fact that this man came with a sense of urgency. He ran to Jesus, kneeled, and addressed Him formally, suggesting respect and sincerity of heart. This question must have pleased Jesus because, up to this point in time, no one had asked such a profound question, not even Jesus' own disciples. This was *the* question that everyone should have been asking. The use of the title "Good Teacher" (not normally used for rabbis) is no doubt sincere and, coupled with his question, reveals a level of spiritual insight. Believing Jesus had mastered spiritual perfection, he desired to learn from Him.

Although this man came to the right place to get his question answered, the question itself demonstrated that he considered eternal life something to be realized by doing good. Jesus therefore had to deal with this misconception. He did so by first addressing the issue of who is truly good, asking him, "Why do you call Me good: No one is good except God alone." It was quite common for rabbis to be addresses by different titles. However, as James R. Edwards notes, "only rarely was a rabbi addressed as 'good teacher,' for fear of blasphemy against God, who alone is good."[13] There are two words in Greek that are translated "good" in English. One is *agathos* and the other is *kalos*. *Agathos* refers to that which is essentially good[14] while *kalos* refers to that which is externally attractive or useful.[15] This is significant, as J. Dwight Pentecost explains:

> The man used the word that refers to intrinsic goodness and addressed Jesus as the intrinsically good Teacher. Christ reminded him that there is only One who is intrinsically good—and that One is God. Jesus Christ had been claiming to be the Son of God. Therefore He claimed to be intrinsically good. He asked His question to see if the man would say that he addressed Him as the intrinsically good Teacher because he believed that He was the Son of God.[16]

Jesus' response was calculated to force the young man to reflect upon who Jesus really was. Jesus' intention was to focus the man on His essential nature. If the man realized this, he would then have to come to grips with the truth of that fact and its demands upon him. Jesus quoted Exodus 20:12–16 and Deuteronomy 5:16–20, "Do not murder, Do not commit adultery, Do not steal, Do not bear false witness, Do not defraud, Honor your father and mother." All of these commands dealt with one's relationship to others.

In this, the young man could honestly say, "Teacher, I have kept all these things from my youth up." Note the change in the man's attitude toward Jesus upon being told to follow the commandments. Instead of referring to Jesus as "Good Teacher" as he had before, he now referred to Him only as "Teacher." By his response the man makes it clear that he recognizes there is still something missing from his life (cf. Matt. 19:20) but also that there may be some question in his mind as to whether or not Jesus can provide the solution.

"And looking at him, Jesus felt a love for him." Jesus beheld him. The Greek word used here is *emblepō* and means "to look at something directly and therefore intently."[17] Jesus set His gaze upon the man. One can only wonder what the man was feeling and thinking as Jesus did this. This suggestion here is that Jesus looked into the man's heart and soul. Perhaps this look brought conviction or perhaps Jesus saw within this man a sincere desire to know God. In any case, we are told that Jesus "felt a love for him." Hiebert writes:

> Mark alone makes reference here to the emotional reaction of Jesus. *Loved him* is probably best rendered "began to love him." Jesus felt strongly drawn to this young man for what he already was, and in love yearned to lead him to the full realization of his quest. *Loved* denotes not mere emotional affection but that high spiritual love which, regardless of the worthiness or unworthiness of the one loved, desires his highest welfare.[18]

In 1 Corinthians 13:5, we are told that love "does not seek its own." Jesus loved this man, but love dictated that He tell the man the truth, so He said to him, "One thing you lack: go and sell all you possess, and give to the poor, and you shall have treasure in heaven; and come, follow Me." Lane remarks:

> The response of verse 21 is not intended to shame him by exposing the real depth of the commandments but is an expression of genuine love for him. The one thing he lacks is the self-sacrificing devotion which characterizes every true follower of Jesus. For this reason Jesus invites him to follow him now and to experience the demands of life and the Kingdom with the Twelve.[19]

With this command and invitation to become a disciple, the man became sad. He was not sad at the invitation, but he was sad at the cost of discipleship. He no doubt believed that his possessions were a sure sign of favor from God and as such he should not be required to do away with them. Moreover, the call for him to deny himself in general was not at all that for which he was looking. His response unfortunately was to go "away grieved, for he was one who owned much property." His disastrous choice revealed two things. First, it revealed that he loved his possessions more than life (cf. Mark 4:19) and second, that he had in fact, sinned the greatest sin in that he did not love God above all things! (cf. Mar. 12:29–31) R. A. Cole provides the following insights:

> His impatient brushing-aside of the expected orthodox Jewish suggestion, that the way to life was by keeping the commandments, shows a spiritual perception far in advance of that displayed by the average scribe (but cf. 12:33). But his spiritual insight was not matched by a readiness for committal which would involve sacrifice, and so he went away sadly. In his case, the impediment was his wealth; sooner than give it up, he gave up Jesus. So he becomes a continual warning to all the disciples of Jesus (verse 23) of the dangers of riches.[20]

Jesus looked into the young man's heart. Though he had indeed been most diligent in trying to keep the Ten Commandments, Christ knew there was one thing in life more important than anything else, his riches—they were his god. He could have had what he had come for, but his riches kept him from becoming Jesus' follower. If there is anything in our lives that is keeping us back from full acceptance of Christ, we must part with it. "The one thing" the rich man lacked was faith. He could not bring himself to believe in Christ to the extent that he would be willing to give up everything (his station in life, his riches, his self-esteem) to find true riches. Salvation is by faith, not by our own works. This illustrates Mark 4:19: "the deceitfulness of riches."

Declaration of Rewards (10:23–31)

(Compare Matthew 19:27–30; Luke 18:28–30)

Mark then adds this phrase, "Jesus, looking around, said to His disciples." As the rich man walked away, Jesus was left with an opportunity once again to teach His disciples.

Those present no doubt wondered at the responses both of Jesus and the man. Surely Jesus could not deny an honored place within His group for such a sincere and honorable man as this! After all, he certainly had the clout and prestige among the people to add credibility to Jesus' cause and most definitely could open doors among those who, like him, were the upper echelon of society. What an opportunity lost!

As Jesus looked round about, He must have realized the questionings that were taking place in the people and especially in the minds of the disciples, because He immediately declared, "How hard it will be for those who are wealthy to enter the kingdom of God!"

The response of the disciples to Jesus' words was that they "were amazed." The verb, *thambeō* is here used as an imperfect passive indicating that they continued to be astonished. This is understandable in that Jesus' remarks shattered contemporary Jewish thinking. In their minds the Old Testament clearly taught that wealth and substance were marks of God's favor. Moreover, it was a commonly held belief that those so blessed of God accrued favor by means of their good works. Therefore, if the wealthy were not able to enter the kingdom of heaven, what hope would there be for those not so blessed?

Jesus, knowing what was in their hearts and minds, again declared, "Children, how hard it is to enter the kingdom of God! It is easier for a camel to go through the eye of a needle than for a rich man to enter the kingdom of God." Upon hearing Jesus repeat this statement, their amazement grew "out of measure," from a different Greek word, *ekplēssō*, meaning literally, "to the point of being overwhelmed." They were dumbfounded! So great was their amazement that they continued to question among themselves, saying, "Then who can be saved? It is important to realize that Jesus' conclusion here is categorically laid out. No amount of twisting the text will change what He said or what He meant. William Hendriksen correctly sums up the matter.

> To explain what Jesus means it is useless and unwarranted to try to change "camel" into "cable,"-see Matthew 23:24, where a real camel must have been meant-or to define the "needle's eye" as the narrow gate in a city wall, a gate, so the reasoning goes, through which a camel can pass only on its knees and after its burden has been removed. Such "explanations" (?), aside from being objectionable from a linguistic point of view, strive to make possible what Jesus specifically declared to be impossible. The Lord clearly means that for a rich man in his own power to try to work or worm his way into the kingdom of God is impossible.[21] (emphasis added)

The disciples had been taught from their youth that wealth was a sign of God's direct blessing and favor. Now Jesus stripped away error and exposed them to truth. This is a painful process, and our willingness to accept truth even when it goes against all we have been taught is a genuine sign of spiritual insight and maturity.

Again Jesus looked upon the disciples. Notice that this expression is key in this pericope. Jesus looked upon the rich man, He looked upon the disciples after making His first declaration, and now He did so again. This was not merely a superficial gaze, but a piercing look designed to expose their hearts, not to Him, for He knew their hearts, but to themselves. For truth to take firm root, it must have good soil within which it can grow. In a manner of speaking, Jesus was weeding their hearts, getting them ready for the truth to come.

Edwards points out that the word of the Lord Jesus comes to them, as to the rich man, not as a word of comfort but as an offense. What Christ said did its job, going inward where they discover their own weaknesses and inadequacies. The commanding words of Jesus makes them aware of what they were *lacking*, as did Jesus' word to the rich man in verse 21. In the same way, Christ brought a certain kind of training to the disciples when He sent them on their mission without provisions, so that they would learn to trust in God (6:7–13). The disciples' sense of inadequacy at the command of Jesus is, in fact, a "severe mercy" (Rom. 11:22), and even a blessing, a beneficial limitation that is intended to draw them away from trust in their own abilities to the one who would be their saving Lord.[22]

As the disciples mulled over what Jesus had just said, He answered their question, saying, "With men it is impossible, but not with God; for all things are possible with God." The point of this response was to bring the disciples to the understanding that salvation is utterly outside the sphere of human capacity.

Neither personal nor corporate achievement will suffice to bring anyone into the kingdom. Salvation is a gift from God and cannot be merited or earned.

The impact of Jesus' words must have brought great concern to the hearts of the disciples. Peter, speaking for the group in verse 28, said, "Behold, we have left everything and followed You." Lane explains: "The disciples were more bewildered than before. They understood that the manner in which Jesus spoke of the rich in fact blocks the way for any man to achieve entrance into the Kingdom, and they were frightened by this implication."[23]

Peter's comments reflect back to Jesus' remarks to the rich man. Unlike him, they had indeed left all to follow Jesus (Mark 1:16–20; 2:14). This comment is at once both an affirmation on his part and a pleading for clarification from Jesus (cf. Matt. 19:27, "what then will there be for us?"). The disciples could find some self-satisfaction in the fact that they had been obedient to the call, but at the same time they were looking for (1) an affirmation of their sacrifices and (2) a guarantee of future reward from Jesus. He did not disappoint them: "Truly I say to you, there is no one who has left house or brothers or sisters or mother or father or children or farms, for My sake and for the gospel's sake, but that he shall receive a hundred times as much now in the present age, houses and brothers and sisters and mothers and children and farms, along with persecutions; and in the age to come, eternal life. But many who are first, will be last; and the last, first." H. A. Ironside remarks:

> Jesus replied with words of assurance, though not at this time fully correcting His followers' carnal ideas of the coming kingdom. He gave the definite promise that no one would lose, but rather gain by sharing His path of rejection. But He warned them, "Many that are first shall be last; and the last first." That is, not everyone who gave promise of being a faithful and devoted follower would continue in the path of self-denial for Christ's name's sake, and some whose devotion seemed questionable, would prove genuine in the hour of trial.[24]

Jesus' warning, "many who are first, will be last; and the last, first," was a caution against a self-seeking spirit. Jesus was telling the Twelve that their priority did not guarantee their supremacy in the future (cf. Matt. 20:1–16). Kingdom benefits and rewards are not bestowed based on human merit. In the end, the One who knows human hearts will judge priority and position.

Death And Resurrection (10:32–34)

(Compare Matthew 20:17–19; Luke 18:31–34)

This was the third and most explicit time that Jesus predicted His resurrection (cf. 8:31–33; 9:30–32). Jesus now at the close of His ministry, proceeded from the region of the dead, the place of the tombs, "up to Jerusalem." He was, "walking on ahead of them," meaning the disciples. This was the normal manner of travel for a rabbi with his disciples.

His disciples "were amazed," but amazed at what? Although the reason is not stated, it seems reasonable to attribute their amazement to the fact that Jesus was determined to go to Jerusalem where they knew danger awaited. Hiebert remarks:

> John's Gospel makes it clear that the raising of Lazarus had brought the hostility of the religious leaders at Jerusalem to a head, and Jesus, to escape their wrath, had withdrawn to Ephraim (John 11:47–57). But now, He was resolutely and energetically leading the way back to Jerusalem; with solemn determination, He was pushing forward in the face of the obvious danger involved. Knowing the danger and struck by their Master's silent preoccupation with His own thoughts as He was walking ahead alone, the Twelve were gripped with a sense of amazement.[25]

The text tells us that "those who followed were fearful." The expression in the Greek is in the present tense and literally, "and the ones continually following, were being fearful." Some have seen in this expression a second group of followers making up a larger procession heading toward Jerusalem. This seems likely because we are next told that Jesus again "took the twelve aside," singling them out from the others.

Realizing the confusion and trepidation they were experiencing, Jesus began again "to tell them what was going to happen to Him." Interestingly, Jesus did not attempt to ease their apprehensions, but instead spoke directly to their concerns, heightening their awareness of what lie ahead.

Jesus got their attention by using the expression "Behold." The Greek word *idou* is used to prompt attention and serves to enliven a narrative by arousing the attention of hearers or readers. It is also used to introduce something new or unusual.[26] By beginning His comments this way, Jesus made it very clear that what was to follow was to be heard, received, and believed.

Jesus continued, "we are going up to Jerusalem." Jesus now more clearly than ever told the disciples where they were headed and what they would encounter. Jesus' choice of pronouns is revealing. By using "we," He united them with Him in what was to come. The Twelve would be present as witnesses when all these things happened!

Next, Jesus told them, "The Son of Man will be delivered to the chief priests, and the scribes." The use of the phrase "will be delivered" pointed to His betrayal (by Judas, unrevealed until later). The fact that He would be delivered to the "chief priests, and the scribes" revealed that His condemnation would be brought about by a judicial process of the Sanhedrin, suggesting that a trial would be held in which they would "condemn Him to death." Once condemned, the Jewish leaders would "deliver Him to the Gentiles." The handing over of Jesus to the Gentiles would be necessary because the Jewish high court did not have the authority to execute a death sentence. It indicated the contempt the Jewish leaders had for Jesus. The highest form of humiliation for a Jew would have been to be handed over to the heathen. Jesus went on to tell the disciples that the Gentiles would "mock Him and spit upon Him, and scourge Him, and kill Him."

In spite of what looked like a hopeless situation, Jesus concluded His comments with, "and three days later He will rise again." The multiple use of the word "and" through out this pericope suggests an order of events. Jesus clearly delineated what was ahead. The last item in the order of events is the most important, namely, Jesus would be resurrected. Luke, writing about the reaction of the disciples, noted that "they understood none of these things, and this saying was hidden from them, and they did not comprehend the things that were said" (Luke 18:34). Why did they have so much difficulty with this? The answer is the same as before: Jesus' words went against everything they had been taught and believed about the Messiah. Because of their personal biases, they could not yet reconcile humility passages concerning the Messiah such as Psalm 22 and Isaiah 53. And Jesus had made it clear previously that further revelation is based upon one's handling of truth already given.

Desire of James and John (10:35–45)

(Compare Matthew 20:20–28; Luke 22:24–27)

Very shortly after Jesus' third and final prediction about His forthcoming passion, perhaps immediately after, the text tells us that "James and John, the two sons of Zebedee, came up to Him, saying to Him, Teacher, we want You to do for us whatever we ask of You." Matthew's account tells us that it was the mother of these sons of Zebedee that came to Jesus with this request. The reality is that this was apparently planned by the three of them.

She came and made the request first with her two sons echoing it to Jesus: "Grant that we may sit in Your glory, one on Your right, and one on Your left." Interestingly, there is a pattern between the two passion accounts contained in 9:30–37 and here. In both instances, Jesus revealed His coming passion, and in both the disciples' inner selfishness is exposed. Also contained in both is teaching concerning humility and true service. Given the similarities between the two accounts, we should not hold James and John over the flames too long. The truth is that all of the disciples were thinking the same way.

With the request now voiced and the inner heart thereby revealed, Jesus declared, "You do not know what you are asking for. Are you able to drink the cup that I drink, or to be baptized with the baptism with which I am baptized?" Clearly, James and John had no idea what they were asking. In the larger sense, no one could drink of the cup that He would drink, nor could anyone be baptized with the baptism ahead of Him. He alone is the spotless Lamb of God. He alone could and would provide the means whereby we might be saved, so in this sense, the expected answer was no. To Jesus' question, James and John ignorantly replied, "We are able," revealing their total lack of understanding of what lie ahead.

Jesus then revealed to the two that there was a sense in which they would indeed partake of His passion. It wouldn't be in the same manner, nor would it have the same result, but yes, they surely would share in His sufferings. Jesus made this clear: "The cup that I drink you shall drink; and you shall be baptized with the baptism with which I am baptized." In fact, all who will be godly shall suffer persecution. In the case of these two disciples, church history records that James became the first apostle martyred (cf. Acts 12:2). John endured great persecution and was finally exiled to the island of Patmos (cf. Rev. 1:9).

Jesus made it very clear that they would participate in suffering for Him, but then told them that "to sit on My right or on My left, this is not Mine to give; but it is for those for whom it has been prepared." Jesus is limited by His submission to the Father (cf. Mark 13:32; Acts 1:7), and therefore any promotion to honor would be determined by the Father.

It is significant that Mark included this event here, for it demonstrates what Luke had indicated, that is, that the disciples were blinded to what Jesus had just said about His passion and also that primary in their minds was their understanding of and place in the messianic kingdom. Lane explains:

> The two brothers are confident that they are prepared to share Jesus' destiny, even in reference to suffering if this is the necessary prelude to glory. Their naive reply only serves to indicate that they were as incapable of understanding the full import of Jesus' reference to his cup and baptism as they were of grasping the real significance of his prophecy of the passion.[27]

Matthew records (19:28) that Jesus had said, "Truly I say to you, that you who have followed Me, in the regeneration when the Son of Man will sit on His glorious throne, you also shall sit upon twelve thrones, judging the twelve tribes of Israel." Not perceiving that this would occur in the distant future, James and John wanted to sit in the places of major prominence, even though Jesus had made this statement about reigning in answer to Peter's question. Jesus had just spoken of His cross in verse 34, but they are still preoccupied with thrones. "The natural interest to advance one's self can show up even in spiritual matters. . . . It is so easy to mistake as zeal something which is really only ambition to be prominent."[28]

We are not told how the other ten disciples became aware of this private discussion, but we are told that when they heard about James and John's request, "the ten began to feel indignant with James and John." The Greek verb translated "indignant" is the same verb that was used in 10:14 to describe the Lord's reaction to the disciples when they refused to allow the children to approach Him. Regarding the indignation of the ten, Edwards writes:

"Their indignation may owe to the fact that they harbor similar ambitions, but it also, and more obviously, owes to the fact that the request of the Zebedee brothers excludes them from the closeness of fellowship in glory that they presently enjoy with Jesus."[29]

Still the patient and loving Teacher gathered the disgruntled disciples around Him and told them: You know that those who are recognized as rulers of the Gentiles lord it over them; and their great men exercise authority over them. But it is not so among you, but whoever wishes to become great among you shall be your servant; and whoever wishes to be first among you shall be slave of all. For even the Son of Man did not come to be served, but to serve, and to give His life a ransom for many.

In this teaching, Jesus set forth two examples before the disciples, one negative and one positive. The negative example He used was that of the way the Gentiles exercised authority over their own. They took their authority to the extreme, lording over and dominating their subjects.

Contrary to this negative example was the example of Jesus Himself. Jesus wanted the disciples to recognize that He, the Messiah, the Son of the Living God, "did not come to be served, but to serve, and to give His life a ransom for many." If they could but see this, then His declaration, "Whoever wishes to become great among you shall be your servant; and whoever wishes to be first among you shall be slave of all," would take root. Then and only then would they be in a position to be honored. Jesus' example of humility was to be imitated by the Twelve and by all who would believe in Him. Jesus taught them that humble service, not exalted prominence, should be their goal, even as it was Jesus' goal at His first coming. Again our Lord set forth His servant-hood as a pattern for us to follow.

Decision of Blind Bartimaeus (10:46–52)

(Compare Matthew 20:29–34; Luke 18:35–43)

The healing of Bartimaeus is the last miracle recorded in Mark's gospel. Both Matthew (Matt. 20:29–34) and Mark indicate that the healing of blind Bartimaeus occurred as Jesus was leaving the town of Jericho. Luke, on the other hand (Luke 18:35–43), implies that the miracle occurred on the way into Jericho. This apparent contradiction is easily resolved when one considers that there were two sites—old Jericho and new Jericho. No doubt this miracle occurred as Jesus traveled between them. Another apparent contradiction is Matthew's account refers to two men, while both Mark and Luke mention only one. Mark's account is the only one that actually names the man, which implies he was the more vocal of the two. Therefore, both apparent contradictions are answered.

As Jesus and the disciples continued on their journey to Jerusalem, they passed through Jericho. On the way a blind beggar, "Bartimaeus, the son of Timaeus," heard that Jesus was coming his way. The Greek construction here allows for direct discourse, that is to say, "when he heard, 'It is Jesus of Nazareth!' he began to cry out and say, Jesus, Son of David, have mercy on me!" This is the first occurrence of the messianic title "Son of David" in Mark's gospel.

We aren't sure why, but many of those around him "were sternly telling him to be quiet." Some have postulated that it was his use of the messianic title that drew their disfavor. Others have seen the apparent class and societal barriers as the reason for their rebuke. Still others believe it was because he was becoming a nuisance. In any event, Bartimaeus was not to be denied, and "he kept crying out all the more, Son of David, have mercy on me!"

Jesus did not attempt to silence Bartimaeus, implying that He did not reject the title "Son of David." In fact, at the cries of Bartimaeus, "Jesus stopped and said, 'Call him here.'" The fickle crowd that had just tried to silence him now eagerly encouraged him saying, "Take courage, arise! He is calling for you." As soon as their words reached his ears, "casting aside his cloak, he jumped up, and came to Jesus." He wanted nothing to hinder his way to Jesus, so he left the one item that would have been most precious to him, his cloak. That cloak kept him warm at night and also served as a blanket upon which others would cast alms to him. Apparently faith had stirred his heart, so he immediately rose up and made his way to Jesus.

Jesus no doubt recognized Bartimaeus's faith, but it was important that that faith should be expressed. Therefore, He did not immediately heal Bartimaeus but asked him, "What do you want Me to do for you?" It seems almost ludicrous that Jesus would ask such a question, yet He had a purpose. The question was designed to stimulate the blind man's faith. Jesus wanted to give the man opportunity to communicate his need and express his faith.

Bartimaeus was not offended by Jesus' apparent lack of concern for his evident need. Instead, he replied, "Rabboni, I want to regain my sight!" In his response he used the Aramaic term *Rabboni* which has an emphatic, personal meaning, literally "My Lord, my Teacher" (cf. John 20:16). This revealed his confidence and trust in Jesus' ability to do what he desired.

Instead of physically touching him, Jesus proclaimed, "Go your way, your faith has made you well." Without hesitation, Bartimaeus, having immediately received his sight by faith, "began following Him [Jesus] on the road."

Bartimaeus's decision was based on his belief in Jesus. God has promised great blessings to every person who puts his or her full trust in Jesus as Savior and Lord. Bartimaeus could have decided to let Jesus pass by, not believing in His messiahship or lordship, but out of his need and by faith, he decided to seek Jesus and went away seeing!

Study Questions

1. Why did Moses allow divorce under the Old Testament Law?

2. What is God's perfect will in the matter of divorce?

3. Are there ever circumstances in which divorce is justified? What about remarriage?

4. What was Jesus' response to the little children being brought to Him? What would this say to parents who are concerned about the salvation of their children?

5. Does God ask everyone who comes to Him to "sell his possessions and follow Him"? Is this about salvation or discipleship?

6. Is it God's purpose that all Christians stay poor? How would you argue for or against this?

7. What did Jesus tell His disciples about His coming visit to Jerusalem?

CHAPTER 11

The Servant Enters Jerusalem as King
Mark 11:1-33

Preview:

The last week of Jesus' earthly ministry with His disciples began with His tri-umphal entry into the capital city of Jerusalem. The King, coming to serve through His sacrifice, was welcomed by multitudes with acclamations of praise, much to the consternation of the religious leaders of the day. After riding in on a colt, Jesus tarried briefly then withdrew to nearby Bethany. Seeing a fig tree with leaves and no fruit, He cursed it—the only negative miracle performed by Christ—and in so doing provided a visual illustration of national Israel barren of real fruit and thus rejected. Also in doing this miracle, He presented a chal-lenge to His followers to exercise faith that could move mountains. Animosity among the leaders was evidenced by hostile questioning, but the Master assert-ed His authority by asking His own question. We find a touch of humor in His handling of these critics.

The Servant "Conquers" Jerusalem (11:1-11)

(Compare Matthew 21:1-11; Luke 19:28-40; John 12:12-16)

After the healing of blind Bartimaeus, Jesus and the ever growing crowd of pil-grims continued on their way to Jerusalem. As they approached Jerusalem, they had to pass close by the smaller towns of Bethphage and Bethany. It was at this time that the Lord took the initiative to prepare for His forthcoming entrance into the Holy City. John 12:1 seems to indicate that Jesus came first to the home of Mary, Martha, and Lazarus in Bethany, where He spent the night before the events recorded in Mark's gospel.

Mark tells us that upon arriving at the Mount of Olives, Jesus sent two of His disciples into a nearby village. There, He told them, "immediately as you enter it, you will find a colt tied there, on which no one yet has ever sat; untie it and bring it here." The description of the colt is important because it reminds us that according to the Law, an animal set aside for a sacred purpose was not to be put to ordinary use (cf. Num. 19:2; Deut. 21:3; 1 Sam. 6:7). This small detail clearly stressed the appropriateness of the colt for its task.

This added to the messianic significance of Jesus' entry. The detail of this account is important because it was designed to cause the reader to reflect on the messianic overtones of His actions. In fact, it seems that Mark's purpose here is to associate Jesus' actions directly with Genesis 49:10–11:

The scepter shall not depart from Judah,
Nor the ruler's staff from between his feet, Until Shiloh comes,
And to him shall be the obedience of the peoples.
He ties his foal to the vine,
And his donkey's colt to the choice vine;
He washes his garments in wine,
And his robes in the blood of grapes.

If someone showed up in your yard and proceeded to walk off with one of your animals, you would take swift action to stop him. Knowing that this could be a problem, Jesus told the two disciples, "If anyone says to you, 'Why are you doing this?' you say, 'The Lord has need of it'; and immediately he will send it back here." We are not told whether the owner of the colt was an acquaintance of the Lord, but it seems likely that he must have been. The two disciples "went away and found a colt," encountered the opposition, and said what Jesus had told them to say; and as Jesus had predicted, they were allowed to bring the colt to Him. Having brought the colt to Jesus, they "put their garments on it; and He sat upon it." It should be noted that Jesus was able to ride this unbroken colt and that by so doing, He demonstrated His authority as Creator over all creation! One wonders if the disciples reflected upon this fact at the time or if they were too caught up with the fervor of the crowd to notice! Jesus' actions were ripe with messianic significance. Warren Wiersbe explains:

Our Lord needed this beast so that He might fulfill the messianic prophecy found in Zechariah 9:9. . . . In fulfilling this prophecy, Jesus accomplished two purposes: (1) He declared Himself to be Israel's King and Messiah; and (2) He deliberately challenged the religious leaders. This set in motion the official plot that led to His arrest, trial, and crucifixion. The

Jewish leaders had decided not to arrest Him during the feast, but God had determined otherwise. The Lamb of God must die at Passover.[1]

As Jesus entered the city, "many spread their garments in the road, and others spread leafy branches which they had cut from the fields." This is reminiscent of respect given to King Jehu in 2 Kings 9:12–13. It is also quite similar to the account of Simon Maccabaeus' entry into Jerusalem after having defeated the forces of Antiochus, as Barclay notes.

> On the twenty-third day of the second month, in the one hundred and seventy-first year, the Jews entered it with praise and palm branches, and with harps, and cymbals, and stringed instruments, and with hymns and songs, because a great enemy had been crushed and removed from Israel (1 Maccabees 13:51).[2]

Mark points out that these actions were instigated both by the crowd that went before Jesus and those that followed along with Him. Although it is clear that neither the disciples nor the crowds understood fully what Jesus was doing, it is also clear that there was some sense in which they understood that His coming to Jerusalem was to fulfill some prophetic mission. Moreover, they had recently witnessed His healing of Bartimaeus, and with this fresh in their minds, they were spontaneously prompted to express honor to Jesus.

John also notes that there were those who "went out to meet Him" (John 12:12–13). No doubt the noise of the approaching pilgrims was heard in Jerusalem, whereby the people came out to meet them bearing palm branches. The text says that they "were crying out, Hosanna!" literally, "Save us now!" This was a prayer taken from the Hallel Psalms (specifically 118:25–26; and 104–6; 111–18; 135; and 146–50) and was traditionally sung as the pilgrims came up to the city of Jerusalem. Although it is true that the expression "Blessed is He who comes in the name of the Lord" was a common greeting and did refer to pilgrims entering the temple sanctuary, Luke makes it clear that the reason the crowd was rejoicing and praising God on this occasion, was directly related to "all the miracles which they had seen" (Luke 19:37). Moreover, Luke also records that the crowds were attributing this blessing to "the King" (v. 38) who was coming in the name of the Lord! This specific terminology referred to the Lord Himself and was a declaration by the people of Jesus' messiahship. *The Theological Dictionary of the New Testament* notes that the word Hosanna is only in the story of Christ entering Jerusalem. Here in Mark 11:9 and following, the crowd met the Lord with great shouts of exaltation that began and ended with Hosanna.[3] "Blessed is He who comes in the name of the Lord" is found in Psalm 118:26. The messianic significance follows in Mark 11:10a: "Blessed is the coming kingdom of our father David." The verse then ends with "Hosanna in the highest." The word Hosanna was known by all of the Jews. Mark wants to emphasize that every messianic expectation was now realized.

Of the Gospel writers, Mark is the only one who adds that the people were crying, "Blessed is the coming kingdom of our father David; Hosanna in the highest!" Clearly the people were under the impression that Jesus was to bring in the kingdom immediately. Why their cries were not picked up by the Roman officials is not immediately evident, but they did not seem to be concerned about it, which leads us to believe that the Romans officials were not threatened and merely regarded these sayings as part of the Jewish tradition.

On the other hand, the Pharisees were seriously offended because of the theological inferences of such statements by the people (cf. Luke 19:39), revealing that they understood Jesus' actions and the people's declarations to be clearly messianic in nature. Jesus did not hinder the people as they attributed this messianic psalm (118) to Him, thereby affirming their declarations that He was indeed their King, the Son of David.

The fact that Jesus had traveled from Jericho up to Jerusalem, (about eighteen miles) suggests that by the time He arrived at the temple, evening was fast approaching. Mark is the only gospel writer who notes this. It appears that due to the lateness of the hour, Jesus merely was "looking all around," making a cursory examination of the temple, and then He "departed for Bethany with the twelve."

The Servant Curses the Fig Tree (11:12–14)

(Compare Matthew 21:19–21)

The following morning as Jesus and the disciples were on their way back to Jerusalem, Jesus noticed a leafing fig tree in the distance. We are told that "He became hungry," and so He approached the fig tree "to see if perhaps He would find anything on it." Unfortunately, the fig tree was not producing figs, "for it was not the season for figs." This is a key statement and reveals that what follows is designed to serve as a living parable.

Jesus then did something that seemed somewhat out of character for Him. He spoke to the tree and said, " May no one ever eat fruit from you again!"

In the area surrounding Jerusalem, it was common for fig trees to produce what was known as early or small fruit (also called buds) during the month of March. This budding preceded the actual leafing of the tree itself, which would occur in April. A fully leafed fig tree in April advertised that fact that the early fruit was ripe. On the other hand, a fully leafed fig tree without figs signaled the fact that the tree would not bear the more valuable fruit that would normally come during the months of August to October.

This explains Jesus' expectation when He saw the fig tree from a distance. He fully expected to find the fig tree burdened with the early fruit, allowing Him to satisfy His hunger. Finding no fruit, Jesus cursed the tree and continued on His journey toward Jerusalem.

This pericope ends with the statement "and his disciples were listening." The verb *akouō* is in the imperfect tense, suggesting that the disciples continually meditated on what Jesus had said and done. It is not clear whether the disciples fully understood the underlying symbolism of Jesus' actions, but it seems plausible that they understood the broader symbolism.

James Edwards explains that in Mark's narration of the cursing of the fig tree, the symbolism points to the fate of Jerusalem and the temple. In the prophetic writings, the fig tree was often used as a symbol of judgment (Isa. 34:4; Jer. 29:17; Hosea 2:12; 9:10; Joel 1:7; Micah 7:1). In the judgment against Judah, the prophet Jeremiah writes, "There will be no figs on the tree, and their leaves will wither" (8:13). The Lord gives a parable with the same idea and point in Luke 13:6–9). This was a dramatization that focused on a specific action that was going to take place (Isa. 20:1–6; Jer. 13:1–11; 19:1–13; Ezek. 4:1–13). In other words, Christ is giving a dramatization of the end of the temple by an enacted parable. As the temple was spiritually deceptive, in like manner the leafy fig tree is with its false promise of fruit. With all of the religious commercialism and monetary activities, the temple was a hiding place for outlaws (Mark 10:17). The cursing of the fig tree was symbolic of God's judgment of the temple.[4]

How much the disciples grasped is unknown, but the events that would immediately follow would begin to clarify Jesus' actions to their minds.

The Servant Cleanses the Temple (11:15–19)

(Compare Matthew 21:12–19; Luke 19:45–48)

The evening before, Jesus had arrived at the temple, looked around, and departed. Apparently He wanted to assess the situation before publicly presenting Himself there. What He most likely found at that late hour were the numerous empty tables of the moneychangers and the booths of those who sold sacrificial animals. Perhaps He arrived as they were closing up shop for the day! Having made His assessment, and having returned the next morning, "He entered the temple and began to cast out those who were buying and selling in the temple, and overturned the tables of the moneychangers and the seats of those who were selling doves." This picture of Jesus does not sit well with those who regard the Lord merely as the "the gentle Jesus," because they cannot understand the holy indignation that made Him act as He did here. Their Jesus is all love and no righteousness, but this is not the Jesus of the Bible!

Mark alone notes that Jesus "would not permit anyone to carry goods through the temple." The indication here is that due to the many gates, the temple proper had come to be used as a shortcut. The Holy place was being dishonored and used for secular purposes.

William Lane comments that by placing the stalls for the sale of animals and other sacrificial requirements, such as wine, oil, or salt, the Court of the Gentiles was turned into an oriental bazaar and a market place for sacrificial animals. Christ was full of righteousness indignation at this desecration of the holy consecrated place that was for the Gentiles who had become proselytes to Judaism. His action in driving out the merchants and their customers, overturning the tables of the moneychangers, and the seats of the sellers of doves, and His standing guard over the court to prevent its use as a thoroughfare, was a profound display of zeal for the honor of the Lord, and for respect for the holiness of the temple mount. Christ was acting in fulfillment of the prophetic obligation given to Him in Zechariah 14:21. "And every vessel in Jerusalem and Judah shall be sacred to the Lord of hosts."[5]

While Jesus cleansed the temple, "He began to teach (*didaskō*), literally "began and continued teaching" and say to them, "Is it not written, 'My house shall be called a house of prayer for all the nations'? But you have made it a robbers' den.'" No doubt Jesus' actions drew a large crowd of earnest worshipers as well as disgruntled merchants. It was to these that he addressed His teaching.

The first part of Jesus' teaching comes from Isaiah 56:6–7:

Also the foreigners who join themselves to the LORD,
To minister to Him, and to love the name of the LORD,
To be His servants, every one who keeps from profaning the sabbath,
And holds fast My covenant;
Even those I will bring to My holy mountain,
And make them joyful in My house of prayer.
Their burnt offerings and their sacrifices will be acceptable on My altar;
For My house will be called a house of prayer for all the peoples.

The second part comes from Jeremiah 7:11: "Has this house, which is called by My name, become a den of robbers in your sight? Behold, I, even I, have seen it, declares the Lord." Both being taken from the Septuagint. This was a real object lesson! R. Alan Cole explains the significance of Jesus' use of these two passages.

> With Isaiah 56:7 is joined here Jeremiah 7:11, a verse which comes in the midst of a searing indictment of the Jews of Jeremiah's day, whose lives were in utter contradiction to the outward worship which they offered. The quotation would gain force from the fact that Jeremiah, too, had preached it in the temple of his day. It came with a warning about the destruction of Shiloh, and the prophecy that, as God had abandoned Shiloh, so He would abandon Jerusalem and His temple there (Jer. 7:14).[6]

The clearing of the temple was a specific reprimand of the chief priests and teachers of the law. It also served to condemn religious exploitation. The result of this confrontation was twofold. First, when the religious leaders heard of what Jesus had done, they "began seeking how to destroy Him; for they were afraid of Him." Second, the people were "astonished at His teaching." Jesus' use of Isaiah and Jeremiah made it clear that His comments were directed against the religious leaders who represented the nation as a whole, and thus the fig tree. They understood this and also that the people were inclined to heed what Jesus had to say. Moreover, the people were hailing Jesus as the Messiah. This was the reason for their fear. H. A. Ironsides explains the actions of the scribes and the chief priests.

> Naturally this aroused an unholy counter-indignation on the part of those who had upheld and profited by this commercializing of sacred things. These scribes and chief priests formed a cabal with the express purpose of seeking to lay hold of Jesus and to destroy Him. But they did not dare act openly as yet, because the people generally were stirred by the teaching and works of Jesus and inclined to think of Him as the promised Messiah. Therefore He was allowed to continue teaching that day in the temple courts. No one dared to interfere.[7]

Jesus courageously continued teaching and ministering to the pilgrims that entire day. Matthew notes in his account that "the blind and the lame came to Him in the temple, and He healed them" (Matt. 21:14) and according to Luke, "all the people were hanging upon His words" (Luke 19:48). Although the leaders wanted to kill Jesus, they were afraid to try to take Him away from the crowds that were eagerly listening to His teaching. When evening finally arrived, Jesus, along with His disciples, "would go out of the city."

Matthew notes that they "went out of the city to Bethany, and lodged there" (Matt. 21:17). It is probable that they retired to the house of Mary, Martha, and Lazarus. "It would scarcely have been safe for Jesus to have spent the night in the city now, with so many foes actively plotting His death; but Bethany was still safe, and so there He presumably returned."[8]

The Servant Completes the Fig Tree Lesson (11:20-26)

(Compare Matthew 21:20-22)

The next morning Jesus and His disciples again headed for Jerusalem and the temple. No doubt taking the same path they had taken the day before, they soon arrived at the location of the fig tree Jesus had cursed. The disciples, remembering the events of the previous day, looked at the fig tree and noticed that it had " withered from the roots up." As the spokesman for the group, Peter implored the Lord to "behold, the fig tree," which had withered. "Peter's words only stated the facts concerning the tree, but they implied the question, How? Matthew indeed recorded that the amazed disciples asked, 'How did the fig tree immediately wither away?' (21:20, ASV)."[9]

In replying to Peter and the rest, Jesus did not openly explain the significance of what had happened but instead told them, "Have faith in God." Grammatically, Jesus here uses the objective genitive telling the disciples to have God as the object of their faith. He does not use the subjective genitive (faith of) here. Jesus is not telling the disciples to "have the God kind of faith" as some teach.

As already mentioned, the fig tree symbolized the nation of Israel (Jer. 8:13; Hos. 9:10, 16; Luke 13:6-9). Jesus had wanted the disciples to meditate on this reality, namely, that like this withered fig tree, Israel was hypocritical, having an outward display of religion but no realistic inner experience.

On the preceding day, Jesus had cleared the temple grounds, declaring that God's house was to be a house of prayer. He was now going to supplement His teaching on prayer. To do so, however, He had to direct their attention away from the miracle and toward its source. D. Edmund Hiebert says:

> They are bidden to have a faith that rests in God. The present imperative *have* demands that they must go on having such a faith. *Faith,* without an article, stressed the quality of the faith as centered in God. His reply was a gentle rebuke of their lack of faith in the power of His word. The withered fig tree gave them a vivid demonstration of its power. Let them maintain that faith amid what lay ahead.[10]

Jesus tells the disciples, "Truly I say to you, whoever says to this mountain, 'Be taken up and cast into the sea,' and does not doubt in his heart, but believes that what he says is going to happen, it shall be granted him." The expression concerning the removing of mountains was a common rabbinical figure of speech suggesting doing what was impossible. The disciples would have been familiar with this. The imagery of this expression would have been heightened, because from where Jesus was teaching, the Mount of Olives and the Dead Sea were visible.

Instead of understanding the direct relationship of the withered fig tree to Israel, the disciples were sidetracked by the miracle and astonished that it had withered so soon. They had missed the significance of Jesus' actions and were focused instead on the wonder of it all. Jesus did not immediately correct their misunderstanding, but instead used this opportunity to rebuke their lack of faith.

Jesus moved from the general to the specific in teaching them about prayer and faith. He began by telling them "whoever says," stressing the fact that effective prayer is available to all! Of course, proper exegesis demands that we understand this verse as a metaphor. No one had more faith in prayer than Jesus, yet He did not go about moving literal mountains. The mountains refer to things considered impossible in this life. Truly, these life mountains will be removed, but at God's will, not ours (1 John 5:14).

After the rebuke, Jesus focused directly on the disciples.

> Therefore I say to you, all things for which you pray and ask, believe that you have received them, and they shall be granted you. "And whenever you stand praying, forgive, if you have anything against anyone; so that your Father also who is in heaven may forgive you your transgressions. But if you do not forgive, neither will your Father who is in heaven forgive your transgressions.

Many have changed the focus of these verses from the object of faith to a formula of faith. They tell us that these verses teach that to receive from God, we must "positively, verbally proclaim what we want from God." They tell us that we can "write our own checks with God." They tell us that Jesus is teaching us that whatever we want, all we have to do is claim it and it is ours, but this simply is not the case.

It is presumptuous to think that I do not have to consider God's will when I come to Him in prayer. The prophet Jeremiah writes, "The heart is more deceitful that all else and is desperately sick; who can understand it?"(Jer. 17:9) Similarly, the apostle James says, "You do not have because you do not ask. You ask and do not receive, because you ask with wrong motives, so that you may spend it on your pleasures" (James 4:2–3). Prayer is not to be a time of haphazardly petitioning God for things that will make our lives easier. No, it is to be a time of offering worship to God and a time of reverent introspection as is indicated by the fact that we are to "forgive, if you have anything against anyone." Yes, God is interested in meeting my needs, but He is most interested in my being "conformed to the image of His Son" (Rom. 8:29). Jesus, having stressed to the disciples the importance of having faith, now emphasized the greater needs to have a right attitude and to maintain right relationships among themselves. As the apostle Paul says, "and if I have all faith, so as to remove mountains, but do not have love, I am nothing" (1 Cor. 13:2).

In addressing the issue of prayer again with the disciples, Jesus declared that faith is not arbitrary, it is basic. He also declared that answered prayer is conditioned on forgiveness. Unless we freely forgive, we cannot expect to be heard no matter how much faith we have.

The Servant Confirms His Authority (11:27–33)

(Compare Matthew 21:23–27; Luke 20:1–8)

No doubt stinging somewhat from Jesus' rebuke, the disciples again headed toward Jerusalem and the temple. Upon arriving, "the chief priests, and scribes, and elders came to Him." One can imagine the ruckus that Jesus must have aroused the day before. More than likely, these leaders were watching for Jesus, hoping to catch Him before He could begin teaching and the crowds began to gather. R. C. H. Lenski remarks:

> On the three groups (high priests, scribes, elders) that composed the Sanhedrin, the Supreme Court of the Jews, see 8:31. It is generally enough to mention only high priests and scribes when the Sanhedrin is referred to. In the present case Matthew names the high priests and the elders because the business in hand was probably executive and not legislative; he does not, of course, intend to deny the presence of the scribes. The main point is that Jesus receives an important inquiry from no less a body than the Jewish High Court, which appeared in person. It must have caused no little stir among the crowds of pilgrims to see all these Sanhedrists, and they wondered what they wanted with Jesus.[11]

The question these men had for Jesus was a simple one, "By what authority are You doing these things, or who gave You this authority to do these things?" In other words, they were demanding to know "in whose name" He taught, that is, under whom He had studied. They also wanted to know what official appointment He had to prove He was legitimate. Theirs was a hidden agenda because it was common knowledge that all rabbis had the right to teach in the temple or elsewhere. Therefore, the expression "these things" must have referred to recent events like His regal entry into the city and His cleansing of the temple. Jesus had on more than one occasion called God His

Father. If they could get Him to do so again, here in the temple proper, then they could arrest Him for blasphemy.

Jesus recognized the intent of their question and instead of giving them a direct answer, replied, "I will ask you one question, and you answer Me, and then I will tell you by what authority I do these things. "Was the baptism of John from heaven, or from men? Answer Me." This question was not specifically designed to entrap these false leaders. In fact, Jesus was giving them an opportunity to confess their wickedness and repent. But as the author of the book of Hebrews has correctly stated, "the word of God is living and active and sharper than any two-edged sword, and piercing as far as the division of soul and spirit, of both joints and marrow, and able to judge the thoughts and intentions of the heart" (Heb. 4:12). If they would not recognize His authority, they would stand condemned because of their constant, willful opposition and chosen blindness (3:29).

Pride is a terrible thing and "to one who knows the right thing to do, and does not do it, to him it is sin" (James 4:17). Instead of humbling themselves and repenting they "began reasoning among themselves, saying, 'If we say, "From heaven," He will say, "Then why did you not believe him?"' 'But shall we say, "From men"?'—they were afraid of the multitude, for all considered John to have been a prophet indeed."

The context makes it clear that they could have answered Jesus' question, but to admit their error was more than they could handle. Pompously, they replied, "We do not know." James Brooks writes:

> The religious officials immediately recognized their dilemma. They did not believe that John was a prophet from God, but they dared not say so publicly because of the high esteem in which John was held. Nor in the present situation could they admit that John's baptism was from heaven because Jesus would castigate them for not repenting and being baptized as a sign of their repentance. The only way out, even though it was not a good one, was to confess inability to decide. What they did not realize was that such inability disqualified them from being religious authorities.[12]

Since the religious leaders were unwilling to answer Jesus' question, He was under no obligation to answer their questions, so He replied, "Neither will I tell you by what authority I do these things." The truth was that both John the Baptist and the Lord worked by the same authority, the authority of the heavenly Father.

At this point the discussion ended. The chief priests and scribes have refused to do the right thing. This prompted Jesus to utter the cutting parables that follow in the next chapter.

Study Questions

1. Why did Jesus ride into Jerusalem on a colt?

2. Why was this entry necessary?

3. Does the Lord have need of us? Why or why not?

4. What does the fig tree typify?

5. Can believers today defile God's work with greed? Explain.

6. What is faith?

7. Is asking God for material things wrong? Explain.

8. Why is forgiveness so important?

CHAPTER 12

The Servant in the Temple
Mark 12:1–44

Preview:
From 11:27 through chapter 12, Jesus and His disciples were in the temple area, where three committees sought to challenge Him or trick Him into making some unwise statement that could be used against Him. A fourth query came from a Pharisee who was "not far from the kingdom of God." Attempts to hang Jesus on the horns of a dilemma over tax payments, to confuse Him about the doctrine of the resurrection, and to disorient Him or negate His teachings failed. The chapter opens with a poignant parable exposing the religious leaders of the Jews as opposing God's Servant. He makes clear their eventual punishment. At the end of the chapter, Jesus compliments a poor widow for her sacrificial gift.

The Servant Applies a Parable (12:1–12)

(Compare Matthew 21:33–46; Luke 20:9–19)

Beginning in Mark 11:27 and continuing through chapter 12, Jesus and the Twelve had been in the temple area. During their time there, three factions— the chief priests, scribes, and elders)—sought to challenge Him or trick Him into some unwise statement that could be used against Him. This chapter begins with Mark's record that Jesus "began to speak to them in parables." The use of the pronoun "them" should be understood specifically to refer to these Jewish leaders. Jesus often used parables, and on this occasion He opened with a poignant parable designed to expose the Jewish religious leaders who were opposing God's Servant. D. Edmond Hiebert explains:

Having silenced them, Jesus was not ready to let them leave; He still had an important lesson for them. His question to them, "But what think ye?" (Matthew 21:28), held their attention. The parable here recorded was an appeal to their conscience and a solemn warning to them of the serious consequences of their hostile efforts. Having silenced the attack upon Him by the Jewish leaders, Jesus with His parable carried the war into the camp of the enemies. Luke notes that the parable was addressed to the people but that the Jewish leaders recognized it was aimed at them (20:9, 19).[1]

Similarly, James Edwards remarks:

> Two points are worthy of note so far. First, the landowner takes vengeance not on the vineyard but on the tenants of the vineyard. That is, the parable cannot be interpreted as a blanket judgment on the Jewish people, but rather on their leaders, particularly the Sanhedrin. Second, the heroic party is not the tenant farmers but the landowner, who justly settles accounts. The parable thus cannot be construed as evidence for a vision or program of a popular uprising against oppression on the part of Jesus. Regardless of popular sentiment about absentee land ownership in Jesus' day, it is the tenants who are defiant rebels against a rightful owner. That must surely be understood as Jesus' judgment on the Sanhedrin and Jewish leadership for confiscating the things of God.[2]

Mark uses the plural "parables," but only records one here. Matthew on the other hand records three parables: this parable, the parable of the two sons, and the parable of the marriage feast (cf. Matt. 21:28–22:14).

Jesus set the stage of this parable by declaring, "A man planted a vineyard, and put a wall around it, and dug a vat under the wine press, and built a tower, and rented it out to vine-growers and went on a journey." Jesus often used agricultural themes in His parables, knowing that the common people could easily relate to them. Moreover, the stage set by Jesus here was a common one mirroring the social tensions that existed between wealthy landowners and those who worked their land. In fact, many Jewish landowners operated in this manner. The husbandmen, or tenant farmers, would live on the land and work it. They were allowed to keep the majority of the fruit but were required to supply the owner his percentage at harvest time. William Lane explains:

> The Parable of the Defiant Tenants reflects the social background of Jewish Galilee in the first century, with its great landed estates and the inevitable tension between the absentee-owners and the dispossessed, land-hungry peasantry who cultivated the land as tenant-farmers. Recent study of the Zenon papyri and of the rabbinic parables has shown that situations very closely analogous to that of the parable actually existed in

Palestine both around 280 years prior to Jesus' ministry and for some time afterward.[3]

Not only did the imagery Jesus established here reflect upon the existing social background, but it also brought to mind the association of Israel as the Lord's vineyard, a theme found in many passages in the Old Testament (cf. Ps. 80:8; Isa. 5:1–7; Jer. 2:21) In fact, by Jesus' day, this idea of the vineyard had become a well-known symbol for Israel.

In this parable, the man represents God; the vineyard, Israel; the servants, the Old Testament prophets; the husbandmen, the Jewish leaders past and present; and the son, the Lord Jesus. Jesus told His hearers that God planted Israel and protected her. He had put a hedge about her and built a tower to watch for enemies. He had also dug a place for the wine vat, a symbol of fruitfulness. Finally, God "rented it out to vine-growers," the Jewish religious leaders. H. A. Ironside remarks:

> Settled by God in the land of Canaan, the Israelites had been cared for in a marvelous way. God had placed them under the care of those who should have watched for their souls and sought to cultivate them spiritually so that there would be abundant fruit for Him.[4]

Jesus continued by stating that when the season was right, the owner of the vineyard "sent a slave to the vine-growers, in order to receive some of the produce of the vineyard from the vine-growers." This of course was the right of the owner. However, instead of fulfilling their agreement with the landowner, these wicked men, "took him, and beat him, and sent him away empty-handed." Mercifully and showing great tolerance, the landowner sent "many others" who were also mistreated and killed. Finally, the landowner decided to send his only son, saying, "They will respect my son," but alas, instead of recognizing the son's authority, they reasoned among themselves and said, "This is the heir; come, let us kill him, and the inheritance will be ours!" Having determined a plan of action, these wicked men "took him, and killed him, and threw him out of the vineyard."

Jesus, knowing that He had the full attention of His audience, then put forth the following question, "What will the owner of the vineyard do?" In Matthew's account the answer comes from the audience, "He will bring those wretches to a wretched end, and will rent out the vineyard to other vine-growers, who will pay him the proceeds at the proper seasons" (Matt. 21:41). It is not a far-fetched possibility that some of those who responded were among the Jewish leaders to whom the parable was addressed. After all, it is most likely that some of them were in fact landowners! They were no doubt engrossed with the story and answered without hesitation. R. C. H. Lenski explains:

Jesus must have told the parable so dramatically that the answer came spontaneously without a moment's hesitation. It is so correct because the minds of these pilgrims are centered on the objective facts as these are stated in the parable and are *not yet directed toward who these vine-growers really are.* The people thus follow their own sense of justice, that justice which will vindicate God's judgments on all unbelievers. The answer thus keeps to the parable. Jesus accepts it as his own, which leads Mark and Luke to write as they do (emphasis added).[5]

Mark notes that before they could reflect upon what they had just said, Jesus repeated their assessment, saying, "He will come and destroy the vine-growers, and will give the vineyard to others." The sudden realization of the significance of what had just been hastily stated suddenly dawned upon them causing others among their group to erupt with "May it never be!" (Luke 20:16).

Jesus, having carefully laid the trap now slammed the door shut by adding, "Have you not even read this Scripture: 'The stone which the builders rejected, this became the chief cornerstone. . . .'?" Finally understanding the significance of the parable, the Jewish leaders realized that they had with their own words, condemned themselves. Jesus brought the climax into view by focusing on the fact that it is God Himself who would bring judgment upon them for, "this came about from the Lord, and it is marvelous in our eyes." Moreover, the son, Jesus Himself, who was to be rejected and killed, would become, "the chief corner stone."

Now fully aware that Jesus had spoken this parable against them, they "were seeking to seize Him." This expression in the Greek indicates that they not only desired to arrest Him, but they actively set about trying to discover means to do so. But this they could not do openly because they "feared the multitude." The only recourse at the present time was for them to leave the scene of their embarrassment and so, "they left Him, and went away."

The Servant Answers Three Questions (12:13–34)

(Compare Matthew 22:15–40; Luke 20:20–44)

After the embarrassment suffered at Jesus' hands, the Jewish leaders, including the Pharisees and the Herodians (cf. Matt. 22:15–16), conspired together along with certain spies (disciples of the Pharisees) who were posing as just men (cf. Luke 20:20). They hoped to "trap Him in what He said" (Matt. 22:15), "trap Him in a statement" (Mark 12:13), or "catch Him in some statement" in order that they might "deliver Him up to the rule and the authority of the governor" (Luke 20:20). Kenneth S. Wuest explains the significance of their actions.

> The defeat which these leaders had sustained, broke them up into separate parties again, each to formulate its own plans. The Pharisees moved first. They sent some of their disciples (Matthew) "who knew how to combine the vigilance of practiced dissemblers (hypocrites), with the apparent innocence of young inquirers" (Swete). They were to entrap our Lord into some remark by which He would fatally compromise Himself. They associated with themselves adherents of Herod. The word "catch" is *agreusōsin* (ἀγρεύω), "to catch wild animals." Their purpose was to hunt and catch Him like some wild animal. Matthew's word is "entangle" Him in His talk (Matthew 22:15). The word is *pagideusōsin* (παγιδεύω), "to snare or trap" birds.[6]

The Pharisees and the Herodians were not friends by any means. Although the Pharisees are well known and appear often in the Gospels, the Herodians appear in the Gospels only on three occasions (Matt. 22:16; Mark 3:6; 12:13). The Herodians were a minor nonreligious political party made up of supporters of Herod and Rome. They were opposed by the Pharisees, who desired complete independence and autonomy for the Jews.

The joining of these two groups together could only be for one purpose—to entrap Jesus. They hatched a plan whereby they acted as if a dispute had arisen between them and they went to Jesus to ask for His help in settling the matter.

When this group of deceivers came to Jesus, they used flattery and presented themselves almost as if they too wanted to become disciples. "Teacher, we know that You are truthful, and defer to no one; for You are not partial to any, but teach the way of God in truth." This of course was done to throw Jesus off guard. However, it was also a clever trap designed to set Jesus up for the question that followed: "Is it lawful to pay a poll-tax to Caesar, or not? Shall we pay, or shall we not pay?" William Lane comments:

> The opening remarks addressed to Jesus were designed to close the way to any possible evasion of a painful and difficult question. By reminding Jesus that he was a man of integrity who paid no attention to the opinions of men but taught absolute commitment to the way of life commanded by God, his adversaries intended to force him to face squarely the issue they had decided upon. . . . In asking if it was allowed by the Law of God to pay the tribute money, it could be assumed that the Pharisees were concerned chiefly in the moral and religious implications of the question, and the Herodians with its political or nationalistic ramifications. In point of fact

the question was insincere. Its object was to force Jesus into a compromising position either theologically or politically. The form of the question ("shall we give, or shall we not give it?") was skillfully designed to thrust Jesus on the horns of a dilemma. An affirmative answer would discredit him in the eyes of the people, for whom the tax was an odious token of subjection to Rome. A negative reply would invite reprisals from the Roman authorities.[7]

But Jesus was not to be trapped so easily for He recognized "their hypocrisy" ("malice" in Matthew 22:18 and "trickery" in Luke 20:23) and replied, "Why are you testing Me?" Jesus recognized that their question was dishonest, because both the Pharisees and Herodians paid the required tax (although for different reasons) as a matter of convenience. Jesus then told them to bring Him a "denarius" so He could look at it. The denarius, or tribute money (Matt. 22:19), was a small silver coin minted by the Roman government. It was the required coin for paying taxes and was also used as the standard pay for a day's work (cf. Matt. 20:1–2).

Those gathered around Jesus must have felt eager anticipation while waiting for the coin to appear. Finally, "they brought one." It does seem somewhat ironic that Jesus had to ask for a coin while those questioning Him about it were able to produce it. Jesus must have held up the coin for all to see as He asked, "Whose likeness and inscription is this?" This seemed a simple and unsophisticated question, and so these hypocrites answered, "Caesar's." After all, what danger could there be in that? They must have thought they had Jesus right where they wanted Him as He held that coin up for all to see.

Calmly, Jesus extricated Himself from their imagined trap by saying, "Render to Caesar the things that are Caesar's, and to God the things that are God's." With this reply, Jesus at once legitimized human government while at the same time quelling any attempt to associate Him with political anarchy. There is an underlying wordplay here that is worthy of consideration. Jesus had asked them, "Whose likeness . . . is this." Clearly the image on the coin revealed who owned it. Jesus therefore told them to give to Caesar that which belonged to him but also to give to God that which belonged to Him. In other words, people bearing the image of God should give themselves to Him. The way in which Jesus answered these foolish hypocrites revealed their hearts and condemned them for their lack of true spirituality!

Once again Jesus had bested them at their own game—so much so that Mark tells us that "they were amazed at Him." Matthew records, "And hearing this, they marveled, and leaving Him, they went away." (Matt. 22:22) while Luke records that "they were unable to catch Him in a saying in the presence of the people;

and marveling at His answer, they became silent." (Luke 20:26). Jesus had out-done them, but they were not yet finished with their attacks on His authority.

Since the Pharisees had failed, the Sanhedrin decided to send in the second team, the Sadducees. The Sadducees came from the most prominent families of Israel and represented Judaism's "holy upper class." They generally looked down with disdain at everybody else. They could afford to do this because the most powerful members of the priesthood and even the high priests were main-ly Sadducees. For them the Pentateuch alone was the only accepted religious authority. This meant that they denied any doctrines that could not be clearly identified within its pages. The *Nelson's Illustrated Bible Dictionary* explains:

> The Sadducees rejected "the tradition of the elders," that body of oral and written commentary which interpreted the law of Moses. This automati-cally placed them in direct conflict with another Jewish group, the Pharisees, who had made the traditions surrounding the Law almost as important as the Law itself. The Sadducees insisted that only the laws that were written in the law of Moses (the Pentateuch, the first five books of the Old Testament) were really binding.[8]

Mark tells us that the Sadducees "say there is no resurrection." And Luke adds that the Sadducees taught "there is no resurrection, nor an angel, nor a spirit" (Acts 23:8). J. E. H. Thomson remarks: "Josephus distinctly asserts (Ant, XVIII, i, 4) that the Sadducees believe that the soul dies with the body. They deny, he says, divine providence (BJ, II, viii, 14). Their theology might be called 'religion within the limits of mere sensation.'"[9]

These men came to Jesus with a hypothetical situation involving the levi-rate law.[10] They initially loosely quoted from Deuteronomy 25:5–10 and then created an elaborate story.

> There were seven brothers; and the first took a wife, and died, leaving no offspring. And the second one took her, and died, leaving behind no off-spring; and the third likewise; and so all seven left no offspring. Last of all the woman died also. In the resurrection, when they rise again, which one's wife will she be?

The first thing that should become immediately clear is the hypocrisy of their question. As already stated, they did not believe in a bodily resurrection or an afterlife. The only reason therefore for asking the question was to try to trap Jesus as the Pharisees and Herodians had attempted to do. Moreover, if they could embarrass and humiliate Jesus, they could in effect kill two birds with one stone, that is, they could also demonstrate their superiority over the Pharisees who had failed in their attempt to silence Jesus! Thinking they had painted Jesus into a corner, they awaited His response.

The Sadducees underestimated Jesus' ability to see through them. They had set up a straw man and now Jesus was going to set them straight. This He did by posing a question which in the original Greek demands an answer in the affirmative. Jesus said, "Is this not the reason you are mistaken, that you do not understand the Scriptures, or the power of God?" What a slap in the face this was! In effect Jesus said, "It really is true that you are in error and also that you do not know anything about the power of God!"

The weight of these words must have caught these Sadducees off guard, but Jesus was not yet finished. After this surprising rebuke, He attacked their theology concerning an afterlife, stating, "When they rise from the dead, they neither marry, nor are given in marriage, but are like angels in heaven." Jesus made it clear that marriage is an aspect of this present life but not a part of the next.

Then Jesus attacks their theology on the doctrine of the resurrection.

> But regarding the fact that the dead rise again, have you not read in the book of Moses, in the passage about the burning bush, how God spoke to him, saying, "I am the God of Abraham, and the God of Isaac, and the God of Jacob"? He is not the God of the dead, but of the living; you are greatly mistaken.

Knowing that the Sadducees would not accept any doctrinal support outside the Pentateuch, Jesus used the incident where God spoke to Moses from the burning bush (Ex. 3:6), to correct their error! He shrewdly demonstrated their ignorance and challenged their understanding of Moses' writings.

The result of Jesus' response was threefold: (1) When the multitudes, including the Sadducees, heard Jesus' words, "they were astonished at His teaching" (Matt. 22:33), (2) Certain of the scribes, no doubt of the Pharisees, commended Him, saying, "Teacher, you have spoken well." (Luke 20:39–40), and (3) He silenced the opposition of the Sadducees (Matt. 22:34).

The text tells us that there was an individual scribe who "came and heard them arguing, and recognizing that Jesus had answered them well, asked Him, 'What commandment is the foremost of all?'" In Matthew's account the Pharisees had "gathered themselves together," no doubt contemplating their next question. "One of them, a lawyer, asked Him a question, testing Him, 'Teacher, which is the great commandment in the Law?'" (Matt. 22:34–36). This man had evidently been elected by the Pharisees to present their question. Concerning this man, Hiebert remarks:

> Mark said nothing about his motive in coming, but Matthew noted that he asked his question "tempting him." The sequel shows that he did not ask his question with a malicious motive, but rather intended to "test" Jesus' skill in answering this much debated question.[11]

Jesus had just silenced the Sadducees and had momentarily won the approval of the Pharisees. It seems that in this instance, the questioning of the Pharisees was not designed to attack Jesus but instead to ascertain His point of view. With this in mind, the scribe approached Jesus without malice. Lenski remarks: "To make the motive of either this scribe or of the Pharisees back of him the hope to entangle Jesus as was done in previous attacks on him is unsatisfactory. The outcome of the questioning is entirely too friendly for that."[12]

In answer to the question, "Which is the great commandment?" Jesus quoted Deuteronomy 6:4-5, "Hear, O Israel! The Lord our God is one Lord; And you shall love the Lord your God with all your heart, and with all your soul, and with all your mind, and with all your strength." This is the great Shema, which was, and even today among pious Jews is, the great confession of faith. Jesus doesn't stop there, however. "The second is this, 'You shall love your neighbor as yourself'," quoting Leviticus 19:18. Jesus then summed up His answer: "There is no other commandment greater than these."

In other words, Jesus said, "If these two commandments are obeyed, all the rest of them will be obeyed." If we truly love God in the manner stated by Jesus, we will find that we are keeping and obeying the first section of the Decalogue, commandments one through four, for they deal with our relationship to God. If we love our neighbor as ourself, we will find that we are keeping and obeying the second section of the Decalogue, commandments five through ten, for they deal with our relationships with our fellow human beings.

Upon hearing Jesus' response, the scribe once again commended Jesus but also demonstrated that he had a level of spiritual insight unseen in the others who questioned Jesus. He said:

> "Right, Teacher, You have truly stated that He is One; and there is no one else besides Him; and to love Him with all the heart and with all the understanding and with all the strength, and to love one's neighbor as himself, is much more than all burnt offerings and sacrifices."

Not only did the scribe express that he was profoundly impressed with the Lord's answer, but he also demonstrated a genuine spiritual acumen by explaining that (1) if love was wanting, the formal sacrificial procedures of the law would be worthless before God and that (2) to unreservedly love God while at the same time loving one's neighbor pleases God most of all. This concept was in no way new or unique (cf. 1 Sam. 15:22; Ps. 51:16-17; Isa. 1:10-17; Hos. 6:6; and Mic. 6:6-8), but the fact that this man was willing to openly affirm it must have been refreshing to the Lord. Finally, here was a man who got it! This was something special.

Jesus recognized that this man had "answered intelligently." This implies that the man had carefully thought about his answer. Jesus' response was immediate and gracious: "You are not far from the kingdom of God." Jesus recognized that here was a Pharisee who actually understood the real intent of the law. The Lord's response was consciously and purposefully ambiguous because He wanted to provoke within this man further reflection. He did not say that the scribe was saved, but that he was close to understanding great spiritual truth. He was, as it were, just outside the door of salvation. To step in he must receive Christ for himself, trusting Him as Savior and owning Him as Lord. James A. Brooks explains:

> In addition to acknowledging the necessity of loving God and humanity, the man evidently committed himself to do just that. He was receptive to Jesus as a person as well as to his teaching. No wonder Jesus indicated that the man was not far from entering the kingdom, from letting God reign in his life. By saying that he was not far, Jesus encouraged him to go the remainder of the way by wholeheartedly following Jesus.[13]

Even among the Sanhedrin there were some who were believers in Jesus (15:43), and we are told that later there were within the church both priests and Pharisees who believed. Perhaps this man was one of them.

Finally, Mark records that "after that, no one would venture to ask Him any more questions." Jesus had competently and expertly exposed His opponent's deep-rooted antagonism and appalling errors. This concluding statement proclaims that Jesus had successfully frustrated all attempts to damage His reputation. Edwards says:

> The wording of v. 34 (particularly in Greek) is strong and unequivocal, signifying that Jesus has prevailed over challenges from the Sanhedrin (11:27–33) and its various constituencies—the Pharisees (12:13–17), Sadducees (12:18–27), and scribes (12:28–34). Jesus has bested the field and debate is closed.[14]

All attempts to hang Jesus on the horns of a dilemma over tax payments, to confuse Him about the doctrine of the resurrection, and to disorient Him or negate His teachings had failed.

The Servant Asks a Great Question (12:35–37)

(Compare Matthew 22:41–46; Luke 20:41–44)

Jesus had endured a long day of confrontation. His opponents hoped to confound him with hypothetical and nonsensical questions. Now it was His turn to ask the questions, and it would soon become clear who exactly was confused!

The preceding attacks on Jesus had occurred the same day while He was teaching in the temple. Mark points out that Jesus' questioning was an immediate continuation of that event. "And Jesus answering began to say, as He taught in the temple. . . ."

Mark records the general circumstances as he introduces this pericope. Matthew on the other hand stipulates that Jesus directed these questions specifically to the Pharisees who were still present (cf. Matt. 22:41). This is significant because Jesus had just commended one of their group, and others may have been justifying themselves for secretly believing as their colleague. It is also likely that the Pharisees were congratulating themselves for "getting it right" where the Sadducees and the Herodians had not.

Jesus was not going to let them off the hook that easily, and so He asked them, "How is it that the scribes say that the Christ is the son of David? David himself said in the Holy Spirit, 'The Lord said to my Lord, "Sit at My right hand, until I put Thine enemies beneath Thy feet."' David himself calls Him 'Lord'; and so in what sense is He his son?"

Jesus first set up the Pharisees by stating the commonly held view of the Messiah. All the scribes taught that Christ would be of the royal lineage of David and hence his son. Jesus then quoted Psalm 110:1, forcing them to deal with David's own words as he spoke by the Holy Spirit. David had clearly referred to the Messiah as Lord! How could David thus speak of his son? A father never spoke of his son in such a way.

No answer is recorded. Indeed, no answer could be given, because although the scribes correctly believed that the Messiah would be a descendant of David, they were blinded to the fact that the promised Messiah must of necessity be both human and divine. Hiebert explains:

> The purpose of Jesus in raising this question was not merely to confound the scribes but to show that to be accepted as reliable interpreters of their own Scriptures, they must have a higher view of the true nature of the Messiah. Their view that the Messiah was simply a human being, the descendant of David, though a conquering king, did not do justice to the teaching of Scripture. For the Messiah to be David's Lord, He must be more than a man.[15]

The answer to the Lord's question was yet a mystery. Messiah would be both the Son of David and Lord—God manifest in the flesh. This would be accomplished by the virgin birth and incarnation of Jesus (cf. Isa. 7:14; Matt. 1:18–25; Luke 1:26–38; John 1:14).

The Pharisees and scribes were baffled and did not dare to discuss the matter further, for doing so would reveal their ignorance, but "the great crowd enjoyed listening to Him." The verb "listening" (*ēkoven*) is in the imperfect, indicating that the great crowd of pilgrims continually received and welcomed His teaching, for they saw in Him humility, sincerity, and truth, characteristics sadly lacking from their pompous Jewish leaders.

The Servant Attacks the Hypocritical Scribes (12:38–40)

(Compare Matthew 23:1–7; Luke 20:45–47)

Each of the Synoptic Gospels records Jesus' solemn condemnation of these same scribes. Matthew's record is the lengthiest and most specific while both Mark and Luke provide a more general record. Matthew (23:1) and Luke (20:45) indicate that Jesus spoke to His disciples in the hearing of the multitude. Matthew records (v. 13) that later Jesus directly addressed the "scribes and Pharisees."

Jesus said, "Beware of the scribes." The imperative, "beware" (*blepete*) was used in 8:15 when Jesus was warning against false teaching. In this instance, He used it to warn against those who would teach such. Jesus is not here condemning all the scribes. This is apparent because He had just commended one of their group in the previous pericope (12:28–34). It is rather those who exhibit the subsequent behaviors that He condemned. Those who received the brunt of Jesus' condemnation were those who "like to walk around in long robes, and like respectful greetings in the market places, and chief seats in the synagogues, and places of honor at banquets, who devour widows' houses, and for appearance's sake offer long prayers."

After explicitly exposing the wickedness of their actions, Jesus issued a final grave judgment upon these deceivers, stating, "These will receive greater condemnation." Walter A. Elwell remarks:

> The scribes were venerated by the people as the representatives of the oracles of God and should have been singularly intent on giving praise to God alone. But Jesus observes that their positions of authority have seduced them from servanthood to egocentric ostentation in dress and desire for public recognition. As the embodiment of truth and wholeness in intent, speech, and acts, Jesus exposes their hypocrisy in making showy and lengthy prayers while devouring widows' houses (the teachers of the law were dependent on gifts and could abuse the patronage of widows). His exposure of their unworthiness begins and ends with strong words of condemnation: "Watch out for the teachers of the law" (v. 38); "Such men will be punished most severely" (v. 40). With this negative word Jesus concludes his public ministry. But he has further words to say to his dis-

ciples that expand upon his condemnation of Israel's leaders, first in the offering of the widow (12:41–44), followed by awesome oracles about the destruction of the temple and coming judgment (chap. 13).[16]

Christ's comprehensive denunciation of the scribes finalized His complete break with the religious leaders and the concluding of His public ministry. The Lord's remaining time spent in teaching would now center upon and be directed to the disciples.

The Servant Affirms Sacrificial Giving (12:41–44)

(Compare Luke 21:1–4)

Jesus had been in the court of the Gentiles while debating with the Jewish leaders. Now, having concluded His public teaching, He along with the Twelve entered the Court of the Women where the temple offerings were collected. Mark begins this pericope by saying "He sat down opposite the treasury." Luke however, notes that Jesus "looked up" (Luke 21:1), indicating that the events that followed happened immediately after the preceding condemnation of the scribes. This pericope provides a sharp contrast between the scribes' façade of righteousness and the unqualified dedication to God characterized by the unidentified widow.

While sitting close by the treasury, Jesus "began observing how the multitude were putting money into the treasury; and many rich people were putting in large sums." According to tradition, the receptacles were placed against the wall in the Court of the Women. They were funnel-shaped with wide, open mouths at the top. Those contributing often stood at a distance, casting their coinage into the receptacles for all present to see. The resulting sound of the coins as they entered and traveled down the neck of the receptacle was quite loud. Many of the rich used this as an opportunity to display their piety before all.

Jesus watched this travesty and noticed that "a poor widow came and put in two small copper coins, which amount to a cent." The Greek copper mite was the smallest coin commercially used, two of which were equivalent to a Roman farthing, or cent. The farthing was the smallest Roman coin, and it took sixteen of them to equal one silver denarius. This means that the value of her gift was one sixty-fourth of a common laborer's daily wage.

Jesus was no doubt moved by this widow's sacrifice, and calling His disciples to Him, He remarked, "Truly I say to you, this poor widow put in more than all the contributors to the treasury; for they all put in out of their surplus, but she, out of her poverty, put in all she owned, all she had to live on." All the rest had given out of their abundance knowing that they would have funds left over for their personal use. This poor widow, in giving her two mites, sacrificed all the money she possessed. This revealed on the one hand her abject poverty and on the other hand her utter faith in God as her last means of support. In the act of giving all she had, she demonstrated that she had completely entrusted herself to God's care.

The contrast is clear. Avarice and nominal religion, with all their pomp and show, are meaningless. Here by contrast is one of the very group who was preyed on by the scribes, a widow who, out of poverty and true devotion to God, made an offering unseen and unnoticed except by Jesus. Together the pictures are a matching pair, emphasizing the strong contrast. Jesus did not deny that the rich gave large sums; He merely said that the widow gave still more, for theirs were only contributions, generous though they might be, while hers was a total sacrifice. God measures giving, not by what we give, but by what we keep for ourselves; and the widow kept nothing but gave both coins, all that she had (vv. 42, 44). This is a lesson that should be taught often and rehearsed regularly.

Study Questions

1. When will it become evident that Jesus is "the chief corner stone"?

2. How did Jesus respond to these questions?

3. Under what conditions should Christians engage in civil disobedience?

4. What are the two root causes of religious error?

5. Why shouldn't marriage be continued in heaven?

6. Do you know what Mormons teach on this subject? Is it right?

7. Should believers in this dispensation keep the first and second commandments?

CHAPTER 13

The Servant Foretells the Future
Mark 13:1–37

Preview:

Jesus' Olivet Discourse appears in all three of the Synoptic Gospels (cf. Matt. 24–25; Mark 13; Luke 17:20–37; 21:5–36). Each account differs somewhat from the others, and each contains information not included by the others. Mark's account is the most condensed of the three, and it is the second of only two extended passages of exposition by Christ in the whole book of Mark (cf. chap. 4). The Olivet Discourse was given two days before the Lord's death (Matt. 26:1–2). It is sandwiched between the censure of the Jewish leadership for failing to recognize Jesus as Messiah (cf. Matt. 23:1–39), and the preparation of the Last Supper (cf. Matt. 26:17–20; Mark 14:12–17; Luke 22:7–14). The purpose of the Olivet Discourse was (1) to answer the disciples' questions concerning when and how Christ's kingdom would appear and (2) to exhort and encourage them to faithful obedience. Beginning with the prediction of the destruction of Jerusalem, Jesus moves swiftly across this present age to the Tribulation and His glorious appearing. He concludes with two parables: the parable of the fig tree and the parable of a man taking a far journey, both of which emphasize the need for vigilance.

Introductory Comments

The Olivet Discourse was given specifically to Israel and is in fact uniquely Jewish. Critical to an understanding of the Olivet Discourse is the realization that neither the church nor the rapture is addressed in it. Furthermore, contrary to what some teach, this discourse does not refer back to the judgment of A.D. 70, which is recorded in Luke 21:20–24.

The Olivet Discourse is eschatological in nature and must be read and studied carefully. To fully understand its message, the reader must connect Mark's record with the parallel passages found in Matthew and Luke. If these simple keys are kept in mind, the reader will have no difficulty understanding what the Lord has to say to us.

Destruction of the Temple Foretold (13:1–2)

(Compare Matthew 24:1–2; Luke 21:5–6)

As Jesus and the Twelve were leaving the temple area, they could not help but notice the beautiful white marble stones and the grandeur of the temple itself. As they reflected upon its wealth and beauty, "one of his disciples said to Him, 'Teacher, behold what wonderful stones and what wonderful buildings!'" This of course was the temple built by Herod the Great. Herod began work on this temple in 19 or 20 B.C., finishing the porch, sanctuary, and Holy of Holies about a year and a half later. Since additions were regularly being made to the temple, it wasn't until A.D. 64, under Herod Agrippa II, that construction finally ceased (cf. John 2:20).

As one of the largest religious structures in existence (covering approximately one-sixth of the entire city area), it was considered one of the great architectural wonders of the Roman world. In fact, some of the stones used to build it were 25 feet by 12 feet by 18 feet and weighed as much as 100 tons! More important, it was there that God's presence dwelt, and for this reason, devout Jewish pilgrims regularly came by the thousands from all across the Roman Empire to worship and sacrifice on the high holy days.

Jesus' response to this disciple's exuberant comment was not at all what the Twelve were expecting. On the contrary, instead of stopping to admire this fabulous structure that represented so much to the children of Israel, Jesus replied, "Do you see these great buildings? Not one stone shall be left upon another which will not be torn down." This was a prediction of the destruction of Jerusalem by the Roman general Titus, which would literally be fulfilled in A.D. 70.

Perhaps anticipating the questions that His words would stimulate, Jesus led the Twelve away from the temple, across the Kidron Valley, and finally up the steep slopes to the top of the Mount of Olives. Although a relatively short distance, it would have afforded the Twelve sufficient opportunity to reflect upon Jesus' words, and it is likely that, as on other occasions, they reasoned among themselves concerning what they meant. Moreover, from the top of the Mount of Olives, they would have had an excellent view of the temple proper, thus providing an appropriate setting for the discussion that would follow.

The Disciple's Questions (13:3–4)

(Compare Matthew 24:3; Luke 21:7)

Upon reaching the top of the mount, Jesus sat down facing the temple area so that He could look out over it. Apparently He had not been there long before "Peter and James and John and Andrew" approached Him to ascertain what it was exactly that He had meant when they left the temple.

Mark records two of the three questions these disciples put to Jesus. They were (1) "When will these things be?" and (2) "What will be the sign when all these things are going to be fulfilled?" Mark's second question actually encompasses two separate questions clarified in Matthew's record, namely, (1) "What will be the sign of Your coming?" and (2) "[what will be the sign] of the end of the age?" (Matt. 24:3). Louis Barbieri explains why these questions were important to the disciples.

> They were wondering about the destruction of the temple. Furthermore, they wanted to know what would be the sign that all these things were going to be fulfilled. In their thinking, they understood from Old Testament prophecies that the destruction of the temple was the final event that would lead to the millennial kingdom of the Messiah. **They did not recognize from Old Testament prophecies any break between judgment and Messiah's kingdom** (emphasis added).[1]

The fact that the disciples did not understand the time frame is significant. It was this misunderstanding that the Lord was about to address, for it was imperative that they understand that there would be an extended period of time between Jerusalem's fall and the end of the age. D. A. Hagner, commenting on the parallel passage in Matthew, writes:

> As far as the apostles were concerned, the ominous words of Jesus concerning the destruction of the temple could point in only one direction: to the experiencing of the eschatological judgment. This was a subject to which Jesus had often alluded in his teaching ministry and therefore something they may well have expected him to indicate. They were accordingly eager to know how soon this might occur and what sign they might anticipate to indicate its approach. Their concern was not one of idle curiosity, for mere information's sake, but concern that they might be properly prepared for the time of judgment. From their perspective, the

destruction of the temple must have meant the coming again of Jesus, not as he now was with them when his glory was veiled but as the clearly revealed Son of God for all to see. Jesus had now to instruct them more closely about these matters, about the future he had intimated in his dramatic oracle of judgment.[2]

The association of the destruction of the temple with the inauguration of the kingdom is a significant point. Jesus had been preparing the Twelve for His forthcoming passion and crucifixion but His statement regarding the destruction of the temple, in their minds, suggested the immediate inauguration of the kingdom. It was necessary for Jesus to establish the correct time frame of these events and thus remove any confusion on this matter.

General Characteristic of the Church Age (13:5–7)

(Compare Matthew 24:46–; Luke 21:8–9)

In preparation to answer the disciples' second and third questions Jesus first provided some general characteristics of the church age. He began by telling the disciples, "See to it that no one misleads you." Jesus warned them that over time "many will come in [His] name." Some will even declare that they are Christ and "will mislead many." This is a critical point. Even though Jesus' disciples would receive and be led by the Spirit of truth, (John 16:13), they would not be immune from error and deception if they failed to saturate themselves in Jesus' teachings. Arnold Fruchtenbaum explains:

> The first general characteristic of the church age would be the rise of false messiahs. Historically, Jesus was the first person who claimed to be the Messiah. After Him, many came claiming to be the Messiah. From the time of Jesus until about the middle of the 1850's, a great number of Jewish men arose claiming to be the Messiah, and indeed led many astray. Gentiles have also claimed the Messianic title. But this was to be a general characteristic of the church age, and the existence of false messiahs in no way meant that the end had begun.[3]

Besides the claims of false messiahs, the disciples would "hear of wars and rumors of wars." The world is in a constant state of change, and thus rulers would come and go. But this was not to move the disciples, for they had His words and the promise of the Holy Spirit. Jesus commanded them, "Do not be frightened; those things must take place." Such things are common to this fallen world. Then He added, "But that is not yet the end." Whether local or foreign, general warfare in no way was to be taken as a sign that the end had begun.

The Sign of the End of the Age (13:8)

(Compare Matthew 24:7–8; Luke 21:10–11)

After addressing the disciples' question from the negative, that is, those things that would not indicate that the end had begun, Jesus addressed their third question, "[what will be the sign] of the end of the age?" He indicated that wars, earthquakes, famines, and troubles on a global level, would signal the end of the age, but He then added that these would merely be "the beginning of birth pangs." The terminology in the previous verse and in this verse revealed to the disciples that the time frame for these events would not be immediate but extended. "This emphasis—'the end is still to come' (Mark 13:7d) and 'these [things] are the beginning of birth pains' (v. 8c)—suggests that an extended period of time will precede 'the end.'"[4]

Apostolic Opposition (13:9–13)

(Compare Luke 21:12–19)

At this point in His answer, Jesus introduced a parenthesis in order to prepare the Twelve for what they could expect to experience before the end of the age. Jesus told them, "Be on your guard; for they will deliver you to the courts, and you will be flogged in the synagogues, and you will stand before governors and kings for My sake, as a testimony to them." Because of their testimony, the gospel would be sent forth to all the nations, and as they were brought before rulers and kings, they were not to concern themselves with what they should say, nor were they to premeditate, for it would not be them speaking but "the Holy Spirit." D. Edmond Hiebert correctly observes:

> The passive *shall be given* points to God as the giver of the appropriate answer, while *whatsoever* leaves open the nature of the thoughts and answers that will be flashed into their minds. *That speak ye* commands obedient utterance of the very thing communicated to them. They must not attempt to mix it with their own ideas as being more appropriate. *In that hour* indicates that the promise is for particular emergencies, when unexpectedly haled into court to defend their faith. **It does not refer to those who have the duty to teach or preach at set times and places** (emphasis added).[5]

Moreover, the apostles could expect to be betrayed by family members and would be hated by all people because of their witness for Christ. Nevertheless, many would come to eternal life. All of this was personally

experienced by the Apostles as related in the book of Acts and other historical records.

The Sign of the Fall of Jerusalem

(See Luke 21:20–24)

Chronologically, it is at this point in His response that Jesus addresses the disciples first question concerning the destruction of Jerusalem. Mark does not
address this, so the reader must go to Luke to find the answer to this question.
He explains that when the Twelve see Jerusalem "surrounded by armies," they
should realize that, "her desolation is at hand." Jesus then goes on to describe
a time of incredible vengeance that is to be visited upon Jerusalem and its
inhabitants. Not only will Jerusalem and the temple be destroyed, but the
Jews themselves will once again be dispersed among the nations, and
"Jerusalem will be trampled under foot by the Gentiles until the times of the
Gentiles be fulfilled."

The Second Half of the Tribulation (13:14–23)

(Compare Matthew 24:15–28)

The doctrine of the tribulation is important and worthy of careful study. This
is true because, as Tim LaHaye and Thomas Ice note:

> there is more space allocated to the Tribulation than the 1000-year
> Millennial kingdom, heaven, hell, or any subject except salvation and the
> promise of Christ's second coming. It is mentioned at least 49 times by
> the Hebrew prophets and at least 15 times in the New Testament.[6]

Since this topic is so well represented in the Bible, it is important to get
the facts straight. One fact that is of utmost importance is that although
Mark's record addresses the second half of the Tribulation, it does not address
the first half of the Tribulation. This will be made clear below. If we want to
get the facts on the first half of the Tribulation, we must go to Matthew's
record, for it is found only there (Matt. 24:9–14).

Due to a failure to make this distinction, many commentators have erred
attempting to find correlations between Mark 13:14–23; Luke 21:12–19; and
Matthew 24:15–28. It must be understood that in spite of the events in these
three accounts being similar, they in fact refer to different time periods. This
is clearly evident when one considers that Mark and Luke record events that

happen before the sign of the end of the age, while Matthew records events that happen after the sign of the end of the age.

This brings us to the third question, "[What will be the sign] of the end of the age?" Mark records Jesus saying that the foremost sign of the end will be the "abomination of desolation." From a study of both Daniel and Revelation, we know that this event begins the second half of the Tribulation. We also know that this event will actually be a process taking place in two phases. The first phase will be when the Antichrist proclaims himself God (cf. 2 Thess. 2:3–10). The second phase will be when the False Prophet sets up the image of the Beast in the Holy of Holies (Dan. 12:11; Rev. 13:11–15).

After introducing the topic of the "abomination of desolation," Jesus cautioned, "let the reader understand." This is a solemn warning which when taken with what follows, stresses urgency. When the Jews during the Tribulation see *this sign*, they must flee Israel (vv. 14–20). The reason for this is that the violence against the Jews of that time will be such that, "unless the Lord had shortened those days, no life [Jews] would have been saved." Thankfully, for the sake of those who are to be saved, God will shorten the days.

In verses 21–23, Jesus informs the disciples that during the second half of the Tribulation, "false Christs and false prophets will arise, and will show signs and wonders, in order, if possible, to lead the elect astray." This is similar to what He told them they could expect in verses 5–7, but the main difference is that during the second half of the Tribulation, these false Christs and false prophets will actually perform lying signs and wonders. This prophecy finds its greatest fulfillment in the persons of the Antichrist and the False Prophet (cf. 2 Thes. 2:8–10; Rev. 13:11–15).

Jesus closed with this warning: "But take heed; behold, I have told you everything in advance." Although this period of violence will be unmatched by any preceding it, Jesus makes it clear that there will yet be those who are saved. It is to these tribulation saints that this warning is specifically addressed. They are not to be misled, for they have been forewarned by Christ Himself!

The Sign of the Second Coming (13:24–26)

(Compare Matthew 24:29–30; Luke 21:25–27)

In verses 24–26 Jesus addresses the disciples' second question, "What will be the sign of Your coming?" (Matt. 24:3). Mark and Matthew both record that after the Tribulation and immediately before Christ's second coming, there will be global darkness and horrific atmospheric instability. Luke adds that there will be "dismay among nations, in perplexity at the roaring of the sea and the waves, men fainting from fear" (Luke 21:25–26). When these things transpire in history, Jesus will return.

Remarkably, in the midst of this global darkness, all the inhabitants of the earth will see "the Son of man coming in clouds with great power and glory." Jesus' return will be personal, bodily, and visible (cf. Acts 1:11; Rev. 1:7; 19:11–16). Note also that His return is not as the meek and lowly Jesus, but with "great power and glory."

The Regathering of Israel (13:27)

(Compare Matthew 24:31)

Mark records that immediately after Christ's second coming, "He will send forth the angels, and will gather together His elect from the four winds, from the farthest end of the earth, to the farthest end of heaven." Most commentators agree that this verse refers to the regathering of the Jews in belief, which culminates in their restoration as a nation at the end of the age. This concept is clearly stated in many Old Testament passages (Deut. 4:29; 30:1–10; Isa. 27:12–13; 43:5–7; Jer. 16:14–15; 31:7–10; Ezek. 11:14–20; Amos 9:14–15; Zech. 10:8–12). Writing on this issue in the parallel passage found in Matthew, J. Dwight Pentecost notes:

> Verse 31 suggests that the event to follow the second advent will be the regathering of Israel. They had been scattered because of the anger of Satan (Rev. 12:12) and the desolation of the Beast (Matt. 24:15), but, according to promise, they will be regathered to the land (Deut. 30:3–4; Ezek. 20:37–38; 37:1–14). This regathering is through special angelic ministries. The "elect" of verse 31 must have reference to the saints of that program with which God is then dealing, that is, Israel (Dan. 7:18, 22, 27).[7]

The Parable of the Fig Tree (13:28–32)

(Compare Matthew 24:32–35; Luke 21:29–33)

Among dispensationalists, there are various views dealing with the parable of the fig tree. The first view is that these verses refer back to the fall of Jerusalem. This is based upon the fact that the symbol of the fig was used in the same manner in chapter 11.[8] The second view is that the parable of the fig tree has a double significance, referring both to the destruction of Jerusalem and the Great Tribulation.[9] The third view is that the parable of the fig tree deals with the nearness of Christ's second coming and therefore applies to the Church.[10] Those holding this view would also see the Rapture in the Olivet Discourse.

Finally, the fourth view, held by Arnold Fruchtenbaum, is that the parable of the fig tree does not refer to Israel but is merely an illustration. Hiebert agrees.

> The definite article, *the fig tree*, does not refer to some well-known fig tree but views the tree as representative of its class. A fig tree may have been close at hand. The fig tree was a recognized symbol of Israel (cf. comments on 11:14), but there is no indication that the reference here has an intended symbolic meaning. The reference seems to be to the literal tree; that Luke so understood the reference seems clear from his added "and all the trees" (21:29). The olive and the fig were common trees in Palestine, but since the olive is an evergreen, only the fig tree could be used to teach the intended lesson. *Learn* (ye) is aorist imperative, bidding the disciples to master the moral parable (cf. 4:2) which the tree taught. This command is another instance of Jesus' insistence that the observant believer can learn valuable spiritual lessons from the most familiar material objects.[11]

The first view is too narrow for the context, basically forcing the reader to ignore other significant points addressed by Jesus. The second view likewise limits the scope of Jesus' discourse. The third view must be discounted, for it places the Church in the Olivet Discourse, robbing it of its unique Jewishness.

The fourth view seems to best fit the requirements of the text, namely, that this parable is being used solely as an illustration. The literal truth then that Jesus is presenting is that when the disciples of "this generation" see these things coming to pass, they can know for certain that His coming is near, "right at the door." Furthermore, the expression "this generation" can only refer to those disciples living when the abomination of desolation is revealed, as has been demonstrated in verses 14–23 above.

In verses 31–32 both Jesus' divine and human natures are revealed: the divine in that, once He had answered the disciples' questions, He eternalized the truth of His words by telling them, "Heaven and earth will pass away: but My words will not pass away," and the human in that He revealed the voluntary limitations of His knowledge (before His glorification) stating that, "of that day or hour no one knows, not even the angels in heaven, nor the Son, but the Father alone" (cf. Acts 1:7; Phil. 2:7). R. C. H. Lenski makes the following insightful observations here:

> The fact that the angels, though they are in heaven, do not know the date and period is no special surprise to us, but the fact that "the Son" should not know day and hour does cause surprise. . . . In their essential oneness the three persons [of the Trinity] know all things, but in his humiliation the second person did not use his divine attributes save as he needed them in his mediatorial work. So the divine omniscience was used by

Jesus only in this restricted way. That is why here on Mt. Olivet (v. 3) he does not know the date of the end. How the incarnate Son could during his humiliation thus restrict himself in the use of the divine attributes is one of the mysteries of his person; the fact is beyond dispute.[12]

The Parable of the Man on a Far Journey Tree (13:33-37)

(Compare Matthew 24:32-35; Luke 21:29-33)

Jesus had already made it quite clear that although the disciples living during the end times would be able to recognize the nearness of the coming catastrophes, no one, not angels nor even the Son Himself, knows the exact moment when that day or hour would arrive (vv. 28-29). Nevertheless, to drive home this point, He gave them another solemn warning (the fourth in this chapter; cf. vv. 5, 9, 23), stating, "Take heed, keep on the alert; for you do not know when the appointed time is." This was then immediately followed by the parable of the man on a far journey, the purpose being to warn the disciples of all ages to stay alert and pay attention to the warnings Jesus had already given. The faithful servant will be watching.

This charge to readiness, however, is contrasted with those who Jesus finds "asleep" when He comes. This contrast is not between vigilant believers and apathetic believers, but rather refers to believers and unbelievers. Readiness in this sense always refers to those who have been saved. Jesus closes this chapter with a command to all disciples to "Be on the alert!." The one watching and heeding Jesus' words will not be caught off guard when the end comes.

Study Questions

1. Are the majority of predicted events between Jesus' first and second advent undesirable or pleasant?

2. What does this chapter teach about Israel?

3. At what time or times is the gospel preached to all the world?

4. When can persecution of believers be expected?

5. Was the destruction of Jerusalem the Great Tribulation?

6. What do these predictions reveal about the attitude of humankind toward Christ?

7. In what ways is Christ's concern and compassion shown in this chapter?

8. What is the difference between the elect from the earth and the elect of heaven?

CHAPTER 14

The Servant Betrayed and Denied
Mark 14:1-72

Preview:
Mary of Bethany broke her alabaster vial of costly perfume and used it to anoint Jesus. She gave all she could, loving Jesus. In contrast, Judas took all he could, betraying Jesus. Christ's final hours before His crucifixion were filled with anguish of soul. All kinds of hatred and indignities were cast upon Him. Both His enemies and even some of His friends turned against Him. Many of His followers forsook Him. Even His disciples fled as cowardly deserters out of fear that persecution might also fall on them. Nevertheless, Christ stood firm as the faithful Servant who remained submissive to His Father's will.

The Servant Anointed by Mary (14:1-9)

(Compare Matthew 26:2-13; Luke 22:1-2; John 12:1-9)

This pericope begins with the Jewish leaders' discussion concerning their urgent desire to do away with Jesus. The dilemma they faced was that the "feast of the passover, and of unleavened bread" was only two days off and it would be next to impossible to take Jesus into custody while the feasts were in full swing. To do so would certainly cause "a riot of the people."

This was a valid concern. Based upon Josephus's historical records, the Roman governor Cestius (c. A.D. 65) ordered the high priest to take a census of the lambs slain at the annual Passover. The number of lambs slain was 256,500. The law established that there must be at least ten persons per lamb, therefore, there easily could have been as many as three million pilgrims in Jerusalem during this time.

It wasn't just the number of people that concerned the Jewish leaders, however; it was also the fact that during the Passover, nationalistic feelings often boiled over. The Romans were well aware of this and augmented the number of troops in Jerusalem to guard against civil or political uprisings. These extra troops were stationed in the Tower of Antonia, which overlooked the temple proper where Jesus would have been teaching.

Concerned about the crowds and the reaction of the Romans, these Jewish leaders "were seeking how to seize Him by stealth, and kill Him; for they were saying, 'Not during the festival.'" Previously Mark had recorded the desire of the religious leaders to kill Jesus (cf. 11:18). Now the only difference was that Jesus' time had come. The Jewish leaders had resolved that Jesus should not be taken on the feast day, but God had already determined this. Monty S. Mills explains:

> The plot the Sanhedrin (for that is who Matt 26:3 describes) decided on did not work out as they planned, for their clear intention was to wait until after the seven day Feast of Unleavened Bread, and then to trick, arrest, and execute Jesus in the relative quiet after all the pilgrims had returned home from Jerusalem. However, in God's timing Jesus was to die at Passover and their plans would be speeded up to comply with His will. Clearly He, not they, was in control; clearly, too, God had the crucifixion in mind when He instituted the Passover fourteen centuries earlier. After all, John had identified Jesus, right at the very beginning of His public ministry, as "the Lamb of God" (John 1:29).[1]

Mark now shifts the focus of this pericope transporting the reader to Bethany and "the home of Simon the leper." Nothing much is known about this man, but it has been speculated that he was a man whom Jesus had in fact healed. This seems likely since, according to the law, no leper would have been hosting a social event. Perhaps Simon had called Jesus to his home to honor Him after being healed. While they were eating, "there came a woman with an alabaster vial of very costly perfume of pure nard; and she broke the vial and poured it over His head."

This incident, also recorded in Matthew 26:6–13 and John 12:1–8, should not be confused with a similar event recorded in Luke 7:36–50. Although similar, there are numerous differences as can be seen in the table, Jesus Anointed by Two Marys.

Israel in the Time of Jesus

Extent of Herod's kingdom

□ Herodian fortress city

◉ Decapolis city (time of Herod)

● Other city

ABILENE

Abila

ITUREA

Abana R.

Sidon

Damascus

SYRIA

▲ Mt. Hermon

Pharpar R.

Leontes R.

Tyre

Caesarea-Philippi

PHOENICIA

GAULANITIS

TRACHONITIS

◉ Raphana

L. Hula

J. Jarmuk ▲ Hazor

GALILEE

Chorazin

Capernaum ● Bethsaida

Ptolemais ●
(Acco)

Gennesaret

Gergesa

TETRARCHY
OF PHILIP

Mt. Carmel ▲

Cana ●

Magdala

Sea
of Galilee

◉ Hippos

BATANEA

Tiberias

Yarmuk R.

AURANITIS

Mediterranean
Sea

Nazareth ▲ Mt. Tabor

● Nain

● Gadara

Abila ●

Kishon R.

Dor ●

Megiddo ●

Bethany
beyond Jordan

Caesarea
(Strato's Tower) ●

Scythopolis ◉

◉ Pella

● Dion

SAMARIA

DECAPOLIS

Sebaste
(Samaria) ●

Salim? ●

◉ Gerasa

▲ Mt. Ebal

□ Amathus

Me Jarkon

Mt. Gerizim ▲ ● Sychar

Jordan R.

Jabbok R.

Joppa ●

Antipatris ●
(Aphek)

● Alexandrium

PEREA

Philadelphia
◉ (Amman)

(SEMI-INDEPENDENT
MUNICIPALITY)

Jamnia ●

Cyprus □ ● Jericho

Emmaus ●

□ Esbus (Heshbon)

Azotus
(Ashdod) ●

▲ Mt. Olivet

Jerusalem ● ● Bethany

● Medeba

Ashkelon ●

Bethlehem ● □ Hyrcania

□ Machaerus

JUDEA

□ Herodium

Gaza ●

● Hebron

● Adora

Dead
Sea

Arnon R.

N
A
B
A
T
E
A

IDUMEA

Masada □

Beersheba ●

● Arad

Besor R.

□ Malatha

Zered Br.

0   10   20   30 miles

0   10   20   30 kilometers

© MAPQUEST.COM

Jesus Anointed by Two Marys

Place	Woman	Action	The Reason	Reference
Galilee	Mary, a prostitute	she anointed Jesus' feet	to express her love to Christ for His gracious forgiveness of her many sins	Luke 7:36–50
Judea of Bethany	Mary, sister of Martha and Lazarus	she anointed Jesus' head	to express her love to Christ because He was going to the cross to die for her	Mark 14:3–9; Matthew 26:6–13; John 12:1–8

Both Matthew's and Mark's accounts mention that this event happened two days before the Passover (cf. Matt. 26:2; Mark 14:1). John's account says six days. Who is right? Actually, both are right. Most commentators agree that the anointing should be dated six days before the Passover. The two-day time reference in Matthew 26:2 and Mark 14:1 should be understood as not dating the anointing but rather the plot to seize Jesus.

Mark notes that a woman came bringing "an alabaster vial of very costly perfume of pure nard." Alabaster is a form of translucent white, gray, yellow, or red gypsum. It is quite soft and was often ornately carved. The container was probably a flask fashioned without handles. This type of flask was common and would have had a long neck that was sealed. The contents of this flask was spikenard, a costly scented ointment or perfume imported from the Himalayas. It was derived from the dried roots and stems of the nard plant and was stored in alabaster flasks for shipment.

Mary's act was shocking to those present for two reasons: first, because women, if allowed to attend a feast where men were present, were not active participants, but servants; and second, because instead of providing the customary few drops of oil for honored guests, she broke the flask and poured out the entire contents!

The reaction of some of the disciples was that they "were indignantly remarking to one another, 'Why has this perfume been wasted? For this perfume might have been sold for over three hundred denarii, and the money given to the poor.' And they were scolding her." It seems that Judas Iscariot was the ringleader on this occasion and was able to influence others in the group (cf. John 12:4–6). The complaint had nothing to do with the act itself or the fact that custom and tradition had been violated. It was supposedly rather that the ointment, equivalent to about one year's wages, could have been sold and given to the poor. John notes that Judas's complaint was insincere because "he said this, not because he was concerned about the poor, but because he was a thief, and as he had the money box, he used to pilfer what was put into it" (John 12:6). Concerning this incident, one commentator writes:

> The closing scenes of the Gospel story are shadowed by the treachery of this "one of the twelve," as he is repeatedly called (Mark 14:10, cf. 14:20; Jn. 6:71; 12:4). He raises the voice of criticism against the action of Mary, who anointed the Master's feet with the precious ointment (Jn. 12:3–5). The comment of the Evangelist is intended to stress the avarice of Judas, who saw in the price of the ointment nothing of the beautiful deed which Jesus praised (Mark 14:6), but only a means by which the apostolic fund would be increased, and thereby his own pocket lined. And even this motive was cloaked under a specious plea that the money could be given away to relieve the poor. Thus to covetousness there is added the trait of deceit.[2]

Mary's act of worship was not to be intruded upon, and so Jesus responded, "Let her alone; why do you bother her? She has done a good deed to Me. For the poor you always have with you, and whenever you wish, you can do them good; but you do not always have Me." Two things stand out here. First, Mary had done a good work and she would be rewarded for it. Second, the poor will always exist, at least until the return of the Lord. There are times when a simple act of worship is needed more than charitable works. This was such a time.

Although Mary had no way of knowing the full import of her actions, Jesus did. He stated, "She has done what she could." Mary had acted out of love and devotion to the Lord, and without her knowledge, her actions were prophetic. Jesus would be crucified very shortly, and because death would occur on a holy day, there would be no time to prepare His body. This explains why He said, "She has anointed My body beforehand for the burial."

Jesus then solemnly declared, "Wherever the gospel is preached in the whole world, that also which this woman has done shall be spoken of in memory of her." What an incredible statement! Mary's act of love so severely criticized by the disciples, was to become a shining example to all those who would hear the gospel message. Hidden in this statement is a wonderful promise that looked beyond the suffering and shame that awaited Him to a time when the gospel was to be preached.

The Servant Betrayed by Judas (14:10–11)

(Compare Matthew 26:14–16; Luke 22:3–6)

Jesus had continually spoke of His forthcoming death with the disciples. After Mary anointed Him, He again reminded His disciples of what was ahead for

Him. Like the other disciples, Judas Iscariot was also looking for a political Messiah. This constant talk of death and suffering did not fit in with his expectations, nor did it allow for his ambitions in the new kingdom. The difference between Judas and the other disciples, however, is one of character. Judas was a thief. This describes not only his activities but also his very nature. He was not interested in God's plan and purposes. He was interested only in enriching himself.

In Judas's eyes it was now apparent that Jesus' would fail to provide a means of personal fulfillment for him and so he "went off to the chief priests, in order to betray Him to them." Believing that there would be no kingdom and having lost any hope of personal fulfillment, Judas devised a plan whereby he would at least come away with some gain. Matthew indicates that Judas approached the Jewish leaders and asked, "What are you willing to give me to deliver Him up to you?" (26:15). Mark says that these leaders "were glad when they heard this, and promised to give him money." Alfred Plummer remarks:

> The offer of Judas freed the conniving ecclesiastical leaders from a grave difficulty. Now they could act before the Feast began. They would not have ventured to make such a proposal to a disciple of Jesus. That one of His most intimate associates should venture to betray Him was an amazing advantage.[3]

Matthew notes that the amount of the "promised" money was "thirty pieces of silver." This was the price of a slave in those days and indicates Judas's complete lack of respect for the man with whom he had spent the last three years of his life. The Jewish leaders were so overjoyed at Judas's proposal that they willingly agreed to his plan. The Greek grammar and structure indicates that they immediately counted out the silver and gave it to him.

Having received his blood money Judas now actively "began seeking how to betray Him at an opportune time."

No Greek dramatist nor Shakespeare ever could have conceived of this amazing and dramatic story line unfolding over a twenty-four hour period. Prophecy would be fulfilled; the world would be changed; millions in every century would be affected.

The Servant Observes the Last Supper (14:12–25)

(Compare Matthew 26:17–29; Luke 22:7–20; John 13:1–35)

The disciples, as they had done on many previous occasions, now set about the task of preparing for the forthcoming Passover feast. As part of that task, it was incumbent upon them to secure lodging so they asked Jesus, "Where do You want us to go and prepare for You to eat the Passover?" Of course, Jesus knew precisely where He would spend these last hours with the disciples, for He was never perplexed by problems or challenged by emergencies. James R. Edwards correctly asserts:

> Jesus is not a tragic hero caught in events beyond his control. There is no hint of desperation, fear, anger, or futility on his part. Jesus does not cower or retreat as plots are hatched against him. He displays, as he has throughout the Gospel, a sovereign freedom and authority to follow a course he has freely chosen in accordance with God's plan. Judas and others may act against him, but they do not act upon him.[4]

In response to their question,

> He sent two of His disciples, and said to them, "Go into the city, and a man will meet you carrying a pitcher of water; follow him; and wherever he enters, say to the owner of the house, 'The Teacher says, "Where is My guest room in which I may eat the Passover with My disciples?"' And he himself will show you a large upper room furnished and ready; and prepare for us there".

Whether this was a miraculous contact and supernaturally perceived on the part of the owner of the place or was prearranged we do not know. The word "chamber" here is the same Greek word translated "inn" in Luke 2:7. At last there *was* room in the "inn." Mark 15:41 indicates that there were many women who accompanied Jesus to Jerusalem. It is reasonable to expect that some of them had children and husbands who came with them. This explains the need for a "large upper room."

The preparation procedures for the Passover were complex and elaborate. William Barclay explains:

> On the afternoon before the Passover evening, came *the sacrifice of the Passover Lamb*. All the people came to the Temple. The worshipper must slay his own lamb, thereby, as it were, making his own sacrifice. . . . Between the worshippers and the altar were two long lines of priests, each with a gold or silver bowl. As the lamb's throat was slit the blood was caught in one of these bowls, and passed up the line, until the priest at the end of the line dashed it upon the altar. The carcass was then flayed, the entrails and the fat extracted, because they were part of the necessary sacrifice, and the carcass handed back to the worshipper. . . . The lamb was carried home to be roasted. It must not be boiled. Nothing must touch it, not even the sides of a pot. It had to be roasted over an open fire on a spit

made of pomegranate wood. The spit went right through the lamb from mouth to vent, and the lamb had to be roasted entire with head and legs and tail still attached to the body.[5]

In addition to the preparation of the lamb was the preparation of the table. On the table there would be unleavened bread, a bowl of saltwater, bitter herbs, a paste called *charosheth,* and four cups of wine. Each item corresponded to some aspect of the Israelites' exodus from Egypt. The unleavened bread reminded them of their rush in leaving. The bowl of salt water reminded them of crossing the Red Sea. The bitter herbs reminded them of their captivity in Egypt, and the *charosheth* paste reminded them of the clay bricks they had been forced to manufacture. Finally, the four cups of wine represented the four promises God made to them in Exodus 6:6–7, namely, (1) I will free you from Egyptian slavery, (2) I will redeem you with an outstretched arm, (3) you will be my people, and (4) I will be your God.

Once the preparations were finished, Jesus and the Twelve disciples went to the upper room to partake of the Passover meal. The actual eating of the Passover meal was a lengthy process. It was divided into four parts, each concluding with a cup of wine. The first part consisted of a blessing. The second part began with a child asking, "Why is this night different from other nights?" This would be answered by retelling the exodus story. The third part consisted of a benediction over the meal, after which those present would begin eating. The final part involved the singing of Psalms 116– 18.

Mark notes that Jesus and the disciples "were reclining at the table and eating," signifying that they were in the third part of the ceremony. As they were in the process of eating, Jesus abruptly and solemnly declared, "Truly I say to you that one of you will betray Me—one who is eating with Me." On numerous occasions Jesus had told the disciples in general terms that He would be handed over to His enemies, but now He specifically revealed that His betrayer was someone in their midst, something that all four Gospels record (Matt. 26:21–25; Luke 22:21–23; John 13:21–30).

The response of those present is understandable. As previously noted, it is highly likely that there were many present, not just the Twelve, and each "began to be grieved and to say to Him one by one, Surely not I?" Jesus' revelation was designed to force each of the disciples to look within themselves. This they began to do, looking from one to the next and asking the same question. As the question of guilt continued to move around the table, Simon Peter asked John to find out who this betrayer was (John 13:24). Jesus responded, "It is one of the twelve, one who dips with Me in the bowl." Jesus' response on the one hand exonerated the larger group, but on the other hand, it added to the sorrow and concern of the Twelve because it was now

clear that this treacherous act would come at the hands of one in their privileged group! Jesus did not name the individual even though He certainly
knew who it was. Perhaps Jesus' answer was purposefully ambiguous to
allow Judas one last opportunity to confess and repent. It may also be that
Jesus, knowing that all the disciples would shortly betray Him, wanted them
to reflect upon their commitment to Him.

John apparently was not satisfied with Jesus' answer and specifically
asked, "Lord, who is it?" (John 13:25). Jesus responded, "That is the one for
whom I shall dip the morsel and give it to him" (John 13:26). By this time the
question of guilt had made its way to Judas himself, who asked, "Surely it is
not I, Rabbi?" (Matt. 26:25) Jesus then dipping the sop and giving it to Judas
(John 13:26) replied to him, "You have said it yourself" (Matt. 26:25).

Jesus continued His revelation: "For the Son of Man is to go, just as it is
written of Him." Jesus was not a helpless victim. He realized that His coming
suffering was a fulfillment of Scripture. Although He had announced that He
was to be betrayed, His suffering and death were not merely due to the actions
of Judas, the Jewish leaders, Rome, or anyone else. It was the fulfillment of
Scripture. God's will was being done. Lenski notes:

> It is all divinely planned and will surely be carried out as Jesus now
> declares. He is not appealing for anything like sympathy for himself, the
> sympathy and the commiseration should go to the traitor. Jesus is indi-
> cating to the Twelve, including Judas, why he does not interfere and make
> this dastardly betrayal impossible.[6]

Even though Scripture must be fulfilled, and even though it was God's
eternal plan for Christ to die (Acts 3:17–18; 4:27–28), Jesus further stated,
"but woe to that man by whom the Son of Man is betrayed! It would have
been good for that man if he had not been born." By this, Jesus was indicating that Judas was morally responsible for his actions. The betrayal was necessary to the fulfillment of God's plan, but Judas was not absolved of his guilt,
for his was not merely a pawn, but an active and willing participant. Warren
Wiersbe explains:

> From the very beginning, Jesus knew what Judas would do (John 6:64),
> but He did not compel him to do it. Judas was exposed to the same spir-
> itual privileges as the other disciples, yet they did him no good. The same
> sun that melts the ice only hardens the clay. In spite of all that our Lord
> said about money, and all of His warning about covetousness, Judas con-
> tinued to be a thief and steal from the treasury. In spite of all our Lord's
> warning about unbelief, Judas persisted in his rejection. *Jesus even washed
> Judas' feet!* Yet his hard heart did not yield.[7]

Although Mark does not specifically mention it, John notes that after Judas had received the sop, "Satan then entered into him" (John 13:27). Luke 22:3 indicates that Satan entered Judas when he made his deal with the Jewish leaders. What should be understood by this is that there was a process happening in Judas's heart that began when he went to the Jewish leaders and culminated when Jesus revealed that He knew he was the traitor.

Once Jesus had exposed Judas's heart, He said to Judas, "What you do, do quickly" (John 13:27). At this point, Judas, with the sop in his hand, left the upper room and went to gather those who would arrest Jesus later that night.

With the traitor now gone, Jesus

> took some bread, and after a blessing He broke it; and gave it to them, and said, "Take it; this is My body." And when He had taken a cup, and given thanks, He gave it to them; and they all drank from it. And He said to them, "This is My blood of the covenant, which is poured out for many. Truly I say to you, I shall never again drink of the fruit of the vine until that day when I drink it new in the kingdom of God."

Here Jesus instituted the Lord's Supper. Many have tried to ascribe a literal meaning to these verses, but even a cursory reading reveals the figurative nature of what Jesus was saying.

Since Jesus was physically present as He spoke these words, there was no way in which the disciples could have literally eaten His body or drunk His blood. Moreover, the consumption of blood was detestable to the Jews and strictly forbidden by the Mosaic Law (cf. Lev. 3:17; 7:26–27; 17:10–14).

How then are we to take these verses? The plain meaning is simply that the bread and the wine represented His body and blood. They were symbolic in nature and were to serve as a memorial of what Christ would accomplish through His suffering and crucifixion. Paul Enns explains:

> The memorial view has much to commend it in the Scriptures. An examination of the passages reveals the significance of the Lord's Supper. It is a memorial to His death (1 Cor. 11:24, 25): the recurring statement, "in remembrance of Me," makes this clear, the bread symbolizing His perfect body offered in sin-bearing sacrifice (1 Pet. 2:24) and the wine His blood shed for forgiveness of sins (Eph. 1:7). It is a proclamation of the death of Christ while waiting for His coming (1 Cor. 11:26): it involves a looking back to the historical event of the cross and an anticipating of His return in the future (Matthew 26:29). It is a communion of believers with each other (1 Cor. 10:17): they eat and drink the same symbolic elements, focusing on their common faith in Christ.[8]

At this moment our Lord gave a promise and uttered a prediction that He would not drink any more of the fruit of the vine until He drank it anew with them in the coming kingdom of God. In other words, the day is coming when our Lord will gather to Himself all of His disciples of all ages, when the kingdom of God will be established in power and might, and then we will celebrate not this feast of remembrance so much as the very marriage supper of the Lamb of God (Rev. 19:7–10).

Another key point in this brief passage is the inauguration of the New Testament (covenant) promised originally in Jeremiah 31:31–37. This new covenant was expressly for the house of Israel and the house of Judah and would not be like the former external Mosaic covenant but would be written on their hearts and minds.

Questions often asked about the new covenant are "Is the church related to Israel's new covenant?" and "Is the church fulfilling the new covenant today?" Scholars are still debating these questions, and among dispensationalists several different views have been set forth, including the view that (1) there are two new covenants—one for Israel and one for the church, (2) the new covenant is expressly Israel's covenant but is applied in general to the church, and (3) the new covenant belongs only to Israel but the blood of the covenant is applied to the Church.

Charles H. Dyer provides a balanced view explaining that the new covenant will have its ultimate fulfillment during the Millennium reign of Christ when the nation of Israel is restored to her God. The new covenant was made with Israel (Jer. 31:31, 33) just as the Mosaic covenant had been (v. 32). One of the most important features of the new covenant is the preservation of Israel as a nation (vv. 35–37). The ultimate fulfillment of this covenant will take place during the earthly reign of Christ, however, at the present the church today is sharing in many of the benefits of that covenant. The covenant was inaugurated by the blood of Christ's at His death (Matt. 26:27–28; Luke 22:20), and the church, by her relationship with Him, is sharing in many of the spiritual blessings promised to Israel (cf. Rom. 11:11–27; Eph. 2:11–22) including the new covenant (2 Cor. 3:6; Heb. 8:6–13; 9:15; 12:22–24). While the present participation of the church in the new covenant is real, it is certainly not the ultimate fulfillment of God's promises. Believers in the body of Christ now are enjoying those spiritual blessings of the new covenant (forgiveness of sins and the indwelling Holy Spirit), however this does *not* mean that spiritual *and* physical blessings will not be realized by the Jews during the Millennial reign. That still awaits the day when Israel will acknowledge her sin, repent, and trust the Lord Jesus, the Messiah, for forgiveness (Zech. 12:10–13:1).[9] (emphasis added).

Though dispensationalists may disagree on this issue, one thing is clear: those who teach that the new covenant refers solely to the church to the exclusion of physical Israel are gravely mistaken.

The Servant Praying in the Garden (14:26–42)

(Compare Matthew 26:36–46; Luke 22:31–46; John 13:36–38)

Jesus and the disciples made their way to the Mount of Olives, a place they knew well (Luke 22:39; John 18:1–2). As they went along Jesus made a three-fold prophecy. First, He predicted, "You will all fall away, because it is written, 'I will strike down the shepherd, and the sheep shall be scattered,'" quoting Zechariah 13:7. Mark records the fulfillment of this prophecy later that night: "They all left Him and fled" (14:50). Interestingly, Mark and Matthew both place Jesus' warning on the way to Gethsemane while Luke and John both place it while still in the upper room. The solution to this apparent contradiction is that two different warnings were given. In Luke and John, the warning is directed to Peter while in Matthew and Mark the warning is directed to all the disciples, and Peter, as usual, acts as spokesman for the group.

The second prophecy related to Jesus' resurrection and reunion with the disciples in Galilee, "But after I have been raised, I will go before you to Galilee." He accomplished both parts of this prophecy before His ascension (Mark 16:7). Finally, He specifically predicted Peter's actions, "Truly I say to you, that you yourself this very night, before a cock crows twice, shall three times deny Me." The fulfillment of this prophecy is found in Mark 14:66–72.

Once they arrived at the Mount of Olives, they entered into Gethsemane, which was situated just east of Jerusalem, across the Kidron Valley and opposite the temple on the Mount of Olives (Mark 13:3; John 18:1). The name Gethsemane is a transliteration of two Hebrew words literally meaning "oil press." This is strangely appropriate considering the agony that was about to press in on the Lord.

The Lord then took Peter, James, and John, His inner circle, with Him into the interior of the grove, leaving the remaining eight disciples at the entrance. This was not considered unusual or a reason for alarm for Jesus had taken these same three men with Him before (cf. Mark 5:35–43; 9:2–9). Moreover, these three men had previously boasted of their strength of character—James and John in Mark 10:38–39 and 14:31, and Peter in 14:29–31—so they would certainly be good friends in such a time of crisis!

When Jesus arrived at the desired location, He "began to be very distressed and troubled. And He said to them, 'My soul is deeply grieved to the point of death.'"

James R. Edwards explains the significance of the expression that said Jesus "began to be deeply distressed and troubled." "Distressed" (*ekthambeō*) and "troubled" (*adēmoneō*) are rare words in the New Testament. The first occurs only in Mark 9:15 and 14:33 and has the sense of "alarm." The second is used in Matthew 26:37 and Mark 14:33 with the meaning "to be troubled or distressed." "My soul is overwhelmed with sorrow to the point of death" is a similar cry of the downcast and heartbroken soul of Psalm 42:6, 12; 43:5. The Greek word for "overwhelmed with sorrow" (*perilupos*) is also a rare word, and in the present context can mean "despair."[10]

What exactly was it that caused the Lord such agony? The answer to this question is complex. Certainly it included the physical suffering He would endure, but it was not the physical suffering that overwhelmed Him. On the contrary, His agony can be explained only by what He would endure on the cross. With this before Him, Jesus told the privileged three, "Remain here and keep watch." What He must do, He must do alone. Lenski explains:

> The battle that Jesus fights in this hour he must of necessity fight alone. He alone must now will "to lay down his life" (John 10:17, 18), "to give his life as a ransom for many" (Matthew 20:28), to be made sin and a curse for us (II Cor. 5:21; Gal. 3:13). The imagination faints before the images thus rising up before it. Who can conceive all this abominable sin, all this damnable curse! The Holy Son of God is to plunge into it all now—the great and awful moment is almost present in the approach of Judas. Shall Jesus go on, or, as his pure and holy nature recoils from the unspeakable ordeal—is there yet a way out? [11]

Mark records that Jesus "went a little beyond them, and fell to the ground, and began to pray that if it were possible, the hour might pass Him by." What Mark presents in a general format, Matthew states as Jesus' own words, "My Father, if it is possible, let this cup pass from Me" (Matt. 26:39). Some have assumed that Jesus' prayer demonstrated weakness and was an attempt on His part to bypass the suffering that lay ahead. Scripture, however, records that John the Baptist identified Jesus' purpose from the beginning, namely, to be the "Lamb of God who takes away the sin of the world" (John 1:29). Moreover, Jesus Himself had said that "the Son of Man did not come to be served, but to serve, and to give His life a ransom for many." (Mark 10:45). So, it was not the physical suffering that Jesus drew back from, it was the realization that He would be forsaken by His Father (cf. Mark 15:34). This was no mere shrinking from physical death—it was all the sins and all the deaths of the human race.

Even in Jesus' prayer there was a superhuman determination to complete the task at hand. He began by addressing God as His dear Father, "My Father" and "Abba, Father." He then conditioned His request, saying, "if it is possible" and "all things are possible for Thee," acknowledging that God indeed had the power to change what lie ahead. He continued, "remove this cup from Me," knowing that if such a possibility existed, the Father would employ it. Jesus knew that the "cup" contained the sins of the world, which He must take into Himself. Finally, recognizing that there was no other way, Jesus took the way of the Servant, determining "not what I will, but what Thou wilt."

Jesus then arose from the ground and went to the three. Finding them asleep, He addressed Peter, the leader of the group, saying, "Are you asleep? Could you not keep watch for one hour?" Jesus had come to the three perhaps for some small bit of encouragement, but instead He found them asleep! He rebuked Peter who had so strongly boasted of his loyalty to Jesus. Then in the midst of His own great agony and turmoil, the Lord, still looking out for Peter, commanded him, "Keep watching and praying, that you may not come into temptation." The Lord had already prophesied Peter's denial, yet Peter had not taken it to heart. Finally, Jesus told him, "The spirit is willing, but the flesh is weak." This is so true. We desire to do God's will yet are so weak in our flesh that we fail to follow through!

Jesus knew there was no point in going to the sleepy disciples, for He could receive no help from them. Consequently, He went back to the only source of help available to Him, "saying the same words."

Hebrews 5:7 indicates that Jesus "offered up both prayers and supplications with loud crying and tears." So great was His agony that Luke records that it was essential for God to send an angel from heaven who "appeared to Him, strengthening Him." (Luke 22:43). As a result of receiving strength, Jesus "pray[ed] more fervently; and His sweat became like drops of blood, falling down upon the ground" (Luke 22:44). As Jesus descended into the waiting maelstrom of divine judgment upon sin, He shrank from the awful contamination of sin and shame and evil that He would have to absorb into His soul. It was the realization of the pangs of sorrow and guilt that had to be vicariously merged into His very being and the subsequent rejection He would have to suffer from the Father that so agonized His being.

Breaking from His prayers, Jesus returned to find the disciples asleep once again. Mark notes that "their eyes were very heavy" while Luke records that they were "sleeping from sorrow" (Luke 22:45). No doubt the disciples heard Jesus' cries and saw His tears. The lateness of the hour and the heaviness of their hearts was more than they could handle. Mark alone records that upon realizing that they had once again failed to maintain vigil, they "did not know what to answer Him." The boldness and self-assurance that all three had so blatantly declared previously was gone, replaced by embarrassment.

Jesus resumed praying. Then, after having completed His time alone with God, He returned to His disciples a third time and again found the three sleeping. Once again Jesus asked, "Are you still sleeping and taking your rest?" His query revealed the weakness of His inner circle to comprehend the severity of the hour.

Jesus' internal conflict was now worked out, and He had resolved within Himself to fulfill the Father's will. With a sense of grave determination, He declared, "It is enough; the hour has come; behold, the Son of Man is being betrayed into the hands of sinners." This no doubt startled the sleeping disciples who upon awaking were immediately commanded to "Arise" and prepare for departure, for, Jesus said, "The one who betrays Me is at hand!"

Three times Jesus prayed, but He remained surrendered to His Father's will. His prayers demonstrated that there was no other way, consistent with the justice of God, for salvation to be provided. Jesus must take upon Himself the sins of the world. He must take the cup of God's judgment and drink it all. He must take our sins into Himself and pass through this awful valley of the shadow of death and die as an outcast on a cross.

The Servant Arrested and Forsaken (14:43–52)

(Compare Matthew 26:47–56; Luke 22:47–53; John 18:2–11)

Jesus' words to the disciples had hardly reached their ears before the traitor, along with his mob, arrived on the scene. Mark tells us that Judas brought with him, "a multitude with swords and clubs, from the chief priests and the scribes and the elders." John notes that Judas had come with "the Roman cohort, and officers from the chief priests and the Pharisees" who carried "lanterns and torches and weapons" (John 18:3). John also points out that the band was lead by a captain. The Greek word for "band" literally means "cohort" while the word for "captain" literally means "tribune." A military tribune normally commanded a cohort of six hundred men, but it is unlikely that the full command of men was used on this occasion due to the confined area of Gethsemane. The scene then is set. The official Levitical temple police with clubs, sent from the Sanhedrin along with a Roman guard carrying short swords, had come to arrest Jesus.

Judas had beforehand indicated that he would give these men a sign as to who they were to arrest. In the dimly lit area surrounded by olive trees, it would be necessary to make absolutely sure that they got the right man. Mark tells us that this sign was to be the intimate and respectful kiss of a disciple to his teacher. Once the sign was given, Judas instructed the mob to "seize Him, and lead Him away under guard."

Judas, seeing that Jesus and the disciples were in the garden, immediately went up to Him and, calling Him "Rabbi," "kissed him." Matthew notes that Judas pretended to be overjoyed at finding Jesus there and called out, "Hail, Rabbi!" (Matt. 26:49) Moreover, when Judas had made arrangements to give them the deadly sign, he had used a form of the Greek word *phileō*. But when he actually kissed the Lord, the intensified form of the word, "*kataphileō*," is used. The idea is that when Judas kissed the Lord, it was an extended, exaggerated action. Apparently, without waiting for a response from Jesus, Judas embraced Jesus, showering Him with supposed affection. Concerning this passage, J. Vernon McGee remarks:

> Here we have recorded one of the basest acts of treachery. It is foul and loathsome. Judas knew our Lord's accustomed place of retirement, and he led the enemy there. A kiss is a badge of love and affection, but Judas used it to betray Christ. This makes his act even more dastardly and repugnant.[12]

When the guards arrived and proceeded to arrest Jesus, according to John 18:2–11, they were at first simply overpowered by Jesus' presence. This illustrated that He freely surrendered Himself, although He could have supernaturally resisted. But as "they laid hands on Him, and seized Him," Peter, impulsive and rash, suddenly "drew his sword, and struck the slave of the high priest, and cut off his ear." No doubt remembering his failure to keep watch with the Lord, along with his boastings of dying for Him, Peter took the initiative to prove that he was true to his word. As the leader of the disciples, his actions were closely watched by the rest, and they would have been moved to imitate his actions. Had Jesus not immediately intervened, a terrible catastrophe may have resulted (cf. Luke 22:51; John 18:11).

Although Jesus offered no physical resistance, He did make it clear that He was in control of the situation. In the presence of all, He confidently told Peter that He could at any time "appeal to My Father, and He will at once put at My disposal more than twelve legions of angels" (Matt. 26:53). Moreover, John notes that Jesus reminded Peter and the eleven others that as He had told them before, this was "the cup which the Father has given Me." Jesus' question, "Shall I not drink it?" again drove home to His disciples what He had been telling them, namely, that His entire life had been leading up to this point in time (John 18:11).

Then Jesus directed His attention to the chief priest and elders (Luke 22:52) who had apparently come along behind the guard but had now made their way to the front of the group. He protested their need to put forth such a show of force, asking them, "Have you come out with swords and clubs to arrest Me, as against a robber?" This show of force was what one might expect for a band of robbers or a group of insurrectionists. He continued rebuking them: "Every day I was with you in the temple teaching, and you did not seize Me." In other words, the treachery of their deed was apparent. When they had opportunity, they failed to take Him because they knew the people would not permit it. With this piercing accusation, Jesus forced all of these men, guards and leaders alike, to examine their motives and the legality of their actions.

But Jesus did one more thing. He revealed to these pawns of the Sanhedrin that although they were the means, God was the author that "the Scriptures might be fulfilled." Here is a clear example of God's sovereignty and man's responsibility! God had predetermined this event, but they had acted willingly, and so all partook of the guilt of the Sanhedrin. This realization did not curtail them, however, for "this hour, and the power of darkness were theirs" (Luke 22:53).

John records that just before Peter cut off the ear of the servant of the high priest, Jesus had asked the mob for the second time who they were seeking. They again told Him that that were seeking Jesus of Nazareth. To this He responded, "'I told you that I am He; if therefore you seek Me, let these go their way', that the word might be fulfilled which He spoke, 'Of those whom Thou hast given Me I lost not one'"(John 18:8-9). Evidently Jesus' request was granted, for it is recorded that "they all left Him, and fled" without being hindered by the armed guard. One can only wonder if in so doing they realized they were fulfilling Jesus' earlier prophecy concerning them (cf. 14:27).

Verses 51-52 are interesting because they indicate that besides the Twelve, "a certain young man was following Him, wearing nothing but a linen sheet over his naked body" who perhaps had been hiding among the olive trees. As the mob moved off with Jesus in custody, "they seized him" but he fought them off and, "left the linen sheet behind, and escaped naked. "

Numerous theories have been advanced concerning the identity of this young man, but none of them can be substantiated. Of the four Gospels, Mark alone records this strange episode, leading many scholars to believe that it is Mark's personal reminiscence. One thing is certain, it could not have been part of Peter's record, for it occurred after he and the other disciples had fled. It is quite probable that this young man was indeed John Mark.

The Servant Tried by the Sanhedrin (14:53-65)

(Compare Matthew 26:57-68; John 18:12-13, 19-24)

Now that they had their prey, the wolves began to assemble. They "led Jesus away to the high priest" where "all the chief priests and the elders and the scribes" were assembled. The high priest at the time was Joseph Caiaphas, son-in-law of Annas (cf. John 18:13), who served as high priest from A.D. 18–36. It was in the palace of Caiaphas that the plot to take Jesus had been birthed (cf. Matt. 26:3–4) and to where they would eventually lead Him. According to tradition, Caiaphas's palace was about a kilometer southwest of Gethsemane on the slopes of Mount Zion.

A Byzantine shrine was erected on this spot in the middle of the fifth century but was later destroyed by Moslem invaders. It was rebuilt by the Crusaders and given a new name: St. Peter's in Gallicantu (cock-crow). In 1931 the Church of St. Peter was erected on this site. Excavations beneath the church have revealed a series of rock-hewn pits, cisterns, and grottos dating from 37 B.C.– A.D. 70. These pits were designed specifically for the purpose of detaining and interrogating prisoners. In fact, one can still see the pillars to which the prisoners and, it is believed, Jesus Himself, was bound and whipped.

Although Jesus was finally led to Caiaphas's palace, John notes that Jesus was first led to Annas (cf. John 18:12–13), who questioned Him concerning His disciples and teaching. This seems to have been more of an informal, private hearing intended to gather evidence for the trial that would follow at Caiaphas's palace. During this hearing, Jesus refused to respond, probably because Annas really had no legal right to question Him. Given Jesus' silence, "Annas therefore sent Him bound to Caiaphas the high priest" (John 18:24), where the formal trial before the Sanhedrin was to convene.

As they led Jesus away to be questioned, "Peter had followed Him at a distance, right into the courtyard of the high priest." Although certainly gripped with fear and concern for what was to become of His master, Peter nevertheless followed the procession from a distance as they made their way to Caiaphas's palace. Where was the boastful man who had so forthrightly proclaimed his loyalty and devotion only hours before?

Arriving at the home of Caiaphas, Peter thought that he could move about incognito, so he "was sitting with the officers, and warming himself at the fire." One is reminded of Psalm 1:1, where we are told, "How blessed is the man who does not walk in the counsel of the wicked, nor stand in the path of sinners, nor sit in the seat of scoffers!" Here we find Peter, walking, standing, and sitting with those who instigated the Lord's suffering and death. Edwards correctly remarks:

> How awkward Peter looks in the courtyard of the high priest, trying to mingle with the henchmen who probably arrested Jesus and who will presently mock and beat him. . . . Peter has forsaken a discipleship of costly following (8:34) for one of safe observation.[13]

As Jesus stood before the hostile Sanhedrin, these wicked men, "obtain testimony against Jesus to put Him to death; and they were not finding any." This is a significant statement demonstrating that they were in search of evidence to support their predetermined conclusions. Mark continues, noting that

> many were giving false testimony against Him, and yet their testimony was not consistent. And some stood up and began to give false testimony against Him, saying, We heard Him say, "I will destroy this temple made with hands, and in three days I will build another made without hands."

The Greek word used for "temple" here is *naos* and is used by Mark only here and in 15:29 and 15:38. It refers to the sacred sanctuary itself, including the Holy of Holies. In the rest of Mark's gospel, the Greek word *hieron* is used, which refers to the entire temple complex (cf. 11:11, 15, 16, 27; 12:35; 13:1, 3; 14:49). The claim on the part of these witnesses was that Jesus had said that He would destroy the Holy Place and replace it Himself!

We have no such statement from Jesus, but we do have something that approaches this. In John 2:19 Jesus stated, "Destroy this temple, and in three days I will raise it up." Clearly the Jewish leaders did not understand Jesus, for they responded, "It took forty-six years to build this temple, and will You raise it up in three days?" (v. 20). John drives this point home by adding, "But He was speaking of the temple of His body" (v. 21). Although Jesus' words were not grasped, neither were they forgotten.

Jesus had made many statements that stirred up His opponents, and it is likely that they were recording His words to use against Him when the time was right. Moreover, they purposefully misconstrued these words recorded by John and blended them with Jesus' recent prediction concerning the destruction of the temple in Mark 13:2. The point of this accusation is clear. They were seeking a charge of blasphemy against Jesus, for to so speak of the Holy Place was to the Jews a crime punishable by death. In spite of their attempts to put words in Jesus' mouth, Mark notes that "not even in this respect was their testimony consistent."

This was problematic for Jesus' accusers because the law required the testimony of at least two witnesses before the accused could be declared guilty and worthy of death (Deut. 17:6), but in their zeal to arrest Jesus, they had not had sufficient time to adequately coach the witnesses. The fact that they could not find any solid witnesses against Jesus was significant and reason for acquittal, but this was not to be.

Since the false witnesses were unable to agree, "the high priest stood up and came forward and questioned Jesus, saying, 'Do You make no answer? What is it that these men are testifying against You?'" Caiaphas's actions reveal that false witnesses or not, Jesus would be found guilty. He was not concerned with the truth, and so he acted as if that which the false witnesses had stated was accurate and true.

The fact that none of the witnesses could corroborate the other's accusations meant that Jesus was not required to respond, so, "He kept silent and made no answer." His silence was foretold in Psalm 38:13–14 and Isaiah 53:7 and later alluded to by Peter (cf. 1 Peter 2:23). Seeing that they were getting nowhere, "Again the high priest was questioning Him, and saying to Him, Are You the Christ, the Son of the Blessed One?" Jesus now responded, but it is not immediately clear as to why. We must go to Matthew's parallel passage to understand this. Matthew notes that "the high priest said to Him, 'I adjure You by the living God, that You tell us whether You are the Christ, the Son of God'" (Matt. 26:63). A. T. Robertson remarks:

> Caiaphas put Jesus on oath in order to make him incriminate himself, a thing unlawful in Jewish jurisprudence. He had failed to secure any accusation against Jesus that would stand at all. . . . The charge that Caiaphas makes is that Jesus claims to be the Messiah, the Son of God. To refuse to answer would be tantamount to a denial. So Jesus answered knowing full well the use that would be made of his confession and claim.[14]

Caiaphas' use of the term "Christ" directly addressed Jesus' claim to be the promised Messiah, but his use of the term "the Son of the Blessed One" clearly addressed His claim to deity. It is clear from Caiaphas's charge that he and the Sanhedrin were fully aware of Jesus' claims. It is important to point out also that these two titles were not synonymous. The significance of their use together is that they bring together both facets of Jesus' claim. He is indeed both Messiah and God, the God-Man.

Having been put under an oath, Jesus replied, "I am; and you shall see the Son of Man sitting at the right hand of Power, and coming with the clouds of heaven." Jesus not only answered Caiaphas's question, but also declared that a day was coming when their roles would be reversed. Jesus' use of the prophetic language contained in Daniel 7:13–14 and Psalm 110:1 could not be misunderstood!

"And tearing his clothes . . ." Caiaphas's response once again demonstrated that he clearly understood Jesus' claims. Although Jesus had openly demonstrated that His claims were valid, they refused to recognize them. Ironically, as the religious leaders judged and condemned Him, they also judged and condemned themselves. John records:

> If I had not done among them the works which no one else did, they would not have sin; but now they have both seen and hated Me and My Father as

well. "But they have done this in order that the word may be fulfilled that is written in their Law, "they hated Me without a cause." (John 15:24–25)

In reality, Jesus' words were not blasphemy. Caiaphas deemed them so because he understood this statement was an assertion of Jesus' claim to both the status and authority of divinity. Edwards, quoting Robertson, explains:

> It is often supposed that Jesus' claim to be the Messiah triggered the explosion from the high priest and his condemnation by the Sanhedrin. This is not the case. It was no crime to call oneself the Messiah, or to be called so by others; . . . It was the claim to be God's Son (v. 62), not Messiah, that sealed Jesus' fate before the Sanhedrin. The charge of blasphemy is powerful, if indirect, proof of Jesus' claim to be the Son of God.[15]

Now that Caiaphas had the "evidence" that he so desperately sought, he cried out, "What further need do we have of witnesses?" No need for further delay! No need to continue with the proceedings! Lenski correctly notes:

> With one sweep he brushes aside the long proceedings in trying to secure false testimony. . . . With his quick turn Caiaphas gets rid of all the ineffectual testimony and inadvertently exposes the hollowness of his previous demand that Jesus make reply to these witnesses. As far as Caiaphas was concerned, Jesus had condemned himself; the whole case is settled here and now.[16]

Then Caiaphas called for immediate judgment, "'You have heard the blasphemy; how does it seem to you?' And they all condemned Him to be deserving of death." What followed was a travesty of the law and a disgrace of such profound depths as to break the heart of the stoutest soul. "And some began to spit at Him, and to blindfold Him, and to beat Him with their fists, and to say to Him, "Prophesy!" And the officers received Him with slaps in the face." These men—made up of the best educated, the most well-bred, and the most privileged—demonstrated their genuine nature. In the holding of an unlawful trial and the passing of this criminal verdict, they revealed that they cared not for God nor for the law they were duty bound to uphold.

> All these legal safeguards, which had been established in the interest of justice, were summarily overthrown. Yet not a single voice was raised in question, to say nothing of protest. The hatred of Jesus, which focused in the passionate demand of Caiaphas, carries away every judge present. "They all" without a single exception by a viva voce vote then and there condemned "him to be guilty of death." No reflection, no careful consideration is needed—all that had, of course, been attended to when the plot for the judicial murder of Jesus had been definitely laid.[17]

The Servant Denied by Peter (14:66–72)

(Compare Matthew 26:69–75; Luke 22:56–62; John 18:16–18, 25–27)

Mark now shifts back to Peter, resuming the narrative begun in Mark 14:54. By so doing, Mark reveals that the timing of Peter's testing corresponded with Jesus' trial. Mark explains that while Jesus stood before the Sanhedrin, "Peter was below in the courtyard . . . warming himself." Although he was concerned for his master, Peter made the mistake of thinking that he could suddenly become a secret disciple. This was not to be, because "one of the servant-girls of the high priest . . . seeing Peter warming himself, . . . said, You, too, were with Jesus the Nazarene." This Greek construction here suggests contempt on the part of the maid, for the word, "you" is emphatically placed and Jesus the Nazarene is more correctly translated "Jesus, that Nazarene." Her statement "You, too," suggests that she knew that John was also one of Jesus' disciples (cf. John 18:16).

Perhaps due to the abruptness of the statement or to the fact that he was afraid of being discovered and either cast out of the palace or, worse, taken before the Sanhedrin, Peter "denied it, saying, 'I neither know nor understand what you are talking about.' And he went out onto the porch." The porch was a covered passageway that led to the street. Peter left the inner court area and moved there to avoid further contact with those who might have recognized him.

Peter's efforts to maintain his anonymity however, were short-lived, because soon, another maid recognized him and exclaimed to those standing within the outer porch, "This is one of them!" More literally, "This man is of them." Peter's response was again to deny (imperfect middle indicative deponent of *arneomai*, literally, "kept on denying") that he knew Jesus. It seems that Peter may have carried on an informal conversation with the bystanders, because he was once again accused of being one of Jesus' disciples due to his regional accent (cf. v. 70). Realizing that he could not cover up this fact, he immediately began "to curse and swear, [both present active infinitives suggesting continual or repeated action], 'I do not know this man you are talking about!'" This does not mean that Peter began to use vulgarity. Actually, the idea here is that he put himself under an oath to attest to the truth of his denial. The irony of this statement is incredible. All of Israel knew of Jesus, yet Peter hoped to save his skin by claiming ignorance! He even refused to speak the name of His master, choosing rather to refer to him as "this man."

Mark tells us that at this point the cock crowed for the second time, and when Peter heard it he "remembered how Jesus had made the remark to him, 'Before a cock crows twice, you will deny Me three times.' And he began to weep."

The crowing of the rooster punctuates Peter's denial as Jesus had predicted (14:30), and the spokesman for the disciples who had himself been like the cock in his prideful self-sufficiency (14:29, 31) breaks down and weeps at what he has done. The contrast between Jesus and Peter in two parallel courtrooms within sight of each other and at the same moment of truth renders a warning to Mark's readers that at whatever the cost they must bear true witness to the One who ultimately matters, or there will be bitter weeping.[18]

Ironically, even as the Sanhedrin was abusing and mocking Jesus, calling Him a false prophet, His prophetic words concerning Peter were being fulfilled within a few feet of them (14:65)!

Study Questions

1. What was Judas's motivation in betraying Christ?

2. What seems to be the deep inner reasons Mary may have anoint the Lord?

3. What connection is there between the Passover meal and the Lord's Supper?

4. Why did Jesus pray three times in the garden? Do the prayers form a progression and build upon each other?

5. Why didn't the soldiers repent when Jesus healed the severed ear?

6. Who was the young man who fled, leaving his garment? What is so important about this fact, and why do you think it is included in Mark?

7. What does it mean to forsake Christ? How could we be guilty of this sin today?

8. What did the high priest do when Jesus finally spoke?

CHAPTER 15

The Servant Obedient unto Death
Mark 15:1-47

Preview:

As Christ stood before Pilate, it was he, not Christ who was really on trial. Christ's blood was on Pilate's hands, and public hand washing could not remove his own guilt. Against his better judgment, Roman law, and his wife's pleas, he, for political expediency, delivered Jesus to be crucified. Turned away by Pilate, spurned by His own people, and forsaken by His disciples, the Servant was obedient unto death (Phil. 2:8) and went to the cross to die for our sins. "He saved others; himself he cannot save," cried a mocking multitude, uttering more truth than they could possibly imagine. After agonizing hours on the cross, the Savior fulfilled His grand design to be made sin for us who knew no sin, "that we might become the righteousness of God in Him" (2 Cor. 5:21).

Christ on Trial (15:1-15)

(Compare Matthew 27:11-26; Luke 23:2-3, 18-25; John 18:28-19:16)

Mark is careful to point out the time frame of the events of Jesus' trial in light of their blatant disregard of Jewish law. At least three aspects of the law were set aside by the Sanhedrin: (1) a trial involving a capital crime and the subsequent verdict for that crime could only take place during the daytime; (2) if found guilty, the accused could not be convicted until the day after the trial; and (3) capital trials were never allowed on the eve of a Sabbath or Holy day.[1]

Since an *official* sentence could only be declared in the daytime, Mark records that "the chief priests with the elders and scribes, and the whole Council met early in the morning" (cf. Matt. 27:1; Luke 22:66). The Sanhedrin had predetermined the death of Jesus during the illegal night trial, but in order to simulate legality, they held a formal meeting as soon as morning dawned.

This meeting was necessary because the Sanhedrin did not have the authority to execute the death sentence (cf. John 18:31). It also served the following two purposes: (1) it informed those members of the Sanhedrin who had not been present the night before of the so-called blasphemy of Jesus; and (2) since the Roman authorities would not have heard a case about religious blasphemy, it gave the Sanhedrin the opportunity to prepare criminal charges that would stand up in the Roman legal system. Once this was accomplished, the Sanhedrin, "binding Jesus, . . . led Him away, and delivered Him up to Pilate." Royce Gordon Gruenler points out the irony of these actions.

> The Sanhedrin, while rejecting Jesus for blasphemy and failure to be their political king, bind Jesus over to Pilate on the dishonest and hypocritical charge that Jesus is a political pretender, which they know to be false. Thus the cost of getting rid of Jesus is a travesty of justice that denies Old Testament jurisprudence.[2]

Pontius Pilate was the fifth Roman to hold the title of prefect of Judea. He served in this capacity for ten years (A.D. 26–36). He was known for his hatred of the Jews, and during his term of office his harsh treatment of offenders was the norm (cf. Luke 13:1–2). As prefect he lived in Caesarea in a permanent residence provided by Rome, but during the Jewish festivals, he traveled to Jerusalem to ensure that order was maintained. When Jesus finally stood before Pilate, he asked him, "Are You the King of the Jews?" to which Jesus responded, "It is as you say."

Jesus' answer was troublesome to Pilate because Jesus had indicated by His response that He was indeed the King of the Jews. Pilate therefore sought out more evidence. The chief priests saw this as a good sign and immediately "began to accuse Him harshly." Since Jesus was before the Roman court, He had the right to defend Himself, but to Pilate's amazement, Jesus "made no further answer." Ironically, just as the high priest had done earlier, Pilate demanded of Jesus, "Do You make no answer? See how many charges they bring against You!" Jesus could have responded and given Pilate clear proof of His innocence, thus saving Himself from the cross, but His silence was prophesied (Isaiah 53) and demonstrated His desire to fulfill the Father's will. Pilate, "was amazed" at the fact that Jesus made no attempt to answer His accusers, for it was unnatural for the accused not to defend himself and even to plead for mercy.

> It was an amazing spectacle, since Pilate expected the usual voluble protestations of innocence. Pilate marveled, continued to feel wonder and astonishment at the refusal of Jesus to bring any pressure to bear on the gover-

nor in His own behalf. He recognized it as a difficult thing to do, and he somehow admired Jesus for it. It did not lead Pilate to conclude that Jesus was guilty as charged.[3]

Pilate began to suspect that Jesus was innocent, and learning that Jesus was a Galilean, he attempted to escape from having to deal with this case by sending Jesus to Herod Antipas, governor of Galilee. Herod, however, returned Jesus to Pilate, forcing him to take the responsibility of the outcome (cf. Luke 23:6–12).

Mark notes that "at the feast [the Passover] he [Pilate] used to release for them any one prisoner whom they requested." The Greek verb "released" (*apoluō*) is in the imperfect tense, thus indicating a customary action, and could better be translated "would release." It appears that this was a custom Pilate may have initiated in order to maintain the good will of the Jews. The fact that it was "whom they requested" makes it clear that the choice was theirs.

Most likely a large group of people had gathered to ask for the release of some prisoner, perhaps Barabbas. The Jewish leaders, knowing that this was Pilate's custom, used this to their advantage, stirring up the people to demand that Pilate should do as he had always done. Verse 10 makes it clear that Pilate understood their motive (envy) for delivering Jesus up to him, and because of this, he had made at least three separate attempts to free Jesus, stating, "I find no guilt in Him" (John 18:38; 19:4, 6). Moreover, in Luke 23:14–16 Pilate called the chief priest and the rulers into a private meeting and told them:

> You brought this man to me as one who incites the people to rebellion, and behold, having examined Him before you, I have found no guilt in this man regarding the charges which you make against Him. No, nor has Herod, for he sent Him back to us; and behold, nothing deserving death has been done by Him. I will therefore punish Him and release Him.

Despite Pilate's efforts, the pressure from the Jewish leaders was relentless. When the multitude (led by the Jewish leaders) began demanding that Pilate fulfill his customary prisoner release, Pilate must have thought he had finally found a solution to his problem. Here was an opportunity for him to extricate himself from what was turning into a legal fiasco. Surely, given the choice between Barabbas, a confirmed murderer (v. 9), and this "pretender to the Jewish throne," the Jewish leaders and the people would choose Jesus! After all, Barabbas stood already condemned, and many think that this Barabbas was in fact the criminal for whom the third cross was actually prepared.

To make their choice easier, Pilate, in what appears to have been an effort to contrast Barabbas and Jesus, asked them, "Do you want me to release for you the King of the Jews?" In other words, Pilate wanted the leaders to recognize the utter absurdity of this whole matter. Although the supposed charges laid against Jesus were serious, they certainly did not compare with the evidence against Barabbas! If Pilate could get them to acknowledge this, then they would also have to acknowledge that the correct choice for release would have to be Jesus, and Pilate could put and end to this debacle!

Offered the choice of Barabbas or Jesus, the people demanded Barabbas. Although surprised, Pilate still hoped to get off the hook and asked the multitude, "Then what shall I do with Him whom you call the King of the Jews?" Pilate, although disappointed with their choice, still desired to free Jesus. It seems that he meant to suggest that he would be willing to release Jesus if that was their desire. Surely this would be seen as a magnanimous offer that none could refuse. They would get Barabbas and Jesus!

The response of the multitude again took Pilate by surprise as they cried out, "Crucify Him!" This was not what he imagined he would hear, and bewildered he replied, "Why, what evil has He done?" Still hoping to release Jesus, Pilate asked for what charge Jesus should be crucified. But mob rule prevailed, and the multitude "shouted all the more, Crucify Him!"

> The mob spirit was beginning to rise, which is a terrible thing especially in the East. The more they yelled, the more agitated the scene became. One word from Pilate could even now have gained control—a sharp military order to the chiliarch of the cohort of 600 legionaries to clear the place of Jews in short order and to protect Jesus from molestation. But Pilate was long past such a courageous course of action. His very vacillation invited this Jewish insistence that he bow to their will. In that loud yelling and its incipient threatening tone we see where the mastery lay.[4]

One of the saddest comments ever made is said about Pilate, who knowing that Jesus was innocent and worthy of release, chose rather "to satisfy the multitude." Politics won out over justice that day and sadly, often does so today. The people now contented, Pilate, "after having Jesus scourged, . . . delivered Him to be crucified." Although Pilate delivered Jesus up for scourging, John notes that he made one final appeal to release Jesus, declaring, "Behold, I am bringing Him out to you, that you may know that I find no guilt in Him" (John 19:4). It was only after the multitude and the leaders saw Jesus in this wretched state that they ultimately cried out for His death. Ray Stedman explains:

> Now I think we have to ask why they chose Barabbas. The answer seems to be that they were disappointed with Jesus. This was the crowd which, just a few days before, had welcomed him into Jerusalem. The city was filled with people Jesus had healed. The eyes of the blind had been opened, the deaf made to hear, and the lame to walk. There must have been hundreds and probably thousands of people in Jerusalem at that time whom Jesus

had touched personally. He had awakened within the people the hope, the flaming desire, that this was indeed the Messiah come to deliver them from the yoke of Rome. All their ideas of messiah-ship centered around the thought that he would be the one who would set them free from the hated bondage of Rome. Now, when they saw him standing helpless before the Roman governor, saw his apparent unwillingness or inability to make any defense, or to get out of this by any means, or to do anything against the Romans, all their loyalty to him collapsed.[5]

Christ Smitten and Mocked (15:16–21)

(Compare Matthew 27:27–32; Luke 23:26–43; John 19:1–16)

Once Pilate had given the order, "the soldiers took Him away into the palace (that is, the Praetorium), and they called together the whole Roman cohort." A cohort consisted of some six hundred men. Where the Jewish leaders had mocked Jesus for claiming to be their Messiah, the Romans now mocked Him for claiming to be the King of the Jews.

As part of this mockery, they "dressed Him up in purple, and after weaving a crown of thorns, they put it on Him; and they began to acclaim Him, 'Hail, King of the Jews!' And they kept beating His head with a reed, and spitting at Him, and kneeling and bowing before Him." The question must be asked why they dealt so with Jesus. Although they may have been familiar with Him and His activities, surely they knew that He was no threat, but "savagery begets savagery."[6] Stedman explains:

> Why this strange mockery? I think the answer is revealed in what they said to him: "Hail, King of the Jews!" They were not angry at Jesus. They probably had never seen him before and knew very little about him. But they were angry at the Jews. All the pent-up hatred and resentment against this stubborn and difficult people came pouring out and found its object in this lonely Jew whom they understood was regarded in some sense as King of the Jews. All the foul mass of bigotry and racial hatred came pouring out against Jesus.[7]

These loyal Roman soldiers welcomed the opportunity to express their anti-Jewish feelings toward this man who claimed to be the King of the Jews. Here was an opportunity to demonstrate in the most extreme manner what they thought about any Jewish expectations for a king and nation outside of the authority of Rome.

This mocking was prophesied in the Old Testament (cf. Isa. 50:6; 53:5; Mic. 5:1) and came after Jesus had been scourged. It is incredible, given the savagery of the scourging itself, that Jesus was able to stand up under the unrelenting inhuman treatment He received at the hands of the soldiers. In describing this mockery, Mark notes that the soldiers smote Jesus, spit upon Him, and pretended to worship Him. In each case, the Greek tense used is the imperfect illustrating the repetitious process involved. In other words, the soldiers lined up and one after another bitterly mocked Jesus. Ironically, their actions foreshadowed the honor Jesus would receive from the Father once He was raised from the dead (cf. Phil. 2:5–11).

John notes that immediately after the mocking and before Jesus was led out to be crucified, Pilate once again presented Jesus to the crowd, hoping it seems, that they would see Jesus in His weakened state and allow Pilate to set Him free. As Jesus came before them, Pilate cried out, "Behold, the Man!" (John 19:5). The chief priests again cried out "Crucify, crucify!" (John 19:6). Pilate once again stated that he had found no fault in Jesus. To this, the Jewish leaders responded that Jesus should be crucified because "He made Himself out to be the Son of God" (John 19:7). Now the truth finally came out. Jesus was not the political person they had made Him out to be. Jesus was delivered up to Pilate strictly for "religious" reasons! This took Pilate by surprise and taking Jesus inside, he again questioned Him, asking, "Where are You from?" (John 19:9). Jesus' remained silent. Pilate remarks that it is in his power to release or crucify Him. Jesus' response again revealed that He was innocent of any crime, and Pilate again sought to release Him (John 19:10–12).

The final decision to crucify the Lord Jesus (John 19:16) came when the Jewish leaders told Pilate, "If you release this Man, you are no friend of Caesar; everyone who makes himself out to be a king opposes Caesar" (John 19:12). Upon hearing this, Pilate set aside any further attempts to rescue Jesus and delivered Him up to be crucified.

Tradition indicates that Jesus carried the crossbeam (weighing about 100 pounds) until He reached the gates of the city. Once there, however, the physical abuse He had undergone began to take its toll, so the Roman soldiers looked into the crowd that had gathered and forced "into service a passer-by coming from the country, Simon of Cyrene . . . to bear His cross."

We know very little about this man, but it is likely that he had traveled from his home in Africa to celebrate the Passover. Some commentators believe that because of his part in Jesus' crucifixion, he may have remained in Jerusalem until Pentecost and may have been among the men who responded to Peter's first sermon (cf. Acts 2:10). In his greeting to the Romans (Rom. 16:13), Paul mentions Rufus, along with his mother. If this is the same person mentioned by Mark, Simon's family must have been well known to the early Church and especially to Mark's audience.

Roman soldiers would never carry a prisoner's cross, so they used their authority to press Simon into service. Interestingly, by compelling Simon to carry Jesus' cross, the soldiers, knowingly or not, forced Simon to become ceremonially unclean, for the Jews regarded the cross as accursed. This defilement would have prevented him from celebrating the Passover, the very reason he was in Jerusalem! Ironically, "Simon had come to Jerusalem to celebrate the Passover (Acts 2:10; 6:9), and he ended up meeting the Passover Lamb!"[8]

Christ on the Cross (15:22–41)

(Compare Matthew 27:33–44; Luke 23:26–49; John 19:17–37)

The Roman soldiers led Jesus, "to the place Golgotha, which is translated, Place of a Skull." The exact location of Golgotha is uncertain, but it was "near the city" (cf. John 19:20). It got its name from the fact that it was a rounded, rocky hill that resembled a human skull. Although we do not know specifically where our Lord was crucified, it is not really important. What *is* important is that He *was* crucified, buried, and resurrected, and that He died for the sins of the world.

Upon reaching Golgotha, the soldiers tried to give Jesus a numbing substance referred to as "wine mixed with myrrh." This was not an act of kindness but was given to make the victim easier to control. Jesus, however, would not drink it, preferring rather to be fully conscious and in possession of all His faculties. He had been tested in the Garden of Gethsemane and had determined to drink fully the cup that the Father had given Him, the cup that would provide salvation for all who would believe.

Perhaps due to the fact that his audience was familiar with the procedures involved in crucifixion, Mark merely states the obvious—that Jesus was crucified and that it was done at the third hour. Luke notes that as the executioners set about to nail Him to the cross, Jesus' only words were, "Father, forgive them; for they do not know what they are doing" (Luke 23:34).

Having completed their task, the soldiers then "divided up His garments among themselves, casting lots for them, to decide what each should take." Little did these Roman soldiers realize that they were fulfilling David's prophecy in Psalm 22:18.

As part of the process of crucifixion, the offender's crime was spelled out in Greek, Latin, and Hebrew and prominently placed for all to see. Mark notes that "the inscription of the charge against Him read, 'THE KING OF THE JEWS.'" The chief priests were offended at this deliberate lack of respect directed toward them and demanded that Pilate change the accusation to read, "He said, 'I am King of the Jews'" (John 19:21) but Pilate refused (John 19:22).

Mark tells us there were "two robbers with [Jesus], one on His right and one on His left," who were crucified with Him. It is likely that these two men were associated with Barabbas, who also was called a robber. This was a direct fulfillment of Isaiah 53:12, a point not missed by Mark, "And the Scripture was fulfilled, which says, 'And He was numbered with transgressors.'"

Now hanging on the cross, Jesus, broken and naked, had to endure the shame of exposure and further humiliation as "those passing by were hurling abuse at Him, wagging their heads, and saying, "Ha! You who are going to destroy the temple and rebuild it in three days, save Yourself, and come down from the cross!" Lenski remarks:

> We learn who "those passing by" were when we listen to what they say. These are Jews from the city, for they repeat the very thing that was said in the night session of the Sanhedrin by the last two false witnesses about destroying the Sanctuary, etc. (14:57–59) . People who came from a distance could not have used words such as these in blaspheming Jesus, these could have been said only by people who were from the city, who had heard some of the details of the night trial before the Sanhedrin.[9]

These people shook their heads as they passed by Jesus, expressing their disapproval of His claim to be King of the Jews. The word that is translated "hurling abuse" is actually the imperfect, active indicative of the verb *blasphēmeō*, meaning "to slander, revile, defame, speak irreverently, impiously, disrespectfully of or about."[10]

In the very same manner, "the chief priests also, along with the scribes, were mocking Him among themselves and saying, "He saved others; He cannot save Himself. "Let this Christ, the King of Israel, now come down from the cross, so that we may see and believe!" How these "religious" men could have stood by the cross watching the Savior's suffering and carrying on so is unfathomable. What is worse, they, unlike those others who had been blaspheming Jesus, ignored Him, speaking of Him in the third person as if He couldn't see or hear them! By so doing they were making a statement that He was a nobody, a nonperson.

It is not only the fact that they mocked Christ but the content of their mocking that is important. The logic they used was that He obviously did not really save (help) anyone because He could not even save (help) Himself. This was a direct attack on Jesus' miracles and His purpose. Finally, they taunted that if He really was the Messiah, He would come down from the cross, and then they would believe. But they did not understand that if Jesus had indeed come down from that cross, their belief would not have mattered, for they would have had no hope of eternal salvation! Because of God's predestined plan, Jesus could not have saved Himself and at the same time saved them!

If this was not enough, even "those who were crucified with Him were casting the same insult at Him." Initially both of the thieves joined in with the rest as they repeatedly reproached Jesus (imperfect, active indicative of *onei-dizō*), "to find fault in a way that demeans the other; reproach, revile, mock, heap insults upon as a way of shaming").[11] However, Luke records that eventually one of these men repented—no doubt due to the way the Lord conducted Himself while on the cross (Luke 23:40–43).

Mark next records that "when the sixth hour had come, darkness fell over the whole land until the ninth hour." That was the first awful sign connected with the crucifixion. It was awful in the sense that it began at noon (the sixth hour) when the sun was at its peak and would have been producing maximum light. Most likely the people had at sometime in their lives seen an eclipse. But this was no eclipse. This strange, thick darkness lasted until three o'clock (the ninth hour). Although the people did not know what this darkness was all about, it is clear that it signified God's judgment (cf. Isa. 5:30; 9:19; Joel 2:31; 3:14–15; Amos 8:9–10) as it was about to fall upon His own Son. Louis Barbieri comments on this verse:

> This could not have been a natural phenomenon, for the Passover of the Jews always occurred at the time of the full moon. It would be impossible for an eclipse to darken the sun, and no eclipse ever lasts for three hours. The darkness was an indication of the judgment of God.[12]

At three o'clock (the ninth hour) in the afternoon, "Jesus cried with a loud voice, '*Eloi, Eloi, lama sabachthani?*' which is translated, 'My God, my God, why hast Thou forsaken Me?'" "*Eloi, Eloi, lama sabachthani*" is Aramaic, not Hebrew or Greek. Whereas Greek was the language used for commerce and trade and Hebrew was the language used for worship, Aramaic was the common language used among the Jews. This will be important in verse 36.

The darkness had rested over the land of Israel for three hours. No doubt many wondered if it would ever lift. This darkness, however, as previously indicated, was not natural. It, like the darkness that covered the land of Egypt, was a curse. Not a curse upon the land, but a curse upon the Son. For the first time in His entire existence, the Son, acting as the Lamb of God, was rejected by the Father and therefore cried, " My God, my God, why hast Thou forsaken Me?"

R. Alan Cole explains that part of the agony is the suffering of one experiencing God abandoning His own, but there is also here the certainty of faith in the final vindication and triumph. But to what was Christ abandoned, and why? There is more than simply the fact that Christ knew all along what was coming. There was the deep spiritual agony which the Lord endured alone in the darkness, an agony which we can never comprehend. No created being has ever endured such rejection. No explanation is adequate other than the old traditional idea that, in that dark hour, Christ was experiencing the wrath of God that was due sinners. This is not an abstract idea. Christ's eternal communion with His heavenly Father was somehow temporarily shattered. Since the Son knew no sin (1 Cor. 5:21), it had to be the sin of those for whom He died that brought about the separation. Here is the heart of the cross. And it is impossible for us to fully realize the actual nature of that punishment for sin. The true agony of the cross could only be understood and borne by Christ![13]

There was a common tradition among the Jews that Elijah would descend from heaven to rescue the righteous in times of crisis. However, Jesus' words could not have been misconstrued to mean that He was calling for Elijah, because they were "cried . . . with a loud voice." Nevertheless, when "some of the bystanders heard it, they began saying, 'Behold, He is calling for Elijah.'" Hiebert points out:

> The assertion is intelligible only as a piece of mockery. It reveals their continued animosity toward Jesus. Their prefatory interjection, Behold, sarcastically calls attention to what they claim is taking place. Jesus' cry, "My God, my God" (Eli, Eli, Matthew), is asserted to be a call for Elijah (Elias).[14]

Mark records that at this outcry, "someone ran and filled a sponge with sour wine, put it on a reed, and gave Him a drink, saying, "Let us see whether Elijah will come to take Him down." The English here is somewhat misleading. Since those who had been crucified were always under guard, it is certain that the one who went for the sponge was a Roman soldier and not one of the bystanders. This Roman soldier, who probably did not understand Aramaic, had heard what the bystanders were sarcastically saying amongst themselves in Greek about Elijah. Not sure whether they were serious or not, He wanted to see if Elijah would come and so he commanded, "Let us see whether Elijah will come to take Him down." This second person plural command (You all) is addressed *to* the bystanders. A very literal translation would be, "Don't hinder me, let's see."

The filling of a sponge with vinegar, according to John, was prompted by Jesus' cry, "I am thirsty" (John 19:28). This sour wine (*oxos*) "relieved thirst more effectively than water and, being cheaper than regular wine, it was a favorite beverage of the lower ranks of society and of those in moderate circumstances"[15] (cf. Ruth 2:14). Unlike the stupefying drink offered to Jesus earlier, this drink contained no myrrh.

All of the synoptists report that " Jesus uttered a loud cry." This was His second loud cry (cf. v. 34). Matthew and Mark merely report this fact. John, on the other hand, actually records the words that made up Jesus' second loud cry: "It is finished!" (John 19:30). Immediately after this victory cry, Luke notes the words of Jesus' calm and final commitment—"Father, into Thy hands I commend My spirit"—after which Jesus "breathed His last" (Luke 23:46). The manner in which Jesus actually died reveals that His life was yielded voluntarily. His was a supernatural death in that unlike others who normally suffered extended periods of collapse and blackout before dying, Jesus was in total control throughout the entire ordeal.

At the very moment of Jesus' death, a simultaneous and instantaneous event took place that was recorded by each of the synoptists, namely, "the veil of the temple was torn in two from top to bottom." Barbieri remarks:

> This event occurred at the very moment that a priest was in the holy place preparing for afternoon prayer. That priest probably thought his life was over as the veil was rent and the way into the holy of holies was there for him to see. He was, of course, in no danger, for the glory of the Lord representing His presence had departed from the first temple before its destruction by the Babylonians in 586 B.C. (see Ezek. 10:18–19; 11:22–25). The glory of the Lord will not return to the temple until it is again built in the millennial age (see Ezek. 43 ff.). The significance of this sign is stated by the writer of the book of Hebrews (Heb. 10:19–20). It is clear that Jesus Christ has inaugurated for all mankind access into the very presence of a holy God through His blood that He offered on Calvary's cross.[16]

At Golgotha, Mark notes that the centurion, observing the manner in which Jesus died, was moved to exclaim, "Truly this man was the Son of God!" What was it specifically that caused this tough soldier to make such a claim? Matthew adds that at the death of Jesus, "the earth shook; and the rocks were split" (Matt. 27:51). These physical events along with the unnatural darkness, convinced this hardened soldier that Jesus was no ordinary man!

> This centurion had doubtlessly seen other men die by crucifixion. But something in this crucifixion—in the very weakness and suffering of Jesus' death—becomes revelatory. The suffering of Jesus on the cross, which utterly contradicts both Jewish messianic ideals and Hellenistic "divine man" conceptions, becomes, by an act of God, the *window* into the heart and meaning of Jesus, the significance of which is only captured in the confession "the Son of God."[17]

The crucifixion pericope concludes with Mark noting that many of Jesus' friends also witnessed these events. Matthew and Mark mention only the women, while Luke notes that "all His acquaintances," literally, "those known to Him" were also present (Luke 23:40). This phrase in Greek is masculine and stands in contrast to the women mentioned. John makes it clear that he was the only one of the Twelve who was present (John 19:26–27), but the plural here clearly indicates that there were also other men. Perhaps this included Lazarus, Nicodemus, and Joseph of Arimathea.

Mark notes some of the key women by name, "Mary Magdalene, and Mary the mother of James the Less and Joses, and Salome." These women are identified elsewhere. Mary Magdalene was famous in her own right given her miraculous deliverance (Luke 8:2). Mary the mother of James the Less and Joses is referred to as "the other Mary" in Matthew 27:61. From a comparison with John 19:25, it is believed that she was sister to Mary the mother of Jesus. Salome is identified as the wife of Zebedee and the mother of James and John (cf. Matt. 20:20; 27:56).

It is significant, given the denial and departure of Jesus' "faithful" disciples, that these women are further designated as those who, "when He was in Galilee, . . . used to follow Him and minister to Him." Unlike His disciples, they had remained loyal to the end. Mark concludes by noting that there were "many other women who had come up with Him to Jerusalem" who were also present (cf. Luke 8:1–3).

Christ in the Tomb (15:42–47)

(Compare Matthew 27:57–61; Luke 23:50–56; John 19:38–42)

Jesus was now dead, and according to Mark, "it was the preparation day, that is, the day before the Sabbath." The Mosaic Law declared that one hanged on a tree must be buried before sunset (Deut. 21:22–23). Moreover, the next day was the Passover Sabbath! It was vitally important therefore that the body of Jesus be interred as soon as possible. But who would do this? The women were not able to take Jesus' body down from the cross, and the disciples were no where to be found. What was to become of the now lifeless body of Jesus? Would it be dragged off with the bodies of the two thieves? Isaiah had the answer to this when he wrote, "His grave was assigned with wicked men, yet He was with a rich man in His death" (Isa. 53:9).

Mark records that "Joseph of Arimathea came, a prominent member of the Council, who himself was waiting for the kingdom of God; and he gathered up courage and went in before Pilate, and asked for the body of Jesus." The term "member" (*bouleutēs*) specifically refers to the fact that Joseph was a member of the Sanhedrin. Concerning this man, John records that Joseph was "a disciple of Jesus, but a secret one, for fear of the Jews" (John 19:38). This was due to the fact that the Jewish leaders had threatened excommunication for anyone confessing that Jesus was the Messiah (John 9:22). Additionally, Luke notes that Joseph, "had not consented to [the Sanhedrin's] plan and action" concerning Jesus (Luke 23:51). Heibert remarks that Joseph now stepped forward to prevent the body of Jesus from being profaned by being thrown rudely into a common grave with the two criminals. He apparently knew that Pilate's order to hasten the death of the crucified meant that the bodies would be dumped into a common grave. . . . *Boldly*, an aorist participle, is perhaps best rendered "having dared" or "become bold." . . . It took courage to face Pilate, who would likely be in a bad mood toward all Sanhedrin members because they had forced him to crucify Jesus. Joseph also knew that to identify himself with the cause of Jesus would bring upon him the hostility of his colleagues. . . . In approaching Pilate he disregarded ceremonial defilement (cf. John 18:28), since success in his decision to secure and bury the body of Jesus would make him ceremonially unclean anyhow.[18]

The rapidity with which Jesus died surprised Pilate, because death by crucifixion was very slow, sometimes taking up to four days. Pilate therefore called the centurion who had overseen the process and "questioned him as to whether [Jesus] was already dead. And ascertaining this from the centurion, he granted the body to Joseph," no doubt glad that this day's events had finally come to an end.

Having been given the body of Jesus, Joseph then hurried about to secure the needed items required to prepare the body. This included "a linen cloth" with which to wrap the body and, "a mixture of myrrh and aloes, about a hundred pounds weight" supplied by Nicodemus (John 19:39). Unlike the Egyptians, the Jews did not embalm; therefore these spices were necessarily used to offset the stench of corruption. The linen was torn into long thin pieces, and the spices were spread between them as they were wrapped around the body.

With the help of Nicodemus, Joseph "took [Jesus] down from the cross." The body was then wound up in the linen and spices "as is the burial custom of the Jews" (John 19:40), after which they "laid Him in a tomb." John notes that the tomb was near at hand (John 19:41–42). Some commentators believe that Joseph and Nicodemus, believing Jesus' words concerning His death, had anticipated Jesus' crucifixion, and purposely purchased a tomb nearby. Matthew notes that the tomb belonged to Joseph (Matt. 27:60), but some scholars do not believe that Joseph intended it for himself. The reason given is that a rich man like Joseph would never have chosen to be buried near a place of execution. But this is speculation at best. What is certain is that by placing Jesus' body in Joseph's own tomb, Isaiah 53:9 was fulfilled.

Mark points out, as does Matthew (Matt. 27:60), that the tomb was "hewn out in the rock." These tombs were common and served as burial sites for entire families. They were cut directly out of the rock and had individual small rooms with shelves where the bodies were laid.

Once Jesus' body was in place, Joseph and Nicodemus "rolled a stone against the entrance of the tomb" sealing it within. The method of sealing was quite ingenious. On the outside of the sepulcher, a grooved, slanted incline was carved. This incline started above the floor of the sepulcher and ended slightly below it. A large, circular, flat stone, weighing up to half a ton, was then rolled down the incline until it was securely in front of the entrance. Grave robbers were thus kept out, because rolling the stone back up the incline required several very strong men.

Mark closes the burial pericope by noting that "Mary Magdalene and Mary the mother of Joses were looking on to see where He was laid." These two women had witnessed Jesus' death (cf. Mark 15:40) and now witnessed where their Master was buried. Donald A. Hagner explains the significance of this fact in his commentary on the parallel passage in Matthew.

> The two Galilean Marys sat . . . "across from the tomb," where they would have been able to watch Joseph put the body in the tomb and seal it with the huge stone. This note functions to certify correct knowledge concerning the specific tomb into which Jesus had been placed. Thus the empty tomb these same two women (i.e., the two witnesses; cf. 18:16) encounter in 28:1, 6 could not have been the wrong tomb.[19]

Given Mark's fast pace of events and the fact that the Sabbath was approaching, these key characters hardly had an opportunity to reflect upon the day's events. They must have been operating in a mental and emotional cloud. But now Jesus' body was sealed in the tomb' and the reality that He was now gone would overcome them like a flood.

Study Questions

1. Why did Jesus not answer Pilate?
2. What was Pilate's reaction to Christ's silence?
3. What was the Praetorium?
4. What Scriptures were fulfilled by Jesus' suffering and death?
5. How long was Jesus on the cross?
6. What did the centurion say about Jesus?
7. What is known about Mary Magdalene?

CHAPTER 16

The Servant's Glorious Triumph ·
Mark 16:1–20

Preview:
On that glorious first day of the week, the Resurrection and the Life emerged from the darkened tomb. The three women at the tomb were the first heralds of the good news. The angels appeared to them first. Jesus Himself then (John 20) appeared to Mary Magdalene, then to Mary the mother of James and to Salome (Matthew 28) on the road. There followed ten or eleven appearances, climaxing with Jesus' ascension, which is described in greater detail in Acts 1. The Gospel of Mark concludes with the gospel being spread abroad. That process is still continuing, and the Servant now intercedes on our behalf before His Father's throne!

The Resurrection of Christ (16:1–8)
(Compare Matthew 28:1–8; Luke 24:1–10; John 20:1–18)

"And when the Sabbath was over" indicates that these events took place on the Sunday immediately following the Sabbath (the Sabbath had ended at sundown on Saturday). "Mary Magdalene, and Mary the mother of James, and Salome" were not expecting Jesus to rise from the dead even though He had mentioned it on several occasions (cf. 8:31; 9:31; 10:34). Compelled by their love and respect for Jesus, these women "bought spices, that they might come and anoint Him." Like the spices used by Joseph and Nicodemus, these included fragrant oils that would be used to anoint the body to neutralize the stench of decay.

In their desire to complete the burial process that had been so hurriedly performed earlier, the women left their homes quite early and headed into Jerusalem. Mark notes that "very early . . . when the sun had risen" they came to the tomb. John and Luke agree, recording that it was still dark, probably just before dawn, when the women arrived at the tomb (Luke 24:1; John 20:1).

As the women entered the garden and moved in the direction of the tomb, they realized that they would not be able to move the great stone that covered its mouth. Concerned about this, they asked one another, "Who will roll away the stone for us from the entrance of the tomb?" Their questioning presupposes their ignorance of the fact that Pilate had given the Sanhedrin a watch of Roman soldiers to guard the tomb. This had been done specifically at the request of the Jewish leaders (cf. Matt. 27:62–66).

The women continued walking and talking until suddenly they found themselves standing at the entrance to the sepulcher. To their amazement, "looking up, they saw that the stone had been rolled away." In keeping with his style, Mark does not record all of the details as to how this came about, but Matthew records that, "a severe earthquake had occurred, for an angel of the Lord descended from heaven and came and rolled away the stone and sat upon it" (Matt. 28:2). The earthquake and the appearance of the angel of the Lord caused such fear in the soldiers who were watching the tomb that they "shook for fear of him, and became like dead men" (Matt. 28:4). It is important to remember that these were not mere weekend warriors. They were hardened Roman soldiers familiar with war and death.

The actions of the soldiers are important in the resurrection story because they add credibility to it. According to military law, if a Roman soldier left his post, he would be executed on the spot. Matthew records that not only did they leave their posts, but as they fled in fear, "some of the guard came into the city and reported to the chief priests all that had happened" (Matt. 28:11). The soldiers knew that they had a death sentence hanging over them, and they knew also that Pilate would not be merciful. This left only one place for them to go if they hoped to retain their lives—to the Jewish leadership. The soldiers' news forced the chief priests to call an emergency meeting to decide how best to suppress this information. The Sanhedrin's answer to the problem was first to make sure that these witnesses had the same story purchased with a bribe, so "they gave a large sum of money to the soldiers, and said, "You are to say, 'His disciples came by night and stole Him away while we were asleep'" (Matt. 28:12–13). Second, the Jewish leaders promised them that in the event that this information should come to Pilate, "we will win him over and keep you out of trouble" (Matt. 28:14). Since this was their only option, the soldiers "took the money, and did as they had been instructed." Matthew then adds that "this story was widely spread among the Jews, and is to this day" (28:15).

In the meantime, back at the garden, the women cautiously entered the tomb not knowing what they would find. Luke records that as they entered in they "did not find the body of the Lord Jesus" (Luke 24:3). This caused much concern on the part of these women. As they thought on these things, "they saw a young man sitting at the right, wearing a white robe; and they were amazed." Interestingly, Matthew and Mark mention the presence of only one heavenly being (identified by Matthew as an angel of the Lord, Matt. 28:2). Luke and John record that there were two men (Luke 24:4; John 20:12). There is no contradiction, however, since Luke and John are interested in substantiating the *number* of witnesses (cf. Deut. 17:6) while Matthew and Mark are concerned with the *message* they were witnessing.

Mark records that this "young man" told the women, "Do not be amazed; you are looking for Jesus the Nazarene, who has been crucified. He has risen; He is not here; behold, here is the place where they laid Him." John D. Grassmick remarks:

> The angel's message clearly identified the Risen One as the Crucified One, both referring to the same historical Person, and it revealed the meaning of the empty tomb. The certainty of the Resurrection rests on the angel's message from God which people then and now are called on to believe. The historical fact of the empty tomb confirms it.[1]

Then the women were commanded, "Go, tell His disciples and Peter, 'He is going before you into Galilee; there you will see Him, just as He said to you.'" This is the command we too have been given: "Go and tell!" Upon hearing and seeing these things, the women "went out and fled from the tomb, for trembling and astonishment had gripped them; and they said nothing to anyone, for they were afraid." D. Edmond Heibert remarks:

> The strong double-negative assertion, *neither said they anything to any man,* is peculiar to Mark. It cannot mean that they never delivered the message as directed (cf. Luke 24:9; Matthew 28:8). Mark's statement stresses that the stupendous events so unexpectedly encountered left them with mingled and confused emotions. *Were afraid* is imperfect tense, marking the duration of the feeling. The verb may denote alarm and fright, especially if the verse is regarded as an incomplete sentence. More probably the meaning here is reverential awe at the amazing message disclosed to them. It was an awesome message which they did not dare to break to others; only after they had found those to whom they were to give the message did they find themselves able to speak of it.[2]

Initially, because of their fear, the women remained silent. But they did not remain so for long, and the message reached the disciples and Peter shortly thereafter.

The Appearances of Christ (16:9-14)

(Compare Matthew 28:9-10, 16-17; Luke 24:9-10, 13-49; John 20:11-31)

In verses 9-14 Mark provides a summary of three separate appearances of the Lord after His resurrection. The emphasis is on the fact that even though there was eyewitness evidence to the resurrection, namely, Mary Magdalene (cf. John 20:11-18) and the two disciples (Luke 24:13-35), the disciples were so overcome with grief that they "refused to believe it." Although from a cultural perspective the dismissal of a woman's testimony was understandable, the fact that the witness of two "disciples" was also rejected radically underscores the intensity of their despair.[3] The only thing that would convince the disciples would be a personal visitation from the Lord Himself. Therefore, when the timing was right, Jesus "appeared to the eleven themselves as they were reclining at the table; and He reproached them for their unbelief and hardness of heart, because they had not believed those who had seen Him after He had risen" (cf. Luke 24:36-43; John 20:19-29). Alfred Plummer explains, "The Apostles may have been allowed to hear of the Resurrection before seeing the risen Christ in order that they might know from personal experience what it was to have to depend upon the testimony of others, as would be the case with their converts."[4]

The Commission of Christ (16:15-18)

(Compare Matthew 28:18-20; Luke 24:46-48)

Verse 15 is Mark's abbreviated account of the Great Commission seen in it's fullest form in Matthew 28:18-20 (cf. Luke 24:44-49; John 20:21-23; Acts 1:3-8). Jesus gives the command to, "Go into all the world and preach the gospel to all creation." Previously, the Eleven were restricted in their witness, preaching solely to the house of Israel (cf. Matt. 10:6) but now the middle wall of partition had been removed and the disciples were commanded to take the Gospel message into all the world (Eph. 2:14). H. A. Ironside remarks:

> The great commission was not given at one time only, but on several occasions, and in each instance there are differences that are of deep interest. In Mark 16:15-18 Jesus set forth His program of world evangelization in no uncertain terms. "Preach the gospel to every creature." The disciples

were to carry the good news of an accomplished redemption not only to Israel, to whom the message of the kingdom had been largely confined during the Lord's earthly ministry (Matthew 10:6), but "into all the world." Every barrier was to be thrown down so that the river of grace might flow out to all.[5]

Jesus assured them that as they preached some would believe and be baptized (v. 16). Some have tried to suggest that this passage teaches baptismal regeneration, but this is not the case. That baptism is an outward sign of commitment to Christ is understood when one considers that it is unbelief that brings damnation, not a failure to be baptized. Saving faith and baptism always go together but the order must never be reversed. Saving faith comes first, followed by believer's baptism. "Baptism is here put for the external signature of the inner faith of the heart, just as "confessing with the mouth" is in Romans 10:10; and there also as here this *outward* manifestation, once mentioned as the proper fruit of faith, is not repeated in what follows (Ro 10:11)."[6]

Verses 17–18 are often pointed to as evidences that believers should manifest supernatural giftings today. However, it should be noted that the Twelve had previously been given power to "Heal the sick, raise the dead, cleanse the lepers, cast out demons (cf. Matt. 10:8; Mark 6:7–13; Luke 10:1–20), and also that Paul regarded these signs as "the signs of an apostle" (2 Cor. 12:12). The only additional signs in verse 17–18 deal with speaking in "new tongues," taking up "serpents" and drinking "any deadly poison." With the exception of drinking deadly poisons, all of these "signs" were recorded in book of Acts as part of the authenticating ministry of the Holy Spirit in the lives of the New Testament apostles and prophets (cf. Acts 2:1–12; 4:30–33; 5:12; 9:12; 10:46; 16:18; 19:6; 28:3–5, 8).

Church history records that even before the end of the first century, these sign gifts were no longer extant. Moreover, the earliest Church fathers confirm that these "sign gifts" were unknown in their time. Some today are teaching that these "sign gifts" are valid today, but the reality in this present dispensation is that the authenticating ministry of the Holy Spirit is effected solely through the test of correct doctrine (cf. 2 John 9–10). There are no equivalent sign gifts today, nor are there equivalent offices of apostle and prophet today. Lenski correctly asserts:

They [sign gifts] followed those that came to faith (*pisteuō*, v. 17, aorist), and even then not promiscuously and like a common thing but in given cases as the Spirit saw fit. *When sufficient attestations were provided, these miraculous gifts ceased; for those recorded in Scripture were sufficient and stand today as signs and credentials for us, just as if they had been wrought before our eyes.* To call for an endless line of signs declares only that the original signs were not enough. But the Lord does not discredit himself and his promised signs in such a foolish way (emphasis added).[7]

The Ascension of Christ (16:19–20)

(Compare Luke 24:50–53; Acts 1:9–12)

Mark records that "when the Lord Jesus had spoken to them, He was received up into heaven, and sat sown at the right hand of God." Mark's comments here are characteristically brief, so the reader must go elsewhere to discover that Jesus actually continued schooling the disciples for an additional forty days before being "taken up into heaven" (cf. Luke 24:50–53; Acts 1:1–11). This is understandable when one considers that Mark's audience was familiar with the details of Jesus' resurrection and subsequent ascension. Mark is more concerned with the fact that his audience should understand that not only was Jesus received up into heaven, but He presently sits "at the right hand of God" (cf. Mark 12:36; 14:62; Acts 2:33–36; 7:56; see also Ps. 110:1).

> To speak of God's right is, of course, anthropomorphic, for as a spirit he has no right or left, nor do the Scriptures ever mention God's left. The right hand of God is his omnipotent majesty. . . . To sit at his right is to exercise that majestic omnipotence most fully. Jesus had exercised it in a limited way here on earth in his miracles. He now rules as the Almighty King and Lord forever. And he now does this in his human nature which alone was capable of such exaltation, and was capable of it only as being joined to the divine nature, for omnipotence, majesty, and all divine attributes were the property of the Son from all eternity.[8]

Mark concludes his gospel by noting that the disciples "went out and preached everywhere." Verse 20 is a summary conclusion to Mark's gospel. He does not fill in the gaps with details that are already known to his audience—specifically the conflicts that the Jerusalem church faced with regard to the question of Gentile inclusion in God's plan or the conflict with the Judaizers. Mark merely sums up the ultimate outcome—having been recommissioned and empowered, the Eleven set about to fulfill Christ's command. Where they had been weak and wavering in their earlier dedication to the Lord, they now went out joyfully, totally committed to Him, eager to tell others the Good News.

Mark also points out that as they went out, they did not go out alone, for the Lord "worked with them." The apostle Paul likewise reminded the Corinthians that they were "working together with [Christ]" (2 Cor. 6:1) and

"God's fellow workers" (1 Cor. 3:9). That the Lord was working with them was evidenced by the fact that He "confirmed the word by the signs that followed." Note that Mark here records the purpose of the sign gifts mentioned above. They authenticated (past tense) their message (cf. Heb. 2:3–4). In Ephesians 2:20 the apostle Paul makes it clear that the foundation for the Church was laid by the New Testament apostles and prophets, the Lord Jesus being the chief cornerstone in that foundation. The foundation could only be laid one time, after which the construction of the building (the body of Christ) formally began.

The work of laying the foundation is finished, and therefore the need for apostolic signs ceased. However, the commission to "Go into all the world, and preach the gospel to all creation" has not ceased. The Lord continues today working in and through His servants, proclaiming life to a lost and dying world.

These eleven apostles alone could not proclaim the gospel to the world, much less to *every creature* in it; but they and the other followers of Christ, seventy in number, with those who should afterward be added to them, would multiply themselves in many ways, and, wherever they went, they would carry the gospel along with them. They would also send others where they could not go. They would then be making it their very lives to send others with the truth throughout the entire world. This would not be a task of amusement or entertainment, but it would be the solemn Word of God to sinful men. "Tell as many as you can, and bid them tell others; it is a message of universal concern, and *therefore*, ought to *have* a universal welcome, because it *gives* a universal welcome."[9]

Study Questions

1. What emotions might have been in the hearts of the women as they discovered the empty tomb?

2. When did Christ arise from the dead?

3. How does this account compare with Matthew 26?

4. How many times did Jesus appear after His resurrection?

5. Why do you think a woman, Mary Magdalene, was selected to first see Jesus?

6. Where did Jesus appear to two disciples? What was the significance of that appearance?

7. What was the initial response of the apostles to the news of Jesus' resurrection?

8. Why isn't baptism essential to salvation? And what is its importance today?

BIBLIOGRAPHY

Barclay, William. *The Gospel of Mark*. Louisville: Westminster John Knox, 2001.

Brooks, James A. *The New American Commentary*: Mark. Nashville: Broadman, 1991.

Bruce, F. F. *The Canon of Scripture*. Downers Grove, IL: Intervarsity, 1988.

Cole, R. A. *The Gospel According to Mark: An Introductory and Commentary*. Grand Rapids: Eerdmans, 1989.

Edwards, James R. *The Gospel According to Mark—The Pillar New Testament Commentary*. Grand Rapids: Eerdmans, 2002.

Enns, Paul. *The Moody Handbook of Theology*. Chicago: Moody, 1989.

Guelich, R. A. *Word Biblical Commentary*: Mark 1:1—8:26. Dallas: TX: Word, 1998.

Hendriksen, William. *Exposition of the Gospel According to Mark*. Grand Rapids: Baker, 1975.

Hiebert, D. Edward. *Gospel of Mark*. Greenville, SC: Bob Jones University Press, 1994.

Lane, William. *The Gospel According to Mark, The New International Commentary of the New Testament*. Grand Rapids: Eerdmans, 1974.

Lenski, R. C. H. *The Interpretation of Mark's Gospel*. Minneapolis, MN: Augsburg Publishing House, 1946.

Pentecost, J. Dwight. *The Words and Works of Jesus Christ*. Grand Rapids: Zondervan, 1981.

Shedd, William G. T. *Dogmatic Theology*. Phillipsburg, NJ: P & R Publishing, 2003.

Sweet, Henry Barclay. *The Gospel According To St. Mark*. London: MacMillian, 1905.

Walvoord, John F. and Zuck, Roy, eds. *The Bible Knowledge Commentary*. Wheaton: Victor, 1985.

Wiersbe, W. W. *The Bible Expositional Commentary*. Wheaton: Victor: 1989.

NOTES

Introduction

1. R.C.H. Lenski, *The Interpretation Of St. Mark's Gospel* (Minneapolis: Augsburg Publishing House, 1946), 463-464.
2. Ibid., 101.
3. Norman L. Geisler, William E. Nix, *A General Introduction To The Bible* (Chicago: Moody Press, 1986), 288.
4. F.F. Bruce, *The Canon of Scripture* (Downers Grove: InterVarsity Press, 1988), 126.
5. Fragments of Papias, *The Ante-Nicene Fathers, Vol. I* (Albany: Sage Digital Library, 1996), 291.
6. Bruce, *op. cit.*, 127.
7. Ibid., 128.
8. Bruce Wilkinson & Kenneth Boa, *Talk Thru the Bible* (Nashville: Thomas Nelson Publishers, 1983), 319.
9. R.C.H. Lenski, *St. Paul's Epistles to the Colossians, to the Thessalonians, to Timothy, to Titus and to Philemon* (Minneapolis: Augsburg Publishing House, 1946), 868-869.
10. John F. Walvoord, and Roy B. Zuck, *The Bible Knowledge Commentary, New Testament* (Wheaton, Illinois: Scripture Press Publications, Inc., 1985), 99.
11. Ibid.
12. John F. MacArthur, Jr., *The MacArthur Study Bible*, (Dallas: Word Publishing, 1997), computer reference, no page given.
13. Wilkinson & Boa, *op. cit.*, 321.
14. Walvoord & Zuck, *op. cit.*, 99–100.
15. Ibid., 100.
16. MacArthur, Jr., *op. cit.*, computer reference, no page given.
17. Wilkinson & Boa, *op. cit.*, 322.

Chapter 1 – The Servant Begins His Ministry

1. James, A. Brooks, *The New American Commentary: Mark* (Nashville, TN: Broadman, 1991), 38.
2. R. A. Guelich, *Word Biblical Commentary : Mark 1-8:26* (electronic ed. Logos Library System; Word Biblical Commentary. Dallas: Word, Incorporated, 1998) Mk 1:9.
3. D. Edmond Hiebert, *Gospel of Mark: An Expositional Commentary* (Greenville, SC: Bob Jones University Press, 1994), 33.
4. See William. G. T. Shedd's, *Dogmatic Theology* , 3 vols. Vol. 2, (Reprint. Nashville: Nelson, 1980), page 330–349 for a thorough discussion of Christ's impeccability.

5. H. A Ironside, *Mark: Ironside Commentaries*, rev. ed. (Neptune, NJ: Loizeaux Brothers, 1994), 16-17.

6. Tim LaHaye Prophecy Study Bible, (AMG Publishers, 2000), 1051.

7. Lawrence O. Richards, *The Teacher's Commentary* (Wheaton, Ill.: Victor Books, 1987), Mk 1:1.

8. Matthew Henry, *Matthew Henry's Commentary On the Whole Bible, Vol. 5* (Peabody: Hendrickson Publishers, 1991), 370.

9. D. A. Carson, *New Bible Commentary : 21st Century Edition.* 4th ed. (Leicester, England; Downers Grove, Ill., USA: Inter-Varsity Press, 1994), Mk 1:35.

Chapter 2 – The Servant Responds to His Critics

1. W. W. Wiersbe, *The Bible Exposition Commentary* (Wheaton, Ill.: Victor Books, 1989) Mk 2:1.

2. Lawrence O. Richards, *The Teacher's Commentary*. Wheaton, Ill.: Victor Books) 1987. Mk 6:1.

3. W.A. Elwell, Editor, *Evangelical Commentary on the Bible*, Baker Reference Library (Grand Rapids, Mich.: Baker Book House, 1989), Mk 2:1.

4. Richards, *op. cit.*, Mk 2:1.

5. D. A. Carson, *New Bible Commentary : 21st Century Edition.* 4th ed. (Leicester, England; Downers Grove, Ill., USA: Inter-Varsity Press, 1994), Mk 2:13.

6. The use of the term "sinners" in v. 15 specifically refers to Jews who did not observe the Mosaic Law. To the Jewish leaders they were no better than Gentiles and were considered outcasts by them.

7. James A. Brooks, *The New American Commentary: Mark* (Nashville, TN: Broadman, 1991), 62.

8. R. C. H Lenski,. *The Interpretation of St. Mark's Gospel* (Minneapolis, MN: Augsburg Publishing House, 1946), 116.

9. D. Edmond Hiebert, *Gospel of Mark: An Expositional Commentary* (Greenville, SC: Bob Jones University Press, 1994), 76.

10. Wiersbe, W. W. *The Bible Exposition Commentary* (Wheaton, Ill.: Victor Books, 1989) Mk 2:23.

11. W. A. Elwell, Editor, *Evangelical Commentary on the Bible, Baker Reference Library* (Grand Rapids: Baker Book House, 1989) Mk 2:18–23.

Chapter 3 – The Servant Chooses the Twelve

1. John Walvoord & Roy Zuck, Gen. Editors, *The Bible Knowledge Commentary: An Exposition of the Scriptures, Vol. 2* (Wheaton, IL: Victor Books, 1985), 115.

2. D. Edmond Hiebert, *Gospel of Mark: An Expositional Commentary* (Greenville, SC: Bob Jones University Press, 1994), 84.

3. Lenski, R. C. H., *The Interpretation of St. Mark's Gospel* (Minneapolis, MN: Augsburg Publishing House, 1946), 134.

4. Walvoord & Zuck, *op. cit.*, 115.

5. Lenski, *op.cit.*

6. Hiebert, *op. cit.*, 86-87.

7. *NET Bible Notes : Study Notes for the New English Translation*, electronic edition (Dallas, TX: Biblical Studies Press, 1998), Mk 3:21.

8. Guelich, R. A., *Word Biblical Commentary: Mark 1-8:26* (Dallas, TX: Word, Inc., 1998), 175.

9. *King James Version Study Bible*, electronic ed. (Nashville: Thomas Nelson, 1988), Mk 3:28.

10. *Barnes' Notes, Electronic Database* (Biblesoft, 1997), Matt 12:31–32.

11. Giesler, Norman, *Bibliotheca Sacra, Issue 544* (Dallas TX: Dallas Theological Seminary, 1979), 342.
12. Lewis Sperry Chafer, *Systematic Theology, Vol VII* (Grand Rapids MI: Kregel, 1976), 48.
13. Paul. P. Enns, *The Moody Handbook of Theology* (Chicago, IL: Moody Press, 1989), 265.
14. Lenski, *op. cit.*, 156–157.
15. Hiebert, *op. cit.*, 104.

Chapter 4 – The Servant Teaches by the Seaside

1. *Theological Dictionary of the New Testament, Vol. 5*, ed. G. Kittel, G. W. Bromiley & G. Friedrich (Grand Rapids: Eerdmans, 1964–1976), 752.
2. W. W. Wiersbe, *The Bible Exposition Commentary* (Wheaton: Victor Books, 1989).
3. James, A. Brooks, *The New American Commentary: Mark* (Nashville: Broadman, 1991), 83.
4. R. A. Cole, *The Gospel According to Mark: an Introductory and Commentary* (Grand Rapids: Eerdmans, 1989), 115.
5. H. A Ironside, *Mark: Ironside Commentaries*, rev. ed. (Neptune: Loizeaux Brothers, 1994), 20.
6. William MacDonald, *Believer's Bible Commentary*, (Nashville: Thomas Nelson Publishers, 1995), 1329–30.
7. John Walvoord & Roy Zuck, Gen. Editors, *The Bible Knowledge Commentary: An Exposition of the Scriptures, Vol. 2* (Wheaton: Victor Books, 1985), 120.
8. MacDonald, *op. cit.*, 1331.
9. William Barclay, *The Gospel of Mark* (Louisville: Westminster John Knox, 2001), 120–122.
10. Ironside, *op. cit.*, 44.
11. Walvoord & Zuck, *op. cit.*, 120.
12. James, R. Edwards, *The Gospel According to Mark – The Pillar New Testament Commentary* (Grand Rapids, MI: Eerdmans, 2002), 143.
13. R. A. Guelich, *Word Biblical Commentary : Mark 1-8:26*, electronic ed., Logos Library System; (Dallas: Word, Incorporated, 1998).
14. Cole, *op. cit.*, 152–153.
15. Walvoord & Zuck, *op. cit.*, 121.
16. William Barclay, *The Gospel of Mark*, pgs. 126–127 (Louisville: Westminster John Knox, 2001), 126–127.
17. Wilbur, M. Smith, *Peloubet's Select Notes on the International Bible Lessons for Christian Teaching*, (Boston: W. A. Wilde Company, 1950), 31.
18. Edwards, *op. cit.*, 144–145.
19. Brooks, *op. cit.*, 85-86.
20. Walvoord & Zuck, *op. cit.*, 121.
21. Brooks, *op. cit.*, 85-86.
22. William Lane, *The Gospel According to Mark*, The New International Commentary of the New Testament (Grand Rapids: Eerdmans, 1974), 173.
23. Barclay, *op. cit.*, 132–133.

Chapter 5 – The Servant Manifests His Power

1. William Lane, *The Gospel According to Mark*, The New International Commentary of the New Testament (Grand Rapids: Eerdmans, 1974), 181.
2. James, R. Edwards, *The Gospel According to Mark – The Pillar New Testament Commentary* (Grand Rapids: Eerdmans, 2002), 155.
3. William Barclay, *The Gospel of Mark* (Louisville, KY: Westminster John Knox, 2001), 136.

4. John Walvoord & Roy Zuck, Gen. Editors, *The Bible Knowledge Commentary: An Exposition of the Scriptures, Vol. 2* (Wheaton: Victor Books, 1985), 122.
5. Kittel, G., Bromiley, G. W., & Friedrich, G., Editors, *Theological Dictionary of the New Testament, Vol.5* (Grand Rapids, MI: Eerdmans, 1976), 462-463.
6. Ibid. *Vol. 1*, 563.
7. Lane, *op. cit.*, 183–184.
8. Albert Barnes, *Barnes' Notes* (Biblesoft Electronic Database, 1997).
9. *The Pulpit Commentary*, (Biblesoft Electronic Database, 2001).
10. Edwards, *op. cit.*, 156–157.
11. Lane, *op. cit.*, 185–186.
12. Barclay, *op. cit.*, 138–139.
13. Edwards, *op. cit.*, 160–161.
14. Ibid., 146.
15. James, A. Brooks, *The New American Commentary: Mark* (Nashville: Broadman, 1991), 96.
16. R. A. Cole, *The Gospel According to Mark: an Introductory and Commentary* (Grand Rapids: Eerdmans, 1989), 161.
17. Lane, *op. cit.*, 195.
18. Edwards, *op. cit.*, 166.
19. Ibid.
20. Walvoord & Zuck, *op. cit.*, 125.
21. Barclay, *op. cit.*, 154–155.
22. Up to eleven and one day a girl was regarded as "a child"; from eleven years and one day to twelve years and one day as "under age"; from twelve to twelve and a half years as "a young daughter"; and from twelve and a half years as "an adult." Lane, William, *op. cit.*, 197.
23. Ibid., 198–199.

Chapter 6 – The Servant in His Great Galilean Ministry

1. D. Edmond Hiebert, *Gospel of Mark: An Expositional Commentary* (Greenville: Bob Jones University Press, 1994), 151–152.
2. J. Strong, *Enhanced Strong's Lexicon* (Ontario: Woodside Bible Fellowship, 1996).
3. Hiebert, *op. cit.*, 154.
4. Louis Barbieri, *Moody Gospel Commentary: Mark* (Chicago: Moody Press, 1995), 135.
5. G. Kittel, *Theological Dictionary of the New Testament*, (Grand Rapids: W.B. Eerdmans, 1985), 1036.
6. Frank E. Gaebelein, Ed., *The Expositor's Bible Commentary* (Grand Rapids,: Zondervan, 1992), *electronic edition.*
7. R. C. H. Lenski, *The Interpretation of St. Mark's Gospel* (Minneapolis: Augsburg Publishing House, 1946), 238.
8. Hiebert, *op. cit.*, 156.
9. William Lane, *The Gospel According to Mark*, The New International Commentary of the New Testament (Grand Rapids: Eerdmans, 1974), 204.
10. *KJV Bible Commentary, electronic ed.* (Nashville: Thomas Nelson, 1994).
11. Hiebert, *op. cit.*, 157.
12. David Hewitt, *Mark – Free to Follow Jesus* (Grand Rapids: Baker Books, 1995), 88.
13. Alexander Balmain Bruce, *The Expositor's Greek Testament, Vol. I* (Grand Rapids: Eerdmans Publishing, Reprinted 1990), 378–379.
14. Lenski, *op. cit.*, 240.
15. Hiebert, *op. cit.*, 158.

16. J. Swanson, *Dictionary of Biblical Languages With Semantic Domains: Greek (New Testament)* (Oak Harbor: Logos Research Systems, Inc., 1997).

17. Ibid.

18. R. A. Cole, *The Gospel According to Mark: an Introductory and Commentary* pg. 167–181 (Grand Rapids: Eerdmans, 1989), 167–181.

19. Lane, William, *op. cit.*, 208.

20. Lenski, *op. cit.*, 245.

21. Hewitt, *op. cit.*, 92.

22. James, R. Edwards, *The Gospel According to Mark – The Pillar New Testament Commentary* (Grand Rapids: Eerdmans, 2002), 189.

23. James A. Brooks, *The New American Commentary: Mark* (Nashville, TN: Broadman, 1991), 103 .

24. Hiebert, *op. cit.*, 173.

25. Ray C. Stedman, *Expository Studies in Mark 1-8: The Servant Who Rules* (Waco,: Word, 1976), 159.

26. A.T. Robertson, *Word Pictures in the New Testament, Vol 1* (Grand Rapids: Baker, 1930), 314.

27. Lenski, *op. cit.*, 262–263.

28. *Theological Dictionary of the New Testament, Vol. 7*, Ed. G. Kittel, G. W. Bromiley & G. Friedrich (Grand Rapids: Eerdmans, 1976), 554-555.

29. Brooks, *op. cit.*

30. Edwards, *op. cit.*, 191.

31. Lane, William, *op. cit.*, 228.

32. Barbieri, *op. cit.*, 149.

33. Hiebert, *op. cit.*, 184–185.

34. Barbieri, *op. cit.*, 152.

35. Lenski, *op. cit.*, 273.

Chapter 7 – The Servant Looks at the Heart

1. Stanley E. Jones, *Growing Spiritually*, Quoted in *Believers Bible Commentary* (Nashville: Thomas Nelson Publishers, 1995), 1337.

2. William Lane, *The Gospel According to Mark, The New International Commentary of the New Testament* (Grand Rapids: Eerdmans, 1974), 245–246.

3. R. C. H. Lenski, *The Interpretation of St. Mark's Gospel* (Minneapolis: Augsburg Publishing House, 1946), 290.

4. William Kelly, *An Exposition of the Gospel of Mark*, Quoted in the *Believers Bible Commentary* (Nashville, TN: Thomas Nelson Publishers, 1995), 1337.

5. Lenski, *op. cit.*, 293.

6. H. A. Ironside, *Mark: Ironside Commentaries* (Neptune, NJ: Loizeaux, 1994), 70.

7. Louis Barbieri, *Moody Gospel Commentary: Mark* (Chicago, IL: Moody Press, 1995), 163.

8. William MacDonald, *Believers Bible Commentary* (Nashville, TN: Thomas Nelson Publishers, 1995), 1338.

9. Lane, *op. cit.*, 259.

10. A. T. Robertson, *Word Pictures in the New Testament* (Oak Harbor: Logos Research Systems, 1997), Mk 7:26.

11. Lane, *op. cit.*, 261.

12. James, R. Edwards, *The Gospel According to Mark – The Pillar New Testament Commentary* (Grand Rapids: Eerdmans, 2002), 226–227.

13. K. S. Wuest, *Wuest's Word Studies from the Greek New Testament : For the English Reader* (Grand Rapids: Eerdmans, 1984), Mk. 7:35–36.

14. Robertson, *op. cit.*, Mk. 7:36.

Chapter 8 – The Servant Announces His Rejection and Death

1. James, A. Brooks, *The New American Commentary: Mark* (Nashville, TN: Broadman, 1991), 125.

2. Frank E. Gaebelein, Ed., *The Expositor's Bible Commentary* (Grand Rapids: Zondervan, 1992), *electronic edition*.

3. R. A. Cole, *The Gospel According to Mark: an Introductory and Commentary* (Grand Rapids: Eerdmans, 1989),193.

4. Louis Barbieri, *Moody Gospel Commentary: Mark*, pg. 174 (Chicago: Moody Press, 1995), 174.

5. Brooks, *op. cit.*, 124–125.

6. H. A. Ironside, *Mark: Ironside Commentaries* (Neptune: Loizeaux, 1994), 75.

7. R. C. H. Lenski, *The Interpretation of St. Mark's Gospel* (Minneapolis: Augsburg Publishing House, 1946), 320–321.

8. Gaebelein,

9. Gaebelein, *op. cit.*, *electronic edition*.

10. D. Edmond Hiebert, *Gospel of Mark: An Expositional Commentary* (Greenville: Bob Jones University Press, 1994), 222–223.

11. James, R. Edwards, *The Gospel According to Mark – The Pillar New Testament Commentary* (Grand Rapids, MI: Eerdmans, 2002), 236.

12. Brooks, *op. cit.*, 127.

13. The author's brother was born blind and thus this insight is offered from one familiar with the blind community.

14. Edwards, *op. cit.*, 246.

15. Lenski, *op. cit.*, 337.

16. Alfred Plummer, *The Gospel According to St. Mark* (Grand Rapids: Baker Book House, 1914), 203.

17. Barbieri, *op. cit.*, 173–192.

18. Hiebert, *op. cit.*, 240.

19. Hugh Anderson, *The Gospel of Mark, New Century Bible*, pg. 220 (London: Marshall, Morgan, & Scott, 1976), 220.

Chapter 9 – The Servant Reveals His Divine Glory

1. W. Arndt, *A Greek-English Lexicon of the New Testament and Other Early Christian Literature.* 3rd ed. (Chicago: University of Chicago Press, 2000), 195.

2. D. Edmond Hiebert, *Gospel of Mark: An Expositional Commentary* (Greenville: Bob Jones University Press, 1994), 241.

3. Arndt, *op. cit.*, 639.

4. R. A. Cole, *The Gospel According to Mark: an Introductory and Commentary* (Grand Rapids: Eerdmans, 1989), 210.

5. Ibid., 211.

6. H. A. Ironside, *Mark: Ironside Commentaries* (Neptune, NJ: Loizeaux, 1994), 84.

7. W. W. Wiersbe, *The Bible Exposition Commentary* (Wheaton: Victor Books, 1989), Mk 8:27.

8. Hiebert, *op. cit.*, 247.

9. R. Kent Hughes, *Mark, Volume Two* (Westchester: Crossway Books, 1989), 17.

10. James, R. Edwards, *The Gospel According to Mark – The Pillar New Testament Commentary* (Grand Rapids: Eerdmans, 2002), 269.

11. Louis Barbieri, *Moody Gospel Commentary: Mark* (Chicago: Moody Press, 1995), 199.

12. Hiebert, *op. cit.*, 249–250.

13. William Lane, *The Gospel According to Mark, The New International Commentary of the New Testament* (Grand Rapids: Eerdmans, 1974), 325–326.

14. R. C. H. Lenski, *The Interpretation of St. Mark's Gospel* (Minneapolis, MN: Augsburg Publishing House, 1946), 377–378.
15. Lane, *op. cit.*, 331.
16. Lenski, *op. cit.*, 382.
17. Lane, *op. cit.*, 335–336.
18. Hiebert, *op. cit.*, 259.
19. Lenski, *op. cit.*, 388–389.
20. Edwards, *op. cit.*, 287–288.
21. Hiebert, *op. cit.*, 263.
22. Barbieri, *op. cit.*, 211.
23. William MacDonald, *Believers Bible Commentary* (Nashville: Thomas Nelson Publishers, 1995), 1344.
24. Henry Barclay Swete, *The Gospel According to St. Mark* (London: Macmillian, 1905), 210.
25. Lane, *op. cit.*, 348.
26. John Walvoord & Roy Zuck, Gen. Editors, *The Bible Knowledge Commentary: An Exposition of the Scriptures, Vol. 2* (Wheaton: Victor Books, 1985), 147.

Chapter 10 – The Servant on His Way to Jerusalem

1. William Lane, *The Gospel According to Mark*, The New International Commentary of the New Testament (Grand Rapids: Eerdmans, 1974), 353.
2. R. C. H. Lenski, *The Interpretation of St. Mark's Gospel* (Minneapolis: Augsburg Publishing House, 1946), 414.
3. D. Edmond Hiebert, *Gospel of Mark: An Expositional Commentary* (Greenville: Bob Jones University Press, 1994), 276–277.
4. James, A. Brooks, *The New American Commentary: Mark* (Nashville: Broadman, 1991), 157.
5. Lenski, *op. cit.*, 419.
6. H. Lubbock, as quoted in the lecture notes of Dr. Jim Combs, Provost of Louisiana Baptist Theological Seminary.
7. C. S. Keener, *The IVP Bible Background Commentary : New Testament* (Downers Grove: InterVarsity Press, 1993), Mk 10:13.
8. W. W. Wiersbe, *The Bible Exposition Commentary* (Wheaton: Victor Books, 1989), Mk 10:13.
9. Louis Barbieri, *Moody Gospel Commentary: Mark* (Chicago: Moody Press, 1995), 223.
10. Hiebert, *op. cit.*, 282.
11. Lenski, *op. cit.*, 426.
12. Lane, *op. cit.*, 360.
13. James, R. Edwards, *The Gospel According to Mark – The Pillar New Testament Commentary* (Grand Rapids: Eerdmans, 2002), 310.
14. W. Arndt, *A Greek-English Lexicon of the New Testament and Other Early Christian Literature.* 3rd ed. (Chicago: University of Chicago Press, 2000), 3.
15. Ibid., Page 504.
16. J. Dwight Pentecost, *The Words and Works of Jesus Christ* (Grand Rapids: Zondervan, 1981), 360.
17. Arndt, *op. cit.*, 321.
18. Hiebert, *op. cit.*, 287.
19. Lane, *op. cit.*, 367.
20. R. A. Cole, *The Gospel According to Mark: an Introductory and Commentary* (Grand Rapids: Eerdmans, 1989), 233.
21. William Hendriksen, *Exposition of the Gospel According to Mark* (Grand Rapids: Baker, 1975), 399–400.

22. Edwards, *op. cit.*, 315.
23. Lane, William, *op. cit.*, 371.
24. H. A. Ironside, *Mark: Ironside Commentaries* (Neptune, NJ: Loizeaux, 1994), 97.
25. Hiebert, *op. cit.*, 451.
26. Arndt, *op. cit.*, 468.
27. Lane, *op. cit.*, 381.
28. M. Gutzkie, as quoted in the lecture notes of Dr. Jim Combs, Provost of Louisiana Baptist Theological Seminary.
29. Edwards, *op. cit.*, 324.

Chapter 11 – The Servant Enters Jerusalem as King

1. W. W. Wiersbe, *The Bible Exposition Commentary* (Wheaton: Victor Books, 1989), Mk 11:1.
2. William Barclay, *The Gospel of Mark*, (Louisville: Westminster John Knox, 2001), 310.
3. *Theological Dictionary of the New Testament, Vol. 9*, Ed. G. Kittel, G. W. Bromiley & G. Friedrich (Grand Rapids: Eerdmans, 1976), 683.
4. James, R. Edwards, *The Gospel According to Mark – The Pillar New Testament Commentary* (Grand Rapids: Eerdmans, 2002), 340.
5. William Lane, *The Gospel According to Mark*, The New International Commentary of the New Testament (Grand Rapids: Eerdmans, 1974), 405-406.
6. R. A. Cole, *The Gospel According to Mark: an Introductory and Commentary* (Grand Rapids: Eerdmans, 1989), 254.
7. H. A. Ironside, *Mark: Ironside Commentaries* (Neptune, NJ: Loizeaux, 1994), 106.
8. Cole, *op. cit.*, 255.
9. D. Edmond Hiebert, *Gospel of Mark: An Expositional Commentary* (Greenville: Bob Jones University Press, 1994), 325.
10. Ibid., 325.
11. R. C. H. Lenski, *The Interpretation of St. Mark's Gospel* (Minneapolis: Augsburg Publishing House, 1946), 500.
12. James, A. Brooks, *The New American Commentary: Mark* (Nashville: Broadman, 1991), 187–188.

Chapter 12 – The Servant in the Temple

1. D. Edmond Hiebert, *Gospel of Mark: An Expositional Commentary* (Greenville: Bob Jones University Press, 1994), 333.
2. James, R. Edwards, *The Gospel According to Mark – The Pillar New Testament Commentary* (Grand Rapids: Eerdmans, 2002), 357.
3. William Lane, *The Gospel According to Mark*, The New International Commentary of the New Testament (Grand Rapids: Eerdmans, 1974), 416.
4. H. A. Ironside, *Mark: Ironside Commentaries* (Neptune, NJ: Loizeaux, 1994), 109.
5. R. C. H. Lenski, *The Interpretation of St. Mark's Gospel* (Minneapolis: Augsburg Publishing House, 1946), 513.
6. K. S. Wuest, *Wuest's Word Studies from the Greek New Testament : For the English Reader* (Grand Rapids: Eerdmans, 1984), Mk 12:13.
7. Lane, *op. cit.*, 422-423.
8. *Nelson's Illustrated Bible Dictionary*, Electronic Database, (Nashville: Thomas Nelson Publishers, 1986).
9. *International Standard Bible Encyclopaedia*, Electronic Database, (Biblesoft, 1996).
10. The levirate marriage law (cf. Deut 25:5; Ruth 4:1–12) was very important because it provided for a widow who had no children to care for her, and because it perpetuated the family of the deceased since the first born son from the levirate marriage, retained

his deceased father's family name and was also regarded as the legal heir of his deceased father's property and goods.

11. Hiebert, *op. cit.*, 350–351.

12. Lenski, *op. cit.*, 534.

13. James, A. Brooks, *The New American Commentary: Mark* (Nashville: Broadman, 1991), 199.

14. Edwards, *op. cit.*, 374.

15. Hiebert, *op. cit.*, 357.

16. W. A. Elwell, *Evangelical Commentary on the Bible, Baker Reference Library* (Grand Rapids: Baker Book House, 1989), Mk 12:38.

Chapter 13 - The Servant Foretells the Future

1. Louis Barbieri, *Moody Gospel Commentary: Mark* (Chicago: Moody Press, 1995), 287.

2. D. A. Hagner, *Word Biblical Commentary : Matthew 14–28* (electronic ed. Logos Library System; Word Biblical Commentary. Dallas: Word, 1998) Mt 24:4.

3. Arnold G. Fruchtenbaum, *Footsteps of the Messiah* (Tustin: Ariel Ministries Press, 1983), 435-436.

4. John Walvoord & Roy Zuck, Gen. Editors, *The Bible Knowledge Commentary: An Exposition of the Scriptures, Vol. 2* (Wheaton: Victor Books, 1985), 169.

5. D. Edmond Hiebert, *Gospel of Mark: An Expositional Commentary* (Greenville: Bob Jones University Press, 1994), 373.

6. Tim LaHaye, and Thomas Ice, *Charting the End Times* (Eugene: Harvest House, 2001), 56.

7. J. Dwight Pentecost, *Things to Come* (Grand Rapids: Zondervan, 1958), 280.

8. James, R. Edwards, *The Gospel According to Mark – The Pillar New Testament Commentary* (Grand Rapids: Eerdmans, 2002), 404-406.

9. Walvoord & Zuck, *op. cit.*, 172.

10. Ritchie, Homer, Ritchie, Omer, and Shipman, Lonnie, *Secrets of Prophecy Revealed* (Springfield, MO: 21st Century Press, 2001), 35.

11. Hiebert, *op. cit.*, 383.

12. R. C. H. Lenski, *The Interpretation of St. Mark's Gospel*, pg. 590-591 (Minneapolis: Augsburg Publishing House, 1946), 590-591.

Chapter 14 – The Servant Betrayed and Denied

1. M. Mills, *The Life of Christ : A Study Guide to the Gospel Record* (Dallas: 3E Ministries, 1999).

2. D. R. W. Wood, *New Bible Dictionary*. 3rd ed. (Downers Grove: InterVarsity Press, 1996), 625.

3. Alfred Plummer, *The Gospel According to St. Mark* (Grand Rapids, MI: Baker Book House, 1914), 315–316.

4. James, R. Edwards, *The Gospel According to Mark – The Pillar New Testament Commentary* (Grand Rapids: Eerdmans, 2002), 419.

5. William Barclay, *The Gospel of Mark* (Louisville: Westminster John Knox, 2001), 387–388.

6. R. C. H. Lenski, *The Interpretation of St. Mark's Gospel* (Minneapolis: Augsburg Publishing House, 1946), 617.

7. W. W. Wiersbe, *The Bible Exposition Commentary* (Wheaton: Victor Books, 1989), Jn 13:18.

8. P. P. Enns, *The Moody Handbook of Theology* (Chicago: Moody Press, 1989).

9. John F. Walvoord & Roy B. Zuck, Editors, *The Bible Knowledge Commentary: An Exposition of the Scriptures, Vol. 1* (Wheaton: Victor Books, 1985), 1171.

10. Edwards, *op. cit.*, 432.

11. Lenski, *op. cit.*, 635.

12. J. V. McGee, *Thru the Bible Commentary, Vol. 4*, electronic ed (Nashville: Thomas Nelson, 1981), 226.

13. Edwards, *op. cit.*, 442.

14. A.T. Robertson, *Word Pictures in the New Testament, Vol 1* (Grand Rapids: Baker Book House, 1930), 218.

15. Edwards, *op. cit.*, 448-449.

16. Lenski, *op. cit.*, 669.

17. Ibid., 669-670.

18. W. A. Elwell, *Evangelical Commentary on the Bible, Baker Reference Library* (Grand Rapids: Baker Book House, 1989), Mk 14:66.

Chapter 15 – The Servant Obedient Unto Death

1. James, R. Edwards, *The Gospel According to Mark – The Pillar New Testament Commentary*, (Grand Rapids: Eerdmans, 2002), 443-443.

2. W. A. Elwell, *Evangelical Commentary on the Bible, Baker Reference Library* (Grand Rapids: Baker Book House, 1989), Mk 15:1.

3. D. Edmond Hiebert, *Gospel of Mark: An Expositional Commentary* (Greenville: Bob Jones University Press, 1994), 441.

4. R. C. H. Lenski, *The Interpretation of St. Mark's Gospel* (Minneapolis: Augsburg Publishing House, 1946), 691-692.

5. Ray C. Steadman, *Expository Studies in Mark 8–16: The Ruler Who Serves* (Waco: Word Books, 1976), 190.

6. R. Kent Hughes, *MARK Vol I: Jesus, Servant and Savior* (Westchester: Crossway Books, 1989), 194.

7. Steadman, *op. cit.*, 193.

8. W. W. Wiersbe, *The Bible Exposition Commentary* (Wheaton: Victor Books, 1989), Mk 15:21.

9. Lenski, *op. cit.*, 709.

10. Arndt, W., F. W. Danker, & W. Bauer. *A Greek-English Lexicon of the New Testament and Other Early Christian Literature*. 3rd ed. (Chicago: University of Chicago Press, 2000), 178.

11. Ibid., Page 710.

12. Louis Barbieri, *Moody Gospel Commentary: Mark* (Chicago: Moody Press, 1995), 357.

13. R. A. Cole, *The Gospel According to Mark: an Introductory and Commentary* (Grand Rapids: Eerdmans, 1989), 321–322.

14. Hiebert, *op. cit.*, 459.

15. Arndt, W., F. W. Danker, & W. Bauer. *op. cit.*, 715.

16. Barbieri, *op. cit.*, 360.

17. Edwards, *op. cit.*, 479-480.

18. Hiebert, *op. cit.*, 465.

19. D. A. Hagner, *Word Biblical Commentary : Matthew 14–28*. electronic ed. (Logos Library System; Word Biblical Commentary. Dallas: Word, Incorporated, 1998), Mt 27:61.

Chapter 16 – The Servant's Glorious Triumph

1. John F. Walvoord & Roy B. Zuck, Gen. Editors, *The Bible Knowledge Commentary: An Exposition of the Scriptures, Vol. 2*, (Wheaton: Victor Books, 1985), 192.

2. D. Edmond Hiebert, *Gospel of Mark: An Expositional Commentary* (Greenville: Bob Jones University Press, 1994), 477.

3. Most textual scholars believe that the most trustworthy manuscripts end with verse 8. However, the overwhelming majority of manuscripts contain the longer ending to

Mark (v. 9–20). Given this scholarly disagreement it is best *not to* base doctrine or experience on the verses found in this pericope.

4. Quoted by D. Edmond Hiebert, *op. cit.*, 483.

5. H. A. Ironside, *Mark: Ironside Commentaries* (Neptune: Loizeaux, 1994), 150.

6. R. Jamieson, A. R. Fausset, A. R. Fausset, D. Brown, & D. Brown. *A Commentary, Critical and Explanatory, on the Old and New Testaments* (Oak Harbor: Logos Research Systems, Inc., 1997), Mk 16:16.

7. R. C. H. Lenski, The Interpretation of St. Mark's Gospel, (Minneapolis: Augsburg Publishing House, 1946), 771,

8. Ibid., 773-774.

9. Matthew Henry, *Matthew Henry's Commentary On the Whole Bible, Vol. 5* (Peabody: Hendrickson Publishers, 1991), 461.

About the Author

Dr. James A. McGowan, a former network engineer, brings his biblical and analytical skills to the exegesis of Mark's gospel. A skilled Bible teacher, Dr. McGowan holds he Th.M. and Th.D. from Louisiana Baptist Theological Seminary. He is an effective minister and classroom professor. His style is both academic and practical, as his excellent commentary reflects.

Dr. McGowan has taught Greek, Hebrew, and Old Testament studies at Tyndale Theological Seminary, the North Houston Bible Institute, and the Bible Institute of Texas. His love of teaching has opened up many opportunities including ministry in Africa, Bolivia, Guatemala, Honduras, and Mexico.

Dr. McGowan married his high school sweetheart, Sandra, also a teacher,. They have two grown daughters. The McGowans live in Houston, Texas. Currently, Dr. McGowan serves as Christian Education Pastor at Sugar Land Bible Church in Sugar Land, Texas.

About the General Editors

Mal Couch is founder and former president of Tyndale Theological Seminary and Biblical Institute in Fort Worth, Texas. He previously taught at Philadelphia College of the Bible, Moody Bible Institute, and Dallas Theological Seminary. His other publications include *The Hope of Christ's Return: A Premillennial Commentary on 1 and 2 Thessalonians, A Bible Handbook to Revelation,* and *Dictionary of Premillennial Theology.*

Edward Hindson is professor of religion, dean of the Institute of Biblical Studies, and assistant to the chancellor at Liberty University in Lynchburg, Virginia. He has authored more than twenty books, served as coeditor of several Bible projects, and was one of the translators for the New King James Version of the Bible. Dr. Hindson has served as a visiting lecturer at Oxford University and Harvard Divinity School as well as numerous evangelical seminaries. He has taught more than fifty thousand students in the past twenty-five years.